Feminism in the Labor Movement

Feminism in the Labor Movement

*Women and the
United Auto Workers, 1935–1975*

Nancy F. Gabin

Cornell University Press

ITHACA AND LONDON

First published 1990 by Cornell University Press.

International Standard Book Number 0-8014-2435-6 (cloth)
International Standard Book Number 0-8014-9725-6 (paper)
Library of Congress Catalog Card Number 90-1571
Printed in the United States of America
Librarians: Library of Congress cataloging information
appears on the last page of the book.

⊗The paper in this book meets the minimum requirements
of the American National Standard for Information Sciences—
Permanence of Paper for Printed Library Materials ANSI Z39.48–1984.

To my grandparents,
Sol and Evelyn Krames,
Pincus and Gertrude Gabin

Contents

Acknowledgments

It is a pleasure to acknowledge the people whose assistance, advice, and encouragement made this book possible. My greatest debt is to Sidney Fine, who taught me how to be a historian. A prodigious researcher, a prolific writer, and a skillful critic, Professor Fine is an inspired and inspiring scholar. The professional standards he sets for himself are ones I will always try to emulate. He also was the project's strongest advocate. His concern for my personal and professional well-being is a constant source of comfort.

I am grateful to Louise Tilly for teaching me how to think about the history of women and work. Several other people have read chapters at various stages. Mari Jo Buhle, Carol Groneman, Robin Jacoby, Jacqueline Jones, Alice Kessler-Harris, Ruth Milkman, Marjorie Murphy, Margaret Rose, and Robert Thomas offered important insights and suggestions. Ava Baron read an early version of chapter 5 and, in helping me to see the study in a different light, immeasurably aided the revision process. Frank Bolles, Ruth Meyerowitz, Ruth Milkman, Douglas Reynolds, and Seth Wigderson, all of whom have done research on the UAW, shared ideas and information and generously provided references to archival material that I might otherwise have missed. I also thank Donald Berthrong and John Contreni, successive heads of the Department of History at Purdue University since my arrival there in 1983. Understanding the demands made on younger scholars, they acknowledged the importance of my research and provided continuing support and encouragement.

The staffs at various manuscript repositories extended courteous and expert service. I particularly thank Jerry Hess of the National Archives and Records Service and David Crippen of the Ford Motor Company Archives. A special thanks goes to the people at the Walter P. Reuther Library, Archives of Labor and Urban Affairs. Philip Mason, Warner Pflug, Joan Rabins, Dione Miles, Carolyn Davis, Michael Smith, and all the others on the staff provided easy and ready access to all material and made my many hours there a genuine pleasure. Margery Long and Thomas Featherstone in the Audiovisual Department of the Reuther Library and Judy Harden in the UAW Public Relations Department at Solidarity House responded graciously and quickly to my requests for photographs.

Fellowships from the University of Michigan Rackham Graduate School, Wellesley College, the Business and Professional Women's Foundation, the National Endowment for the Humanities, the Rockefeller Foundation, and the Purdue University Research Foundation provided much-appreciated financial assistance for the research and writing of this book.

It is also my pleasure to acknowledge the efforts of the staff at Cornell University Press in producing this book. Peter Agree, my editor, has been honest, fair, and supportive. The manuscript is better for the talents and skills of Jo-Anne Naples as copy editor.

Friends and family members assisted in the creation of this book in myriad ways. I acquired an abiding respect for unions from my grandparents, Sol and Evelyn Krames and Pincus Gabin, my parents, George Gabin and Ellen Gabin, my sister, Carol Papagiannis, my husband's uncle, Bernard Morrison, and my husband, Michael Morrison. Their involvement in the labor movement has sparked and confirmed my interest in labor history.

My mother-in-law, Joan Morrison, tolerated the clacking of a typewriter for weeks at a time and provided bed and board during research trips. She and my sister-in-law Christine Kosdrosky cared for my son, Nathaniel, while I attended conferences. Suzanne Larson, Denise Hakenewerth, and Susan Waananen loved and nurtured him and offered me friendly concern and encouragement. Nathaniel has never known me not to be writing this book. Although there were moments when he lost patience for his mother's other labor of love, Natty generally tolerated it with good cheer, forbearance, and a disregard for the project that was a refreshing reminder of the more important things in life. I hope that when he is old enough to understand, he knows that throughout those many hours when I was at work away from home, he was always in my mind and heart. My daughter, Katie, was born in time to keep me company through many hours of late-night and early-morning proofreading. Without the willingness of my husband to shoulder more than an equal share of domestic and parental responsibilities, this book would not have seen the light of day. He is my sternest taskmaster, my staunchest supporter, and my best friend; his companionship ineffably enhances my work and my life.

NANCY F. GABIN

West Lafayette, Indiana

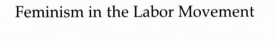

Feminism in the Labor Movement

Introduction

This book examines women's relationship to and experience of unionism, using the United Auto Workers (UAW) as a case study. Since its origins in the middle 1930s, the UAW has been regarded as one of the most liberal and egalitarian labor organizations in the United States. The union, however, would not seem to have been a setting especially conducive to or receptive of women's activism. Women historically have composed a small proportion of the labor force in the automotive and aerospace industries. As a result, women have not represented much more than 15 percent of the union's membership, except during World War II.

Despite the male dominance and to a certain extent the male orientation of the UAW, however, women's activism and union efforts in behalf of women have long been hallmarks of the history of women and the union. The UAW's Women's Department, established in 1944, was the first of its kind. To facilitate and augment the work of the department, a 1962 amendment to the UAW constitution mandated the organization of women's committees at the local union level. The union also compiled a respectable record of collective bargaining in the interest of gender equity. The UAW's image as an advocate of women's rights in particular and women generally derives, moreover, from its relationship to the contemporary women's movement. Two UAW leaders were founders of the National Organization for Women (NOW) in 1966, and Olga Madar, a UAW vice-

1

president, served as the first president of the Coalition of Labor Union Women (CLUW). In 1970 the UAW became the first union in the nation to endorse the Equal Rights Amendment. The UAW has provided an arena for the collective action of working women. The uses UAW women have made of that arena offer the evidence for an important chapter in the history of American women and American labor.

The period between the enfranchisement of American women in 1920 and the resurgence of feminism in the 1960s has received increasing scholarly attention in the past two decades. In seeking the sources of stability and change in women's lives in these decades, historians have generally been concerned to explain and assess the growing importance of employment for married women on the one hand and the resurgence of feminism in the 1960s on the other. Although valuable and important, the twin concerns of these studies have created something of a blind spot in the historical literature on this period. Because the most noticeable increase in female labor-force participation has occurred among middle-class wives and because contemporary feminism to a large extent reflects the concerns of middle-class women, historians have traced middle-class experience backward through time, emphasizing female employment in the tertiary sector, since middle-class women tend to hold white-collar jobs. As a consequence, women in blue-collar occupations have been almost wholly ignored by historians.[1]

Labor history for its part generally has been concerned with men. For example, most historians who have examined the emergence of mass-production unionism and the rise of the Congress of Industrial Organizations (CIO) in the 1930s, arguably the most important chapter in the history of American labor in this century, have not considered gender a category for analysis.[2] To a certain extent, this oversight reflects the fact that the most of the CIO unions organized workers in predominantly male-employing industries. The focus on the male majority, however, has produced a distorted history of workers and their families in modern America.[3] Historians of work-

1. Works that emphasize middle-class experience include William Chafe, *The American Woman* (London, 1972); Winifred Wandersee, *Women's Work and Family Values, 1920–1940* (Cambridge, Mass., 1981); Lois Scharf, *To Work and to Wed* (Westport, Conn., 1980); Eugenia Kaledin, *Mothers and More* (Boston, 1984).

2. One notable exception to the rule is Ronald Schatz, *The Electrical Workers* (Urbana, 1983).

3. The large literature on the UAW pays scant attention to gender issues and gender relations within the quintessential industrial union. There is as yet no satisfy-

ing women have been busy in the past two decades challenging the androcentrism of the field. Although most attention has been paid to women's relationship to wage earning and unions in the period before 1930, the outlines of recent women's labor history are becoming clear. A handful of published and unpublished studies of women and the United Electrical Workers, the Packinghouse Workers of America, clerical workers' organizations, the Hotel Employees and Restaurant Employees, and cannery workers' unions have greatly advanced our understanding of women in unions in the 1930s and 1940s.[4] Very little work, however, has been done on the post–World War II period with respect to women and unions.[5]

ing one-volume history of the UAW. Until this gap is filled, the following works must be consulted: John Barnard, *Walter Reuther and the Rise of the Auto Workers* (Boston, 1983); Sidney Fine, *The Automobile under the Blue Eagle* (Ann Arbor, Mich., 1963); Fine, *Sit-Down* (Ann Arbor, Mich., 1969); Peter Friedlander, *Emergence of a U.A.W. Local, 1936–1939* (Pittsburgh, 1975); Martin Halpern, *UAW Politics in the Cold War Era* (Albany, N.Y., 1988); Irving Howe and B. J. Widick, *The UAW and Walter Reuther* (New York, 1973); Steven Jeffreys, *Management and Managed* (Cambridge, England, 1986); Roger Keeran, *The Communist Party and the Auto Workers Unions* (Bloomington, Ind., 1980); Nelson Lichtenstein, *Labor's War at Home* (Cambridge, England, 1982); Lichtenstein, "Auto Worker Militancy and the Structure of Factory Life, 1937–1955," *Journal of American History* 67 (September 1980): 335–53; August Meier and Elliott Rudwick, *Black Detroit and the Rise of the UAW* (Oxford, 1979); William Serrin, *The Company and the Union* (New York, 1974).

    4. For the nineteenth and early twentieth centuries, see, for example, Thomas Dublin, *Women at Work* (New York, 1979); Mary Blewett, *Men, Women, and Work* (Urbana, 1988); Susan Levine, *Labor's True Woman* (Philadelphia, 1984); Nancy Schrom Dye, *As Equals and as Sisters* (Columbia, Mo., 1980); Alice Kessler-Harris, "Where Are the Organized Women Workers?" *Feminist Studies* 3 (Fall 1975): 92–110; Patricia Cooper, *Once a Cigar Maker* (Urbana, 1987); Kessler-Harris, "Problems of Coalition-Building: Women and Trade Unions in the 1920s," in Ruth Milkman, ed., *Women, Work, and Protest* (Boston, 1985), pp. 110–38. Studies of the CIO era include Dorothy Sue Cobble, " 'Practical Women': Waitress Unionists and Controversies over Gender Roles in the Food Service Industry, 1900–1980," *Labor History* 29 (Winter 1988): 5–31; Bruce Fehn, "Women of the United Packinghouse Workers of America, 1946–1956," unpublished paper in author's possession; Dolores Janiewski, *Sisterhood Denied* (Philadelphia, 1985); Milkman, *Gender at Work* (Urbana, 1987); Vicki Ruiz, *Cannery Women, Cannery Lives* (Albuquerque, 1987); Sharon Hartman Strom, "Challenging 'Woman's Place': Feminism, the Left, and Industrial Unionism in the 1930s," *Feminist Studies* 9 (Summer 1983): 359–86; Strom, " 'We're No Kitty Foyles': Organizing Office Workers for the Congress of Industrial Organizations, 1937–50," in Milkman, ed., *Women, Work, and Protest*, pp. 206–34. The UAW is the most studied of the CIO unions with respect to women. See Ruth Meyerowitz, "Organizing the United Automobile Workers: Women Workers at the Ternstedt General Motors Parts Plant," in Milkman, ed., *Women, Work, and Protest*, pp. 235–58; Lyn Goldfarb, *Separated and Unequal*, Union for Radical Political Economics pamphlet, 1976; Sheila Tobias and Lisa Anderson, "What Really Happened to Rosie the Riveter: Demobilization and the Female Labor Force, 1944–47," *MSS Modular Publications* 9 (1973).

    5. For a summary of women and unionism since 1950, see Philip Foner, *Women and the American Labor Movement from World War I to the Present* (New York, 1980), pp. 417–

This book has several goals, one of which is to fill a gap in the historical literature on women wage workers. Highlighting the place of women in the organization and structure of work in the auto industry, the book explores an important but largely unexamined aspect of the history of the foremost mass-production industry in the United States until the 1970s. Similarly, it contributes to our under-standing of the diversity of the female experience, focusing on a heretofore relatively invisible group of working women from the 1930s to the 1970s. Investigation of the character and the sources of change and continuity in women's place in auto plants also offers insight into the dynamics of gender hierarchy and inequality in American industry.

Another goal of the book is to assess the relationship of women to the traditionally male-dominated and male-oriented labor move-ment. Like the record of organized labor generally, the UAW's record in regard to women was decidedly mixed. On the one hand, the UAW tended to marginalize women in the union hall and on the shop floor, denying them equal access to positions of leadership and power within the organization, never making gender equality a cen-tral demand of its collective-bargaining agenda, and at times assert-ing the interests of the male majority at the expense of women auto workers. In these regards, the UAW example confirms the view that organized labor obstructs rather than facilitates working women's collective action.[6] On the other hand, however, the UAW acknowl-edged the problem of sexual discrimination in employment early in its history, institutionalized an advocate for women within the union structure in the middle 1940s, and already had made some important collective-bargaining gains in the interest of gender equity by the time the civil rights and feminist movements began to legitimize the principle of equality in the labor market in the 1960s.

The contradictory evidence raises two questions. How were

572. See also Deborah Bell, "Unionized Women in State and Local Government," in Milkman, ed., *Women, Work, and Protest*, pp. 280–99; Cobble, " 'Practical Women' "; Margaret Rose, "Women in the United Farm Workers: A Study of Chicana and Mex-icana Participation in a Labor Union, 1950 to 1980," Ph.D. diss., University of Califor-nia–Los Angeles, 1988.

6. For this view, see Heidi Hartmann, "Capitalism, Patriarchy, and Job Segregation by Sex," *Signs* 1 (Spring 1976): 137–69; Kessler-Harris, "Where Are the Organized Women Workers?"; Ruth Milkman, "Organizing the Sexual Division of Labor: Histor-ical Perspective on 'Women's Work' and the American Labor Movement," *Socialist Review* 10 (January–February 1980): 95–150.

women able to mobilize within the UAW and to shape the union's policies on issues of importance to female auto workers? And why, despite the indifference and at times hostility of men toward them and those issues, did women continue to look to the UAW to defend them? The answers to these questions indicate that union membership serves not only as a constraint on but also as a resource for female collective action. They also suggest that at least some working-class women experienced the period 1935 to 1975 quite differently than did most middle-class women. Despite—or because of—the ideologically conservative climate of the 1940s and 1950s, UAW women took advantage of the democratic principles of industrial unionism and its implicit challenge to discrimination on the basis of sex and convinced the union at least to acknowledge the legitimacy of their goals and purposes. Although the tensions between women and men in the UAW should not be minimized and the extent of the success of women in the years before they found an important ally in the resurgent feminist movement should not be exaggerated, the experience of women in the UAW demonstrates the significance of the trade union as an important arena for working women's collective action.

The third goal of this book is to evaluate the significance of feminism for women in blue-collar occupations. Having long regarded the terms *feminism* and *unionism* as incompatible and contradictory, scholars now are integrating them in analyses of working women. Historians, however, have focused on the nineteenth and early twentieth centuries.[7] Comparatively less effort has been made to examine the decades since the 1920s in regard to union women's relation to feminism.[8] While the misfortunes of the feminist move-

---

7. Blewett, *Men, Women, and Work*, pp. 97–319; Dye, *As Equals and as Sisters*; Maurine Weiner Greenwald, "Working-Class Feminism and the Family Wage Ideal: The Seattle Debate on Married Women's Right to Work, 1914–1920," *Journal of American History* 76 (June 1989): 118–49; Robin Jacoby, "The Women's Trade Union League and American Feminism," *Feminist Studies* 3 (Fall 1975): 126–40; Alice Kessler-Harris, "Organizing the Unorganizable: Three Jewish Women and Their Union," *Labor History* 17 (Winter 1976): 5–23; Kessler-Harris, "Problems of Coalition-Building"; Susan Levine, "Labor's True Woman: Domesticity and Equal Rights in the Knights of Labor," *Journal of American History* 70 (September 1983): 323–49.

8. For the post–1920s, see Myra Marx Ferree, "Working Class Feminism: A Consideration of the Consequences of Employment," *Sociological Quarterly* 21 (Spring 1980): 173–84; Foner, *Women and the American Labor Movement*, pp. 478–536; Ruth Milkman, "American Women and Industrial Unionism during World War II," in Margaret Randolph Higgonet et al., eds., *Behind the Lines* (New Haven, 1987), pp. 168–81;

ment may help account for the inattention to the 1930s through the 1950s, the resurgence of organized feminism in the 1960s and 1970s has not prompted much consideration by scholars interested in women's labor history. In this absence, students of the women's movement have assessed it as though it were a wholly middle-class phenomenon that only gradually and incompletely found a working-class audience.[9] The evidence from the auto industry and the UAW indicates the presence of feminist values, attitudes, and action during years and in a context in which they were not presumed to have existed. An evaluation of the origins and character of gender advocacy in the UAW, therefore, illuminates an overlooked aspect of the history of both the labor movement and American feminism.

The importance of feminism for women auto unionists is best understood in the context of the persistent (although episodic) attacks on the sexual division of labor that occurred after the 1930s. The first significant action took place during the period of reconversion to peacetime production at the end of World War II, when, to protest wholesale dismissals, women unionists challenged the validity of sex-based job classifications and seniority lists. A second wave of union activity occurred in the 1950s, when auto industry developments reduced the number of so-called women's jobs, thereby raising anew the issue of women's place in auto plants. In the 1960s and early 1970s, high employment and the potential power of Title VII of the 1964 Civil Rights Act altered the context for the struggle to expand women's access to auto jobs and provided the basis for an assault on state laws regulating the employment of women. As the UAW's endorsement of the ERA in 1970 suggests, most auto unionists advocated sex-blind treatment as a strategy for gaining equality for women in the workplace. Examination of the debates over

---

Milkman, "Women Workers, Feminism, and the Labor Movement since the 1960s," in Milkman, ed., *Women, Work, and Protest*, pp. 300–22; Strom, "Challenging 'Woman's Place.'"

9. Most studies of the women's movement in the 1960s and 1970s do mention, for example, the role of UAW activists in the formation of NOW or refer to the union's early endorsement of the ERA. But none of these works pursue the question of union women's participation in the movement. See Myra Ferree and Beth Hess, *Controversy and Coalition* (Boston, 1985); Jo Freeman, *The Politics of Women's Liberation* (New York, 1975); Judith Hole and Ellen Levine, *Rebirth of Feminism* (New York, 1971). The few treatments of women in unions and of the feminist movement usually begin with the formation of the CLUW in 1974. For an exception, see Diane Balser, *Sisterhood and Solidarity* (Boston, 1987), pp. 87–216.

women's place in the auto industry and the appropriate strategies to pursue in gaining equality, however, indicates that in the UAW, as elsewhere, advocates of women's rights alternated between the poles of special protection and equal treatment.[10] What distinguished female auto unionists from middle-class women, however, was the unionists' simultaneous commitment to unionism. Female activists often found it difficult to negotiate the competing, although not necessarily mutually exclusive, terms of feminism and unionism. The complex and contingent character of the mediation process within the UAW prompts an assessment of the prospects for a convergence of feminist and class consciousness.

10. Nancy Cott, *The Grounding of Modern Feminism* (New Haven, 1987); Alice Kessler-Harris, "The Debate over Equality for Women in the Workplace: Recognizing Differences," in Laurie Larwood, Ann Stromberg, and Barbara Gutek, eds., *Women and Work: An Annual Review*, vol. 1 (Beverly Hills, Calif., 1985).

CHAPTER ONE

"No Woman's Land":
The UAW-CIO in the 1930s

During the 1937 convention of the UAW, the delegates debated whether a working woman who was a union member was also eligible for membership in a women's auxiliary. A majority were inclined to agree with Evelyn McGinnis, president of the Milwaukee Women's Auxiliary, who defended the proposal. "After all," she said, "they are active members of the union and are the ones that keep the women [in the auxiliaries] on the right track." Katherine Wilk, an auto-worker delegate from Local 174 of Detroit, then issued a challenge to her fellow unionists. "I am speaking and demanding and pleading for the women of the labor movement," she explained. "I notice, and everyone else here knows, that there has been a great error made. There are women who have been very active in the labor movement and as we all know we haven't even a woman on the Executive Board." Demanding that the UAW encourage women workers to participate in the union as full-fledged members rather than relegating them to a supportive role in the auxiliaries, Wilk urged the convention to "take up the matter of having a woman member on the Executive Board."[1]

The 1937 convention debate on the status of women in the UAW occurred amid the turbulence of the union's early history. Strikes for

1. *Proceedings of the Second Annual Convention of the International Union, United Automobile Workers of America, August 23–29, 1937* (hereafter cited as *1937 Convention Proceedings*), p. 255.

recognition, the consolidation of organizational gains, and internal factionalism preoccupied women as well as men in the UAW in the late 1930s. But as the comments of McGinnis and Wilk suggest, men regarded women as less than equal partners in the effort to unionize the auto industry. The union's strategic emphasis on auto-body and assembly plants, where women were a small minority of those employed in production jobs, meant that organizing energy was focused on men. Some attention was paid female auto workers, particularly when efforts were made to organize auto-parts and accessories factories, where women composed a much more significant part of the labor force, but the UAW never systematically developed a program to organize women. The male orientation of the new auto union extended past the initial phase of organization and into the period of institutional consolidation. Women's rights to and interests in strong representation on the shop floor and at the negotiating table were not wholly ignored. The sexual division of labor, however, was confirmed rather than challenged by the union in the 1930s. In its approach to wage, job-classification, and seniority issues, moreover, the UAW tended to promote the interests of the male majority at the expense of those of female union members.

The statement made by Katherine Wilk at the 1937 convention bespoke the dilemma confronting women auto unionists in the 1930s. Wilk did not demand that the UAW challenge sexual inequality in the auto industry. Rather, she emphasized the shared concerns of all auto workers regardless of sex and asked only that the union recognize and respect women for their dedication to unionism. But although women were no more difficult to organize than men and demonstrated their commitment to the union time and again in the 1930s, the UAW did not reciprocate their loyalty and enthusiasm. The willingness of UAW men to grant working women membership in the Women's Auxiliary and the fact that almost thirty years passed before Wilk's specific call was heeded indicated the importance of women challenging sexual inequality in the union and in the factory.

Women have always been part of the auto labor force. In 1910 approximately 1,000 of the nearly 42,000 people employed in production jobs in the industry were women. By 1920, owing both to the expansion of the industry in the 1910s and to the increased employment of women during World War I, more than 15,000 women were employed in auto factories and they represented 7 percent of the

labor force. The relative and absolute number of women auto workers increased slightly during the 1920s and grew more substantially
in the 1930s. In 1940, of the 288,570 operatives and laborers employed, 30,445, or 10.5 percent, were women.[2]

The sexual division of labor has historically defined the structure
and organization of work in the automobile industry, with women
being confined to a small number of occupations. According to a 1925
Bureau of Labor Statistics study, women were employed in twenty of
fifty-five occupational categories in auto plants, but two-thirds of
them were clustered in just four categories. Fully a third of the
women were sewing-machine operators, 14 percent were trim bench
hands, 13 percent were inspectors, and 9 percent were final assemblers. The extent of sexual segregation was further revealed in the
proportion of women in each occupation. Three of every four sewing-machine operators and one-half of all trim bench hands were
women, whereas the proportion of women among all workers in
each of the other categories averaged only 2 percent.[3]

There was little change in the auto jobs held by women during the
next fifteen years. Women were employed chiefly in the upholstery
departments of auto-body plants and in the manufacture and assembly of small parts and accessories. A 1940 Bureau of Labor Statistics
survey of 448 automobile-assembly, automotive-stamping, and auto-

2. Janet Hooks, *Women's Occupations through Seven Decades*, U.S. Women's Bureau
Bulletin No. 218 (Washington, D.C., 1947), pp. 221, 237. Absolute figures for female
employment in the auto industry vary, but the number of employed women relative to
the total labor force is remarkably consistent. The 1939 Census of Manufactures
counted 499,490 production workers in the automobile and automobile-equipment
industry, of whom 37,261, or 7.4 percent, were female; a 1940 Bureau of Labor Statistics study of the motor-vehicle and motor-vehicle-equipment industry counted 35,969
women (7.6 percent) out of a total of 471,360 wage earners. The five midwestern states
that constituted the center of the industry—Michigan, Ohio, Indiana, Illinois, and
Wisconsin—accounted for 94.6 percent of the 7,928 women employed in auto-body
and assembly plants and 78.5 percent of the 28,041 women working in parts plants in
the nation and 59 percent of those in the Midwest. Of the 6,063 women employed in
parts plants located outside the Midwest, 5,640 worked in New England and in the
Middle Atlantic states. Bureau of the Census, *Sixteenth Census of the United States: 1940,
Manufactures, 1939*, vol. 1 (Washington, D.C., 1942), table 2, pp. 70–71; Harold R.
Hosea and George E. Votara, *Wage Structure of the Motor-Vehicle Industry*, Bureau of
Labor Statistics (BLS) Bulletin No. 706 (Washington, D.C., 1942), table 10, pp. 23–24,
and table 12, pp. 30–31.

3. BLS, *Wages and Hours of Labor in the Motor-Vehicle Industry: 1925*, Bulletin No. 438
(Washington, D.C., 1927), table 1, pp. 2–3. The survey included ninety-nine plants in
the eight most important auto-manufacturing states: Illinois, Indiana, Michigan, New
York, New Jersey, Ohio, Pennsylvania, and Wisconsin. The BLS counted 3,432 women
working in these plants.

motive-equipment plants indicated that women represented only 2.5 percent of the 322,941 workers in assembly and body plants. Although women were found in twelve of the forty-nine processing occupations, more than three-quarters of the them worked in just four job classifications. Nearly a third of the 7,346 women were sewing-machine operators, a quarter were trim bench hands, 12.3 percent were small-parts assemblers, and 10.6 percent were body assemblers and trimmers. Moreover, women accounted for 73 percent of all sewing-machine operators, 48.5 percent of all small-parts assemblers, and 25.5 percent of all trim bench hands. The percentage of women in each of the other processing occupations averaged only 2.4.[4]

According to the same survey, women composed 19 percent of the 148,329 employees in the automotive-parts division of the industry. And in contrast to the auto-body and assembly plants, where one-third of the women worked in one predominantly female job classification, auto-equipment plants employed women in one-third of all processing occupations and as a significant proportion of the labor force in several classifications. Women composed 58.5 percent of the small-parts assemblers; 45 percent of the packers and craters, paint-shop workers, and miscellaneous machining-process operators; and 40.8 percent of the inspectors. Women were also well represented among punch-press operators (31 percent), subassembly sheet-metal assemblers (29.8 percent), and spray painters (24.4 percent). Even here, however, women tended to cluster in a few jobs: 40 percent of the 27,801 women were engaged in small-parts assembly, another 4,854 women (17.5 percent) were inspectors, 3,661 (13.2 percent) were machining-process operators, and 3,599 (12.9 percent) were punch-press operators.[5]

Assumptions about the physical characteristics and capacities of women and men underlay the sexual division of labor not only in the auto industry but in other durable-goods industries as well. Since the early years of the auto industry, women's work typically was described as requiring less physical strength and greater dexterity and tolerance for monotony than men's work. Ford Motor Company officials, for example, believed women's nimble fingers were well suited for winding wire and for sewing, and so hired three hundred

4. BLS Bulletin No. 706, table 10, pp. 23–24.
5. Ibid., table 16, pp. 38–39.

women to work only in the magneto, top-making, and upholstery departments of the pathbreaking mass-production plant in Highland Park, Michigan, in the 1910s. The same gender differences were asserted in the 1930s. Joseph Geschelin wrote in the industry's trade journal in 1939 that most of the operations at the AC Spark Plug plant in Flint "involve the handling of extremely small, if not minute, parts; require the integration of small parts into small, precision assemblies; demand dexterity and exceptional skill on high repetitive tasks." The AC plant, Geschelin contended, "provides at least one excellent answer to the oft-repeated question—what is the place of women in the industry? . . . It is axiomatic . . . [that] women not only are desired but as a matter of fact [are] indispensable since men's thicker fingers and more volatile temperament could not hope to cope with the problem." The employment of women as operators of such heavy equipment as thirty-ton punch presses and the use of men on the assembly line—the epitome of accelerated, mind-numbing monotony—indicate the internally inconsistent rhetoric of sex typing in the auto industry. State and regional variations in job assignments further attest to the arbitrary basis for the labeling of jobs as female or male. The 1925 Bureau of Labor Statistics survey, for example, found that more than one hundred women were working as punch-press operators in Michigan and New Jersey but that not one woman was so employed in six other states. Despite such contradictions, the sexual division of labor had an aura of legitimacy that few people associated with the auto industry challenged in the period before World War II.[6]

Although women and men occupied separate spheres in the auto industry, they shared similar working conditions and had similar complaints. Management's arbitrary and capricious employment practices affected both sexes. Yet women had special problems to confront in this regard. The status of married or pregnant women, for example, always was precarious, with job security dependent on the health of the economy and the prejudices of employers. Women also were subject to sexual harassment by foremen, who extorted dates and other favors in exchange for employment. The physical environment was unpleasant for both sexes; men and women worked in

6. Ruth Milkman, *Gender at Work* (Urbana, 1987), pp. 12–26; Stephen Meyer III, *The Five Dollar Day* (Albany, N.Y., 1981), p. 140; Joseph Geschelin, "Method Study Promotes AC Operating Economics," *Automotive Industries* 80 (June 1, 1939): 647; BLS Bulletin No. 438, p. 33.

extremes of heat and cold in summer and winter. Women employed at a General Motors parts plant in Anderson, Indiana, worked on a balcony suspended over foundry equipment. "When you would go in in the morning at 7:00, it would be way over 100 degrees," Geneva Hartley recalls. "We had to stand on cardboard to keep from burning our feet." In the winter, Hartley adds, "we had to work with our coats and hats on." Other occupational hazards stemmed from the specifications of the job. Punch presses and drill presses, of course, caused injuries to both men and women. But the upholstery, or cut-and-sew, departments of auto-body and assembly plants had their own dangers. Sewing machines were just as capable of maiming workers as were other kinds of industrial equipment. Women working with cloth on auto interiors held tacks in their mouths while firing a charged hammer. "Tack spitting," as the job was called, not only could harm the digestive tract but was, as one woman stated dryly, "very hard on the teeth."[7]

Methods of wage payment were another source of discontent among auto workers. Bonus systems for piecework were so perversely complicated that no one understood them. Many firms did not pay workers for the time they spent in the plant waiting for work. But whereas male auto workers were at least putatively among the highest paid in American industry, female auto workers by comparison received very low wages. A 1925 Bureau of Labor Statistics survey found that women's hourly rate averaged 26 cents, or one-third less than that of men, in the industry as a whole. Moreover, 88 percent of women, as compared to only 18 percent of men, were at the bottom of the industry's wage structure, earning less than 60 cents per hour. As wage levels declined during the Great Depression, the gap between men's and women's rates widened. In 1932 female factory workers received an average hourly rate of 36.1 cents, which was 56.6 percent of the 63.8-cent average hourly rate for males. The

7. Interview with Helen Russell, pp. 1, 4, Women's History Coalition Oral History Project, Anderson Public Library, Anderson, Indiana; interview with John W. Anderson, pp. 4–5, UAW Oral History Project, Institute of Labor and Industrial Relations, University of Michigan and Wayne State University, Detroit, Michigan; interview with Geneva Hartley, pp. 4–5, Women's History Coalition Oral History Project; interview with Nellie Hancock, pp. 1–3, ibid.; transcript, Women's Bureau Labor Advisory Committee meeting, June 1940, United States Women's Bureau Papers, Record Group 86, Box 1714, June 4, 1940 Conference Folder, National Archives, Washington, D.C. (hereafter cited as RG 86/NA). For a general discussion of auto work and workers' complaints, see Joyce Shaw Peterson, *American Automobile Workers, 1900–1933* (Albany, N.Y., 1987); Sidney Fine, *Sit-Down* (Ann Arbor, Mich., 1969).

specification of a minimum wage by the automobile-manufacturing code under the National Industrial Recovery Act had the effect of raising women's wages. Approved on August 26, 1933, the code provided six minimum hourly rates for nonsalaried employees, ranging from 35 to 43 cents per hour and graded according to the sex of the worker. Although the minimums were below prevailing wage rates in the industry, women in particular benefited because their wages were so low. GM, for example, had to raise the wages of 18.5 percent of its female employees but only 3.3 percent of its male workers, and Chrysler had to raise the pay of 7.37 percent of the women in its Detroit plants as compared to only .825 percent of the men in those plants. Briggs of Detroit had to increase the wages not only of 22.5 percent of its male employees but of all its 1,788 women workers. By September 1934 predepression wage levels had been restored in the automobile industry: women factory workers were receiving an average of 47.6 cents per hour, 65.7 percent of the average hourly rate of 72.4 cents paid to men. Women, however, remained concentrated at the bottom of the industry's wage scale. During April 1934, 85.5 percent of the women in the industry but only 22.5 percent of the men had average earnings of less than 60 cents an hour.[8]

In addition to the differential between male and female jobs, women also received less pay than men for the same work. A 1925 Bureau of Labor Statistics study found that wages for men and women in the same occupational classification were consistently unequal. On jobs performed by both men and women, women's hourly rate averaged 65.6 percent that of men. Female inspectors, sewing-machine operators, and trim bench hands, who composed 59 percent of the women surveyed, received, respectively, 53 percent,

8. BLS Bulletin No. 438, table A, pp. 26–36, and table 3, pp. 6–7; "Wages and Hours of Labor in the Motor-Vehicle Industry, 1932," *Monthly Labor Review* 36 (June 1933): 1369; N. A. Tolles and M. W. LaFever, "Wages, Hours, Employment, and Annual Earnings in the Motor-Vehicle Industry, 1934," *Monthly Labor Review* 42 (March 1936): 529, 547; Sidney Fine, *The Automobile under the Blue Eagle* (Ann Arbor, Mich., 1963), p. 123. Although NRA administrator Hugh Johnson, Secretary of Labor Frances Perkins, Women's Bureau director Mary Anderson, the National Women's Trade Union League, and Eleanor Roosevelt all opposed sex-differentiated wages, one-quarter of all the codes, covering nearly 17 percent of the workers in code industries, provided lower wages for women. Alice Kessler-Harris, *Out to Work* (New York, 1982), pp. 262–65. In assessing the impact of the auto code on women's wages, it is useful to note that 34.3 percent of the women and .55 percent of the men in eighteen specified occupations in the motor-vehicle industry in 1925 earned less than 40 cents per hour. BLS Bulletin No. 438, table 3, pp. 6–7.

59 percent, and 63 percent of the hourly rate earned by men in the same occupations. Female drill-press operators received 57.3 cents per hour, the highest hourly wage of all women surveyed; but their rate still fell 20 percent below that paid male drill-press operators. It is noteworthy that these women, the most favored in the female automotive labor force, constituted just 1 percent of all drill-press operators and only 3 percent of all female workers included in the study.[9]

The terms and conditions of employment in the auto industry helped fuel the rise of the UAW in the 1930s. In the space of six years, the UAW grew from a weak and ineffectual labor organization in an industry noted for its antiunionism into one of the largest and most important of the new industrial unions affiliated with the Congress of Industrial Organizations (CIO). The UAW had only 22,687 dues-paying members when the American Federation of Labor (AFL) united the industry's federal labor unions in August 1935. Within a year the UAW threw off the jurisdictional limitations imposed by the AFL and joined the newly formed Committee for Industrial Organization. Using the sit-down strike as an organizational weapon, the UAW-CIO proceeded to win a number of important victories, most notably over General Motors following a forty-four-day strike during the winter of 1936–1937. The success of the sit-down strategy was evidenced by the tremendous increase in the union's dues-paying membership, from about 88,000 in February 1937 to nearly 400,000 by the middle of October. The UAW won recognition from Chrysler Corporation in 1939 and, after a protracted, bitter, and at times bloody struggle, from Ford Motor Company in the spring of 1941. In the fall of 1941, on the eve of America's entrance into World War II, the UAW claimed more than a half million dues-paying members, 8 percent of whom were women.[10]

9. BLS Bulletin No. 438, table A, pp. 26–36, and table 3, pp. 6–7.

10. Membership figures for 1935 cited in Fine, *The Automobile under the Blue Eagle*, p. 407; for 1937 in Fine, *Sit-Down*, p. 327; and for 1941 in *Proceedings of the 1941 Convention of the International Union, United Automobile Workers of America, August 4–15, 1941* (hereafter cited as *1941 Convention Proceedings*), p. 3. In 1935 the motor-vehicle industry ranked first among all manufacturing industries in the United States in terms of the number of wage earners it employed. A total of 387,801 women and men worked in the industry's 946 factories. Although each of the forty-eight states contained at least one auto-manufacturing establishment, the industry was concentrated in eight states, which together included 73 percent of the nation's auto plants and 90.5 percent of the industry's wage earners. New York, Pennsylvania, Illinois, Wisconsin, and California contained 56,788 auto workers, 15 percent of the national total. The second and third most important states in the manufacture of motor vehicles were Ohio and Indiana, which had, respectively, 34,861 and 22,856 auto workers, or 8.5 percent and 6 percent

The birth of the UAW was a prominent feature of the emergence of unionism in the mass-production industries during the 1930s. Only 3 million workers, representing 6 percent of the total labor force, were members of unions in 1933. Labor strength was limited to a few industries, principally coal mining, building construction, the railroads, the public utilities, and the garment trades. Within eight years the number of workers belonging to unions tripled and their proportion of the wage-earning labor force rose to 18 percent. The breakthrough occurred in the mass-production industries. Under the aegis of the AFL's Committee for Industrial Organization and, after 1938, the independent CIO, workers in the iron and steel, rubber, electrical-products, food-processing, and automobile industries for the first time formed successful and durable unions, which gained a central place in the American economy by 1945.[11]

The birth of the CIO promised to change the historically negative relationship between women and the labor movement. Although women constituted about 25 percent of the labor force in 1930, less than 3 percent of all wage-earning women were union members and less than 9 percent of the AFL's members were women. The AFL's practice of organizing workers by craft accounted in part for the limited extent of unionization among women, long excluded from skilled trades. In contrast to the AFL's exclusivity, the CIO adopted an inclusive organizing policy. Committed to organizing all workers on a plant- and industrywide basis, the CIO ignored distinctions among workers based on skill and job assignment as well as differences based on ascriptive characteristics such as race and sex. This democratic organizing principle combined with the decision to unionize workers in the largely unorganized mass-production industries brought thousands of women into the ranks of organized labor. Female membership in unions increased threefold in the 1930s, from

---

of the industry's manufacturing wage earners. Michigan was the center of the industry, with 157 factories and 238,845 wage earners—61 percent of all auto workers in the United States. The industry was further centralized within Michigan; half of the state's auto-manufacturing establishments were located in the Detroit area, and these plants employed 154,462 wage earners—65 percent of all Michigan auto workers and two-fifths of all auto workers in the nation. Bureau of the Census, *Biennial Census of Manufactures: 1935* (Washington, D.C., 1938), pp. 34, 1150.

11. For the history of the labor movement during the 1930s, see Irving Bernstein, *The Turbulent Years* (Boston, 1970); Walter Galenson, *The CIO Challenge to the AFL* (Cambridge, Mass., 1960); Robert H. Zieger, *American Workers, American Unions, 1920–1985* (Baltimore, 1986), pp. 3–99.

265,000 to 800,000, and the proportion of the female labor force that was unionized rose to 6 percent.[12]

The CIO, however, did not accord the organizing of women a high priority in the 1930s. Its principal concern was to unionize the heretofore unorganized basic industries, and in none of them did women represent more than a minority of production workers. The CIO did not exclude women, but neither did it actively and conscientiously recruit them.[13] Auto-assembly and body plants, for example, were the focus of the UAW's first campaigns in the mid-1930s. The heart of the industry, these plants employed relatively few women. Representing just 5 percent of the operatives in auto-assembly plants and 10 percent of those in body plants, women also were segregated in one or a few nearly all-female departments. At best, women were an afterthought. "We must not only remember the stock boys," suggested a male worker at the close of a strategy meeting for union organizers of the Fisher Body plant in Cleveland, "we must take the girls in the sewing room into consideration." At worst, male organizers decided that the low number and isolation of women did not warrant efforts to mobilize them in support of a union.[14]

The treatment accorded women by the men who organized the Midland Steel Products Company in Detroit in 1936 typifies the attitude toward female workers of the CIO generally and the UAW particularly. According to Henry Kraus, the local union debated whether to approach the women working in the plant, but "a stool pigeon who was very influential in that local was able to scotch it." Recalling that John Anderson, the local leader, had opposed the decision not to organize the women, Kraus observes, "It seems strange . . . that stronger efforts hadn't been made to do something about it. . . . [Anderson] certainly could have said 'To hell with that. . . . Our principle is to bring women into the union, and we should.'" Although Anderson supported the proposal to organize the women in the plant, he likely did not deem it an important priority for the fledgling local union, since nearly all the women

12. Gladys Dickason, "Women in Labor Unions," *Annals of the American Academy of Political and Social Science* 251 (May 1947): 71.

13. Sharon Hartman Strom, "Challenging 'Woman's Place': Feminism, the Left, and Industrial Unionism in the 1930s," *Feminist Studies* 9 (Summer 1983): 359–86.

14. William H. McPherson, *Labor Relations in the Automobile Industry* (Washington, D.C., 1940), p. 9; minutes of the First Meeting of Trim Shop Employees, n.d. [1930s], Charles Beckman Collection, Box 10, Folder 13, Walter P. Reuther Library, Archives of Labor and Urban Affairs, Wayne State University, Detroit (hereafter cited as ALUA).

employees were segregated in one predominantly female department.[15]

When workers at Midland Steel staged a sit-down strike on November 27, 1936, the men on the strike committee told the female employees to leave the plant. Never having been approached by organizers, the women were confused by the directive and distressed by the strike. Dorothy Kraus recalls that the women workers were "actually bewildered. They didn't know what in the world was going to take place, they were concerned about whether they were going to be able to start working again soon." Assuming responsibility for mobilizing the women workers, Kraus encouraged them to participate in the strike kitchen she organized to provide food for the sit-downers. Had Kraus not taken this action, the women at Midland Steel would have been unable to share with their male co-workers the pride of having contributed to what the UAW described at the time as "the most significant union victory in the history of the automobile industry in Detroit."[16]

The treatment accorded female workers in sit-down strikes, a principal organizing tactic in 1936 and 1937, indicates that the UAW ignored women for reasons other than the pragmatic management of limited resources. The common practice of ordering women workers to leave plants during the sit-downs was, to a certain extent, a justifiable precautionary measure. Organizers rightly feared that employers would exploit the presence of women in the struck plants to their own advantage, sensationalizing the sharing of living quarters and discrediting the union in the eyes of the public. They also were aware of the importance of maintaining the morale of the sit-downers' wives and families outside the plants and did not want to arouse their jealousy and suspicion. Although understandable from the point of view of public relations, the exclusion of female workers from body and assembly plants during sit-down strikes also betrayed the UAW's insensitivity toward the desire of women to be involved in strikes and its ambivalence about promoting intergender solidarity.

For their part, many female workers preferred to leave the plants to attend to their domestic responsibilities. Other women, however,

15. Interview with Dorothy and Henry Kraus, September 7, 1978, pp. 31, 43, The Twentieth Century Trade Union Woman: Vehicle for Social Change Oral History Project, Institute of Labor and Industrial Relations, University of Michigan, Ann Arbor.

16. Ibid., p. 29; Fine, Sit-Down, pp. 129–30. (Throughout the book I have reproduced quoted material accurately, including grammatical and other errors.)

notably those who were not ignored during organizing drives, objected to being excluded. At the GM Fisher Body plant in Cleveland, Ohio, for example, a concerted effort was made to organize the hundreds of women employed in the trim department. So committed were the women to the union by the time of the sit-down strike that many of them resisted leaving the plant. "We had a problem getting them out," recalls Charles Beckman, a founder and long-time leader of Local 45. During a January 1937 sit-down at Bohn Aluminum in Detroit, women were so adamant that they flatly refused to leave the factory. Patricia Wiseman, who had been employed in the Fisher 1 plant in Flint, Michigan, for six years at the time of the GM sit-down strike, indicated her resentment at being excluded from the plant. Asserting that her proper place was with the workers inside the plant, not in the strike kitchen, Wiseman refused to assist with food preparation and instead assumed daily picket duty outside the plant. When a male picketer taunted her for such unfeminine behavior, Wiseman retorted, "You're getting fifteen dollars a week more than I am for the same number of hours and I'll be damned if I don't work as hard as you do!"[17]

Automotive-parts plants employed a greater absolute and relative number of women than did auto-body and assembly plants. Representing 20 percent of the industry's parts workers and an even greater percentage of the workers in particular plants, women in such plants constituted an important source of union strength, and their participation could prove crucial to the success of organizing drives and strikes. The UAW, however, initially preferred to sacrifice organizational gains in parts plants with a predominantly female work force. At the height of the drive in 1937 to organize the workers of General Motors, for example, the UAW had no plans to organize the Ternstedt plant, the largest plant on Detroit's west side. A division of General Motors that produced small auto parts and accessories, Ternstedt was the largest single employer of female auto workers in Detroit. When Stanley Nowak, the union's Polish language organizer, who had been successful in organizing women cigar makers in Detroit, suggested that Ternstedt be organized, the executive board of the UAW's west side local (Local 174), believing women

17. Interview with Charles Beckman, July 25, 1961, p. 8, UAW Oral History Project; interview with Catherine Gelles, July 7, 1961, ibid., pp. 2–3; Henry Kraus, *The Many and the Few* (Los Angeles, 1947), pp. 97–98; Patricia Yeghissian, "Emergence of the the Red Berets," *Michigan Occasional Papers in Women's Studies* 10 (Winter 1980): 18.

to be unsympathetic to unionism, expressed doubts about the chances for success, since nearly half the plant's twelve thousand employees were female.[18]

The union's reluctance to organize female parts workers also was evident in its dilatory and, in some respects, inept attempt to organize the AC Spark Plug Division of General Motors in Flint. At the time of the GM strike, about half of AC's 4,900 workers were women. Because AC Spark Plug employees were largely unorganized, the UAW did not call on them to strike. Although the strike committee explained the decision to the men working at AC, it did not bother to provide a similar explanation to the women. Laura Hayward, an AC worker at the time, recalls, "The men told the men that, and they kind of sent it through to stay on the job." Toward the end of the strike, the UAW, realizing the importance of unionizing all the General Motors plants in Flint, began to pay attention to the problems of women working at AC Spark Plug. A special AC edition of the strike newspaper, *Punch Press*, issued on February 11, 1937, stressed the need for equal pay for equal work, criticized management's treatment of women, called attention to the unionizing of women in the Kelsey Hayes plant in Detroit, and appealed to women to join the union. The strike committee, however, did little more to demonstrate its interests in the problems of women workers.[19]

Despite the disinterest of the UAW's male leadership, women themselves, working alone or with the encouragement and assistance of a few sympathetic men, undertook the organization of auto-parts plants. After the GM strike was settled in February 1937, Irene Mitchell, Laura Hayward, Rose Webber, and Nellie Besson, a group described by Henry Kraus as "the best missionaries at the AC plant," enlisted the support of their fellow employees for the UAW. Several weeks after the Local 174 executive board reluctantly appointed

18. McPherson, *Labor Relations in the Automobile Industry*, p. 9; Ruth Meyerowitz, "Organizing the United Automobile Workers: Women Workers at the Ternstedt General Motors Parts Plant," in Ruth Milkman, ed., *Women, Work, and Protest* (Boston, 1985), pp. 235–58. On the organization of female cigar makers in Detroit in the 1930s, see Jane Dobija, "Voices of Struggle: Working Women in Detroit," *Ms.*, September 1982, p. 21; Steve Babson, *Working Detroit* (Detroit, 1986), pp. 76–77.

19. Joseph Geschelin, "Improved Working Conditions Cut Costs in New AC Plant," *Automotive Industries* 74 (February 1, 1936): 151; Geschelin, "Method Study Promotes AC Operating Economics," p. 644; Fine, *Sit-Down*, p. 119; Hayward quoted in Ruth Meyerowitz, "Women in the UAW, 1935–1945," unpublished manuscript in author's possession, pt. 1, pp. 37, 47, 100–2; *Punch Press* 1 (February 11, 1937), UAW Local Union 156 Collection, Miscellaneous Publications Box, *Punch Press* Folder, ALUA.

Stanley Nowak as organizer at Ternstedt, management was forced to negotiate with the new union. Nowak had recruited a core group of union-minded women from the plant to mobilize their co-workers. They were so successful that the plant was organized by the unusual means of a slowdown, a strategy that depended on the willingness of women to cooperate in reducing production. The results of NLRB elections held at General Motors plants in April 1940 demonstrated the effectiveness of female organizers and confirmed women's commitment to unionization: 60 percent of the 3,667 AC workers and 88 percent of the 8,439 Ternstedt employees who voted in the election cast their ballots for the UAW-CIO.[20]

The successes of women organizers compelled male unionists to reassess their ideas about the prospects of organizing women in auto plants. Recognizing the effectiveness in this regard of female organizers, the UAW employed women unionists in organizing drives at several auto-parts factories. Margaret Purnia, recording secretary of Local 12 in Toledo, Ohio, assisted with an organizing campaign at Buckeye Spring and Bumper, a factory in Springfield, Ohio, which employed a significant number of women, helping to ensure the victory of UAW Local 402 in a September 1940 NLRB election. Irene Young, a veteran of the organizational drive at Ternstedt in Detroit, recruited female parts workers during 1940 NLRB election campaigns at New Departure plants in Connecticut and at the Ternstedt factory in Trenton, New Jersey. Speaking "woman to woman," Young emphasized the particular benefits of unionization for female employees, such as contractual provisions for maternity leave without loss of accumulated seniority.[21]

As they undertook the task of bringing women into the UAW, female organizers displayed greater sensitivity toward women's needs than did men. Certainly women were no less organizable than men, the attitudes of the Local 174 executive board and other male leaders notwithstanding. Too, women in auto plants had the same grievances as men, such as low wages, speedups, and arbitrary

20. Kraus, *The Many and the Few*, p. 172; Meyerowitz, "Organizing the UAW"; Interview with Stanley Nowak, June 2, 1960, pp. 11–13, UAW Oral History Project; *Detroit News*, April 16, 1937; *Detroit Free Press*, April 16, 1937; National Labor Relations Board (NLRB), *Decisions and Orders of the NLRB*, vol. 24 (Washington D.C., 1940), pp. 159–203.

21. *United Auto Worker (UAW)*, October 1, 1940; Irene Young, "As Woman to Woman!" *Local 110–Local 626 New Departure Employee News Bulletin* 1 (March 23, 1940): 6, Walter P. Reuther Collection, Box 22, Folder 4, ALUA.

hiring and firing practices; and these grievances became the basis for unionization. Women, however, seemed to require special organizing methods, particularly in plants where they were completely separated from men. Nellie Besson recalls that women at the AC Spark Plug plant in Flint "were sort of timid, even after they had the strike and we'd won the point. . . . They were still a little bit afraid." Given the antiunion practices of GM and the desultory efforts of the union strike committee with respect to organizing the women, such a response was not surprising. Although many men were fearful of unionizing, some women had to acquire the confidence to challenge the precepts of gender ideology as well as the prerogatives of management. Women unionists dealt with these obstacles by organizing exclusively female social activities to provide arenas in which women could assert themselves without fear of male criticism or condescension and develop the feelings of solidarity that collective action requires. "That was about the best way to do it with the biggest share of them," Besson explains. "The only way you could win someone was to get them out on social activities and from there they emerged." By contrast, the labor force at Ternstedt was sexually integrated, women and men working side by side. Female organizers were an important factor in unionizing Ternstedt, but no single-sex social activities were required to convince women of the importance of labor organization. The familiarity between the sexes on the shop floor must have served to erase the barriers and ease the concerns that separated women from men at AC Spark Plug.[22]

The struggle to organize two automobile-parts and accessories plants in Anderson, Indiana, in the late 1930s further illustrates both the prospects and the problems of women's relationship to unionism in the 1930s. Part of the GM empire, the Delco Remy and Guide Lamp plants together employed 11,000 production workers, of whom 40 percent were women. Anderson was the site of much antiunion violence during the 1936–1937 strike against General Motors. The union headquarters were sacked, local police threatened out-of-town organizers with arrest and injury, pickets suffered harassment and assault, and a UAW victory meeting was held under siege without police protection by an antiunion crowd for almost twelve hours. In

22. Besson quoted in Meyerowitz, "Women in the UAW," p. 117; Geschelin, "Improved Working Conditions Cut Costs in New AC Plant"; "Production High Spots at Ternstedt," *Automotive Industries* 73 (July 13, 1935): 42, 45.

light of its experience during the strike, it is not surprising that the UAW found it difficult to secure its position in the Anderson plants after the strike was settled. After two years of union-building efforts, the UAW launched a vigorous membership drive in anticipation of the April 1940 corporationwide NLRB election. Although men also were the target of the intensive campaign, women received some special attention. Astutely noting that women had concerns that men did not, Bob Travis, the UAW organizer sent to Anderson during the union drive, called a meeting for women only and invited a Detroit physician to discuss women's health problems and answer questions about the safety of pregnant and postpartal women at work. In the final weeks before the election, a series of women's meetings were held and a flyer was circulated by the union calling upon women to "protect your own interest [and] vote UAW-CIO" and vowing to press for "equal pay for women who perform the same work as men." In the April election, a majority of Guide Lamp workers voted for the UAW-CIO. At Delco Remy, however, 2,454 voters chose the UAW-CIO, 688 the contending UAW-AFL, and 2,774 neither of them.[23]

Confronted with its failure to win the support of a majority of Delco Remy production workers, the UAW-CIO tried again. This time, greater efforts were made to recruit female workers. In contrast to the Guide Lamp factory, where women worked alongside men, Delco Remy segregated most of its female labor force in two huge departments. Seeking to improve its chances with these women, the UAW dispatched Patricia Wiseman to Anderson especially to organize them. Wiseman, who in June 1940 became the UAW's representative on the United States Women's Bureau Labor Advisory Committee, wrote to Mary Anderson, director of the bureau, describing how she applied the lessons she and other union women had learned about the way to mobilize female workers. "They seem to be a little slower to grasp the need of Unionism then the men," Wiseman stated, "but tonite we are putting on a Style Show . . . and have all Remy girl

23. Fine, *Sit-Down*, pp. 211–16, 313–17; minutes of GM Sub Council 4 meeting, December 10, 1939, and January 7, 1940, Cecil Roeder Collection, Box 3, GM Sub Council 4 Minutes Oct. 29, 1939–Nov. 3, 1940 Folder, ALUA; Walter Reuther to Leroy Roberts, January 11, 1940, Walter Reuther Collection, Box 25, Folder 16; George Berkebile reports to UAW GM Department, January 20, 1940, February 19, 1940, and March 6, 22, 27, 1940, ibid., Box 20, Folder 5; "Everybody's Doing It—Vote UAW-CIO," flyer, n.d. [April 1940], Roeder Collection, Box 2, Local 662 Union Shop Drives Education Material Folder; NLRB, *Decisions and Orders of the NLRB*, vol. 24, pp. 159–203, and vol. 27, (Washington, D.C., 1942), pp. 591–98.

doing the modeling, and of course their friends and family's come out to see them and that promotes good will and from there we do the rest." The presence of Wiseman and her use of methods designed not only to appeal specifically to women but to encourage women to identify with a largely male-oriented organization were effective. In November 1940 the adverse representation decision at Delco Remy was reversed in favor of the UAW-CIO, which received 62 percent of the 6,292 valid votes cast. At the election victory celebration, Arnold Atwood, the UAW regional director, praised "the splendid work" of Wiseman.[24]

The success of organizing drives in auto-parts plants demonstrated that women auto workers were organizable. The UAW, however, did not apply the lessons learned by its female organizers in any thoroughgoing or systematic way in the years before World War II. "I think," a UAW male organizer stated candidly at the 1939 convention, "there is altogether too much a feeling in this organization that the women are rather a nuisance except during a strike or some time when we need their help." Some defended the inattention to women by emphasizing their paucity in the most important divisions of the auto industry. Others alleged the greater difficulty, if not impossibility, of organizing women. Few, however, cared to assess either the reasons for the gender difference or the validity of the arguments. George Addes, secretary-treasurer of the UAW in this period, came close when he commented in retrospect, "Women seemed to feel that a union was an organization for men, consequently, it was hard to bring them into the fold." Female unionists recognized that the UAW was regarded as "no woman's land" in the years before World War II and sought by various means to circumvent the problem, organizing meetings and social events that provided women with their own space within the male-dominated union. Organizers also addressed issues of particular concern to women to demonstrate the value of unionization to female workers. The UAW, however, did not take advantage of these insights to formulate a specific program for interesting women in unionism. In contrast to the attention it paid to organizing the industry's black workers, who were overwhelmingly

24. Minutes of GM Sub Council 4 meeting, February 4, 1940, Roeder Collection, Box 3, GM Sub Council 4 Minutes Oct. 29, 1939–Nov. 3, 1940 Folder; Local Union 662 Report, May 20, 1944, RG 86/NA, Box 1703, Union Schedules Folder; Winifred P[atricia] Cooper [Wiseman] to Mary Anderson, December 3, 1940, ibid., Box 867, Auto Workers Folder; *UAW*, November 1, 1940.

male, the UAW employed female unionists as organizers only on an ad hoc rather than a permanent basis and generally left the task of organizing women to the women themselves.[25]

After the organizational period, women again confounded their detractors and actively participated in the establishment of local unions. Although information about women's activity as local union officers and shop-floor leaders is scanty, available evidence indicates that such activity, if not extensive, was neither uncommon nor insignificant. Active involvement in successful organizing drives inspired women to seek election to local union office. Proudly announcing that Local 431 had just won an NLRB election granting it exclusive bargaining rights at Fry Products in Detroit, Josephine Pazik delightedly told the delegates to the 1939 convention: "I am very glad to be here, boys. This is the first time I have been in a convention and I can't express my appreciation to be here." Buoyed by her experience, Pazik successfully ran for the office of vice-president in the first election at Local 431. Like Pazik, other women who played key roles in organizing auto-parts plants achieved prominence as leaders in their locals. Irene Young, for example, was elected recording secretary of Local 174 in March 1938; represented Ternstedt in the Local 174 delegation at the 1937, 1939, and 1940 conventions; and was a member of the Detroit delegation at the International GM Council meetings held in Detroit in June 1940. The union's neglect of women during organizing campaigns in body and assembly plants, furthermore, delayed but did not preclude the entry of women into the leadership ranks. Patricia Wiseman, to cite a notable example, was one of eight delegates elected to represent Local 156 at the 1937 convention. Wiseman, whose "deep voice . . . command[ed] as much respect as that of any male in the union's councils," also achieved distinction as the sole woman on the union's bargaining committee during the General Motors–UAW conference that followed the 1936–1937 strike.[26]

---

25. *Proceedings of the Special Convention of the International Union, United Automobile Workers of America, March 27–April 6, 1939* (hereafter cited as *1939 Convention Proceedings*), p. 722; interview with George Addes, June 25, 1960, p. 5, UAW Oral History Project; *UAW*, March 1, 1943. For an account of the UAW's efforts to organize black workers, see August Meier and Elliott Rudwick, *Black Detroit and the Rise of the UAW* (Oxford, 1979), pp. 34–107. Black women were not employed in production work in the auto industry until World War II.

26. The poor quality of local union records for the late 1930s precludes a precise determination of the extent to which women held leadership positions. I have culled

Other women became involved in local union affairs after the initial period of organization and recognition. The sex-segregated structure of work in body and assembly plants to a certain extent proved an advantage to women seeking union posts in those plants. Among the many women elected stewards or bargaining-committee representatives by co-workers in predominantly female departments were Mary Michael of Midland Steel Local 410 and Helen Gage of Packard Local 190. Conversely, women in such plants rarely served on local executive boards as presidents or vice-presidents, since elections for these positions were conducted on a plantwide basis. Women in body and assembly plants did serve, however, as recording secretaries and secretary-treasurers, jobs likely viewed as particularly appropriate to women. The greater absolute and relative number of women in auto-parts plants improved the prospects for women interested in attaining leadership positions. The predominantly female membership of Local 431 in February 1940 elected not only Josephine Pazik as vice-president but Hilda Elliott as secretary-treasurer, Magdalene Salmeto as sergeant-at-arms, and Mary Wegenech and Josephine Jordan as trustees. The leadership of Local 651, which represented the employees at AC Spark Plug, included a number of women; Irene Mitchell, an organizer in the plant in 1937, was elected recording secretary in 1939 and financial secretary in 1940, a position she held throughout the 1940s.[27]

Women served their constituents well, providing strong and effective union leadership. It was not an easy task. "These women don't need a steward," Ellie Cox told the president of Local 45 in 1937. "They need someone with a *club*." The challenge provided by a tough managerial stance did not daunt Cox and her fellow steward in the trim department, Rose Jalovec. During a meeting of the Local 45

information about women unionists from a variety of sources, including union convention proceedings, union newspapers, and local and international union records. Information on Pazik comes from *1939 Convention Proceedings*, p. 585, and *UAW*, February 28, 1940; on Young from *UAW*, March 19, 1938, *1937 Convention Proceedings*, *1939 Convention Proceedings*, *Proceedings of the Fifth Annual Convention of the International Union, United Automobile Workers of America, July 29–August 6, 1940* (hereafter cited as *1940 Convention Proceedings*), and Delegates Expense Report, UAW General Motors Department Collection, Series I, Box 1, Letters to Locals 1940 Folder, ALUA; on Wiseman from *1937 Convention Proceedings*, from Kraus, *The Many and the Few*, p. 97, and from *UAW*, June 12, 1937.

27. Information on Michael comes from *UAW*, April 2, 1938; on Gage from *UAW*, March 4, 1939; on Local 431 from *UAW*, February 28, 1940; on Mitchell from *UAW*, March 13, 1939, and *UAW Fair Practices Fact Sheet* 1 (August–September 1947): 3.

negotiating committee with the management of the Fisher Body plant in Cleveland in 1938, Jalovec contested a reduction in the piece rate for women who sewed auto headlinings. Management's response indicates that women as well as men exercised control over their work by collectively restricting production. "Probably the fact that each of these girls on this job produced the same amount every day during last year," one manager contended, "shows that they controlled production and that might have something to do with the cut." Pat Wiseman, then chief steward in the cut-and-sew department at the Fisher 1 plant in Flint, boasted similarly at a UAW GM Council meeting in 1940: "We have no set rate of production. They tried to make us do so much per hour, but we just come in and do what we feel is a fair day's work, and that is all we do and all we are going to do." Women's militancy did not go unrecognized. Congratulating Local 190 for having obtained "one of the finest pacts in the industry" from the Packard Motor Car Company, the *United Auto Worker* applauded the contribution of local activists such as Helen Gage and noted that among the local's eleven thousand members were five hundred women who "are as staunch unionists as their male fellow workers." Eager to impress upon the members of the Women's Bureau Labor Advisory Committee the important role played by women in establishing the UAW in the auto industry, Wiseman explained that "since labor has been organized in auto the women have been a very militant group of people." "We had three shut-downs in my department in two weeks," she added, "and raised the standard of women's wages." Declared Wiseman, "If you want to see some militant union people, come up to Flint."[28]

Although women were not absent from the ranks of the union's leadership, they did not hold office in proportion to their numbers at either the local or international level of the UAW.[29] Women's domestic responsibilities accounted in part for the discrepancy between rates of male and female office holding. Another reason for women's

28. Cox to Beckman, April 7, 1937, Charles Beckman Collection, Box 3, Folder 7, ALUA; minutes of Negotiating Committee Meeting with Plant Management, September 22, 1938, p. 2, ibid., Box 10, Folder 2; Job Lists Fisher Body 1, n.d. [1940], UAW Local 602 Collection, Box 1, Folder 29, ALUA; *UAW*, December 10, 1938; transcript of Labor Advisory Committee conference, June 1940, pp. 11, 15, RG 86/NA, Box 1714, June 4, 1940 Conference Folder.

29. Although they represented 8 percent of the union's membership, women composed, for example, only 3.6 percent, 4.1 percent, and 2.5 percent, respectively, of the delegates to the 1936, 1937, and 1939 conventions.

lesser activity was the opposition of husbands and fathers to the participation of wives and daughters. But consistent with the union's general neglect of such matters, the union did not address the barriers to women's participation, failing, for example, to arrange for child care during union meetings. Despite evidence that women as a group were no less capable as leaders than men, the UAW did not consider formulating a special program to interest and encourage women as officers. Concern was occasionally expressed about more fully integrating women into the union. The Local 45 executive board, for example, once offered Ellie Cox encouragement and promised to "make her feel at home and to give her all the aid we possibly can, in order to get the women to take a more active part in the Union."[30] Neither the predominantly male leadership of Local 45 nor that of the UAW in general, however, made any systematic effort to increase the number of female leaders in the union in the years before World War II.

The limited voice and influence of women in the UAW meant that their collective-bargaining interests were generally defined by men. Male unionists, however, did address some issues of exclusive concern to women, such as sexual harassment by foremen. A woman worker at the Midland Steel plant explained to Frank Marquart that she had joined the UAW local in the plant not, as he expected, because of her higher wages but because "when you belong to a union, the foreman can't screw you." "Last month my foreman asked me to go out with him," she told Marquart, "[and] I told him 'to hell with you, Charlie, I know what you want.' He got mad, but he didn't try to spite me. He knew damn well the union would be on his neck if he did."[31] Men also were not wholly indifferent to women's interest in responsible leadership on the shop floor, and they pressed women's grievances concerning low wage rates and bad working conditions. But although the UAW's stand on issues such as sexual harassment and its advocacy of female members' job interests promoted trade-union loyalty among women, its policies with regard to wage determination, job classification, and seniority tended to protect the interests of men, often at the expense of those of women.

The UAW, for example, was not unmindful of the problem of

30. Minutes of Local 45 Executive Board meeting, April 29, 1939, Beckman Collection, Box 10, Folder 1.
31. Frank Marquart, *An Auto-Worker's Journal* (University Park, Pa., 1972), p. 72.

women auto workers' low wages and publicly emphasized the fact. Walter Reuther called the announcement by the Yale and Towne Company in May 1937 that it would close its Detroit plant if its striking employees did not return to work "a piece of supreme treachery toward a group of underpaid, exploited women" and denounced "the adamant and niggardly attitude" of the company in regard to wages. Because the wages of so many female auto workers were at the bottom of the auto-industry wage scale, the early successes of the UAW in raising wage minimums in plants under contract with the union were especially beneficial to women. The *United Auto Worker* reported that as a consequence of the new hourly minimums of 62 cents for women and 72 cents for men established by the 1939 agreement between UAW Local 9 and the Bendix Corporation plant in South Bend, Indiana, "the 750 women workers all get raises and many men also benefit by the new minimums." By 1940 not only had wage rates in the auto industry increased substantially but the differential between women's and men's wages had diminished somewhat. Women workers in auto-body and assembly plants in that year received an average 72 cents per hour, or 74 percent of the men's average hourly rate of 96.7 cents. Women employed in automotive-parts plants earned an average 61.9 cents per hour, giving them 70 percent of the average male rate of 88.6 cents per hour.[32]

Despite the UAW's success in narrowing the sex differential, however, women's wages remained concentrated around their average to a greater degree than did men's. The wages of women employed in 1940 in all processing occupations were all within 4 cents of the 72.2-cent-per-hour average for the women in these occupations, but just half of the men in processing jobs earned within 3 cents of the 95.5-cent-per-hour average for their jobs. The practice of differentiating wages on the basis of sex was of course historically prevalent in all industries. The idea that women's work by definition merited lower wages than work performed by men was almost universally accepted despite the fact that the judgment rarely was derived from any objective standards of evaluation. According to William McPherson, a specialist on labor-management relations in the automobile industry, since some male occupations were the least skilled in any auto plant, the differential between male and female wages could be

32. *UAW*, May 22, 1937, and September 13, 1939; BLS Bulletin No. 706, table 10, pp. 23–24, and table 16, pp. 31–38.

accounted for only to a small degree by the difference in the relative skill requirements of women's and men's jobs. The amount of time required to learn an auto job also was irrelevant, since, by the 1930s, most work in the auto industry was not of a highly skilled character. Of all the occupations in the industry, 26.9 percent required no experience and only 9.8 percent required more than one year of training or experience. Commenting on the seemingly arbitrary methods of wage determination in the auto industry in the 1930s insofar as gender was concerned, McPherson concluded that the sex differential "must be explained largely in terms of custom." Like most other unions, the UAW fully endorsed this custom and the notion of gender hierarchy on which it was based. On occasion the UAW even invoked the principle of the differential to justify its demand for higher wages for male workers. The *United Auto Worker* printed a photograph in 1935 showing four men dressed in women's clothing and carrying signs reading "Help the Poor Woikin Goil—Vote CIO" and "Vote CIO—Restore Our Manhood." The accompanying caption explained that the men were "dressed in girl's clothes because the company paid them women's rates" and noted that the victory for the CIO union in an NLRB election "brought a new contract and men's wages." The UAW's fundamental commitment to the principle of gender hierarchy in the organization of work meant that the union would not seek pay equity for auto workers regardless of sex and that it would not press in any thoroughgoing way even for equal pay for strictly equal work.[33]

Management resistance was admittedly responsible in large part for the persistence of unequal wages for women and men. A suit brought by twenty-nine women employed at the Olds Motor Works in Lansing, Michigan, against GM in 1937 illustrates how resolute was employer opposition to the principle of equal pay for equal work. Charging GM with violating a 1931 state law stipulating that women and men who performed the same work were to receive equal pay, the women contended that management used arbitrary standards in job classification and wage determination. Although four women who worked on the touch-up and stripe job in the paint shop had trained the new male employees the company assigned to

33. BLS Bulletin No. 706, table 10, pp. 23–24, and table 16, pp. 31–38; McPherson, *Labor Relations in the Automobile Industry*, pp. 8, 84; United States Employment Service, *Job Specifications for the Automobile-Manufacturing Industry, June 1935*, 3 vols. (Washington, D.C., 1935); Milkman, *Gender at Work*, pp. 33–48; *UAW*, September 13, 1939.

this work, the men received higher wages. Most of the women had operated punch presses in the small-press room, a subdivision of the sheet-metal department. Although disinterested witnesses attested that the women produced the same quality and quantity of work as the men similarly employed in the room, the women were receiving 75 cents per hour and the men 97 cents per hour in 1937. To add insult to injury, male employees received raises whenever women did, but women did not always receive raises when men did. In 1937, for example, all the men in the sheet-metal department received a raise, but not one women did. So concerned was GM to preserve the wage differential that in September 1937, after the Michigan Department of Labor and Industry investigated the women's original complaint against the company, the plant management transferred all female workers to a newly created Women's Division in hopes of reifying a sexual division of labor.

In his decision upholding the women's claim, Judge Charles Hayden concluded, "Any differentiation urged as between the employment of men and women [by management] exists only in theory, rather than in fact; in form rather than in substance." Judge Hayden deemed the establishment of the Women's Division a wholly arbitrary and deceptive action, stating that not only were the jobs in the division previously performed by men but many women merely continued to do work in the new department which they had done elsewhere in the plant. Judge Hayden also dismissed GM's argument that because women had two fifteen-minute rest periods and the women's bathroom had a hot plate, a cot, several rocking chairs, and a mirror, women merited lower wages. Noting that regardless of the rest periods women were required to produce the same quality and quantity of work as the men on the same jobs, the judge added, "I am not impressed that the operation of [the equal-pay] statute is to be avoided by any difference in the appointment of toilets."[34]

Employer responsibility for the persistence of unequal wages for women and men performing the same work notwithstanding, union policy and practice tended to sanction rather than challenge management's line of action. During its first collective-bargaining conference with General Motors, the UAW demanded a uniform, companywide

34. "Opinion of the Court," in *Florence St. John v. General Motors Corporation*, Circuit Court, Ingham County, Michigan, May 29, 1942, RG 86/NA, Box 1469, AA Work for Equal Pay Folder. Judge Hayden ruled in favor of the plaintiff and awarded the twenty-nine women $55,690 in back pay.

minimum wage rate for all employees regardless of job classification, skill, sex, or race and, "in the name of justice and common sense," equal pay for equal work. "We hold," UAW vice-president Wyndham Mortimer stated, "that a woman doing the same work as a man (or just as valuable work) and a Negro doing the same work as a white man should be paid equally for that work, all other conditions being equal. Their services have equal value to the company—their compensation should be the same." General Motors successfully resisted the inclusion of both demands in the contract, refusing to redress the unequal-pay-for-equal-work grievance until the National War Labor Board compelled the company to do so in 1942. But despite its verbal commitment to equal pay for equal work, the UAW was inconsistent in its advocacy of equal pay for comparable or even equal work, tending to overlook or avoid the problem of unequal wage rates when men were not directly threatened. Because the union's support for the equal-pay principle was a defensive measure intended to protect the wages and jobs of men, the union pressed the issue only when employers attempted to replace male workers with women in order to reduce labor costs.[35]

A grievance filed by Local 212 in May 1941 exemplifies the UAW's approach to the issue of equal pay for equal work. Discovering that a woman in the predominantly female cut-and-sew department was receiving the female rate of 80 cents an hour on a job that was performed only by men elsewhere in the plant, the chief steward demanded that management properly classify the operation as male and accord it the male rate of $1 per hour. At the shop-committee meeting, the plant manager maintained that the woman's satisfactory performance of the job proved that it was a "girl's job" and that she should continue to receive the female rate. Although the union contended that the reclassification was necessary because the job was "[un]healthy for a woman," Don Sniveley, the shop-committee chairman, indicated the union's primary purpose when he stated, "I'm anxious . . . to perhaps give another man a job at a regular man's rate—not only that it is going to protect our classification here." Recognizing that Sniveley suspected management would continue to replace men with women and pay them the lower female rate, the plant manager warned: "You or I don't know what is coming. Maybe

35. "GM-Labor Conference Nears End," Automotive Industries 76 (March 6, 1937): 386; Fine, Sit-Down, pp. 324–25.

in the next couple of years we'll have girls on your job." This threat forced Sniveley into the uncomfortable position of defending the right of the woman to hold the job. "It's the question of the job," he stated. "If you can get a woman tough enough to run it and take a chance on physical conditions and everything, all the angles involved, I don't care who runs the job, but I do want to see the proper rate on it." Management, however, refused to pay the woman the higher rate. "As far as the job is concerned," the plant manager contended, "we're satisfied it is a girl's job." Sniveley quickly retreated from his defense of the equal-pay-for-equal-work principle and insisted once again that the job was too difficult for a woman. Conceding the argument, management replaced the female employee with a male worker and paid him the contractual rate of $1 per hour.[36]

Since both labor and management acted in defense of gender hierarchy, it is unsurprising that the wage differential between women and men in the same job classifications had narrowed but had not been eliminated by 1940. Women's hourly wage rate for jobs performed by both sexes in that year averaged 75 percent that of men. In auto-body and assembly plants, female small-parts assemblers and trimmers received 75.5 percent of male assemblers' and trimmers' rates; women employed as trim bench hands earned only 64 percent of the $1.028 per hour paid to male trim bench hands. The average differential between men's and women's wages in auto parts plants was 17 cents per hour. Female small-parts assemblers, who were nearly two-fifths of the women working in the parts division, earned 76 percent of the hourly rate paid men so employed (61.7 cents for women and 81.4 cents for men); and female punch-press operators, the fourth-largest category of women workers in this division, received 68.6 cents per hour, which, compared with the 85.3 cents per hour paid to male operators, meant a difference of 16.7 cents, or 20 percent.[37]

The same concern for men's jobs and wage standards shaped the UAW's approach to seniority rules. The new union set a seniority system governing transfer, layoff, and recall procedures in the auto industry as a major goal. Instead of the divisive, arbitrary, and some-

36. Grievance 1999, May 8, 1941, and Shop Committee meetings, May 12 and 19, 1941, in UAW Local 212 Collection, Box 11, Mack Ave. Grievances–1941 Folder, ALUA.
37. BLS Bulletin No. 706, table 10, pp. 23–24, and table 16, pp. 31–38.

times capricious standards imposed by employers, the UAW wanted length of service to be the sole consideration in determining job rights. Although the union's objective was best served by plantwide seniority, the more common arrangement was for seniority to be determined not only by length of service but by job classification or department as well. This formula, known as noninterchangeable occupational group seniority, in effect reinforced gender segregation, since jobs were labeled "male" or "female"; but most contracts nevertheless also specified separate noninterchangeable seniority lists for women and men. Although the policy was not intended to exclude women from the industry, it did serve to limit women's job opportunities in auto plants. But the UAW, despite its interest in plantwide seniority, did not question the institution of sex-differentiated lists. Indeed, the UAW became a staunch defender and advocate of separate lists as a means of preventing management from replacing men with women to realize savings in labor costs.[38]

The UAW's concern about the replacement of men by women was reinforced by the observations of contemporaries. The substitution of women for men had been a phenomenon in the auto industry since World War I, when labor shortages made necessary the increased employment of women. The practice persisted in the 1920s. In his critical study of the auto industry, Robert Dunn implied that the hiring of women at lower rates on jobs usually performed by men was extensive; he cited examples from the Packard, Murray Body, and Ford plants in the Detroit area and from the AC Spark Plug and Buick factories in Flint. High unemployment in the industry during the Great Depression intensified fears about the replacement of men by women. Elizabeth Christman, of the National Women's Trade Union League, warned Hugh Johnson, director of the National Recovery Administration (NRA), that auto manufacturers had sub-

38. Jonas Silver and Everett Kassalow, "Seniority in the Automobile Industry," BLS investigation, April 1944, copy in UAW War Policy Division Collection, Box 22, Seniority in Detroit UAW Locals Folder, ALUA. A study of collective bargaining published in 1960 described the origin and purpose of separate seniority lists for women and men. "This sex distinction, which usually was intended to restrict the competitive seniority status of women vis-à-vis men, was widespread twenty years ago. . . . These agreements were most common in the food industries . . . and in transportation equipment agreements. Under these seniority rosters, men competed only with men, and women competed for status only with women." The study added, "In these industries, the alleged noninterchangeability among occupational groups account[ed] for the separate seniority rosters for men and women." Sumner H. Slichter, James J. Healy, and E. Robert Livernash, The Impact of Collective Bargaining on Management (Washington, D.C., 1960), p. 135.

stituted women for men to reduce wages in striping, taping, core making, upholstering, spot welding, assembling, punch-press operating, and other machine operations. Auto workers themselves complained to the NRA that women were displacing men. Confirming this testimony, the NRA's own study of the auto industry reported, "There are many women now doing work that men did either a year ago or some years back." The overall stability in the proportion of women in the auto labor force in these years, however, belies claims for the great extent of substitution in the auto industry. Women's share of the auto labor force did increase from 7 to 10.5 percent during the 1930s, but not as much as one would expect if auto employers had a general policy of reducing the wage bill by replacing men with women.[39]

Regardless of the limited extent of displacement, the UAW acted on its perceptions of the problem. Delegates to the 1939 UAW convention adopted a resolution instructing union negotiators always to include a demand for "separate non-interchangeable seniority classification in the shop for men and women so that men cannot displace women and women cannot displace men on work." Not a single delegate dissented from the view that women's employment should be restricted. However, a male delegate from Local 7, which represented workers at the Chrysler Jefferson plant in Detroit, objected to the clause prohibiting men from replacing women. "It should be our utmost aim at all times," he stated, "to replace women with men on certain jobs that are undermining the health of women." The delegate, actually, was not so much concerned about the health of women auto workers as he was about Chrysler's increased use of women on machines, a practice that limited the number of jobs available to men. "This should not be allowed," the delegate stated. Joseph Mattson, one of the resolution's authors, assured the delegate that adoption of the resolution would not preclude a local union from insisting on the displacement of women by men. "The problem of the work itself,

39. David Gartman, *Auto Slavery* (New Brunswick, N.J., 1986), pp. 255–57; Robert K. Dunn, *Labor and Automobiles* (New York, 1929), p. 76; Christman to Johnson, February 28, 1934, Papers of the National Women's Trade Union League, Container 6, Library of Congress, Washington, D.C.; Fine, *The Automobile under the Blue Eagle*, pp. 362–68; Milkman, *Gender at Work*, pp. 31–32. Ruth Milkman explains the increase in women's share of the auto labor force as an artifact of shifts in product demand during the depression; demand declined less in the more significantly female auto-parts branch than in the predominantly male auto-assembly and body divisions of the industry. Milkman, *Gender at Work*, p. 32. See also Milkman, "Women's Work and Economic Crisis: Some Lessons from the Great Depression," *Review of Radical Political Economics* 8 (Spring 1976): 73–97.

and how it is done," Mattson explained, "is naturally up to the Bargaining Committee or whatever group they have that will take care of that specific case."[40]

Local 9 also objected to the seniority resolution because of a concern for its male members. "We have seen in the last five years," a delegate explained, "a steady encroachment of women on drill presses, punch presses and on the assembly line, where formerly only men did the work." This local preferred a single seniority list that included both women and men, as a means of restoring to men the jobs that management had given to women with less seniority. In proposing the institution of a single seniority list, Local 9 was challenging the rigid sexual division of labor in the auto industry. Rather than seeking a reclassification of so-called female jobs to make them available to men, as Mattson advised Local 7 to do, Local 9 rejected the very notion that jobs should be assigned on the basis of sex. But although the proposal had the potential to widen women's access to jobs in a plant, it was not intended to serve that purpose. In concluding his remarks, the delegate stated that the implementation of a single seniority list would eliminate "the female trouble in the shop." Although variations in local conditions may have prompted different devices to deal with the problem or threat of increased employment of women, the goal of male unionists was the same.[41]

The UAW's approach to wages and seniority reflected its acceptance of gender hierarchy in the workplace; the debate within the UAW over the employment of married women demonstrated the commitment of auto unionists to the same principle outside the plants. Although some employers preferred not to employ married women, either because they did not want to violate conventional notions of woman's proper place and arouse contemporary anxiety about men's unemployment or because they regarded wives and mothers as unstable and unreliable employees, more married than single women worked in auto plants in the 1930s. In Michigan, for example, of the 15,406 women employed in 1940 in production at auto plants, 4,316, or 28 percent, were single and 9,349, or 61 percent, were married.[42] Hiring practices, however, varied from plant to

40. *1939 Convention Proceedings*, p. 180.
41. Ibid., pp. 180–81.
42. The remaining 11 percent (1,741) were widowed or divorced. Bureau of the Census, *Sixteenth Census of the United States: 1940, Population*, vol. 2, pt. 3 (Washington, D.C., 1943), table 14, pp. 630–31.

plant, and many women concealed or lied about their marital status in order to obtain and retain their jobs. Once in the plants, married women remained insecure. Women whose husbands were employed were criticized either for taking away jobs from men who were the sole support of their families or for selfishly seeking to enhance the standard of living of their families at the expense of self-supporting single men and women. "All these married women working in the shop do not have children," two single women who themselves had been laid off asserted in a letter to the *United Auto Worker*. "They have a double income and luxuries, swell furnished homes, and all drive nice cars," they complained. "There should be action to put these women in their place, which is home, seniority or no seniority."[43]

Married women workers had few defenders in the UAW in the late 1930s. In response to the wife of a Local 2 member who asked, "Why doesn't the union eliminate the working wife from the Murray Corporation and why aren't others laid off immediately upon getting married?" Mike Manini, the local vice-president, explained that although he agreed that "the working wife whose husband is employed should be barred from industry," regrettably the union contract required him to protect the seniority rights of married female employees at Murray Body. Asking the woman "to understand my futile position in this dilemma," Manini offered his fervent hope that "we will reach the economic ideal where the married woman will find her place in the home caring for children, which is God's greatest gift to woman and her natural birthright." With such advocates as Manini, it is not surprising that the presence of married women in auto plants often was tolerated only until a layoff occurred, when, following jointly negotiated agreements, they were the first to be dismissed regardless of seniority.[44]

The UAW's official policy regarding the employment of married women was at best ambivalent. Although the resolutions committee at the 1940 convention recommended nonconcurrence on a resolution submitted by Local 165 which would have required the international to "take steps immediately to prohibit employers from hiring married women," its action was not based on principle. "This is such

---

43. *UAW*, January 29, 1938.
44. *UAW*, Local Union 2 edition, November 15, 1939, clipping in Joe Brown Collection, Box 34, Women-Employment Folder, ALUA.

a controversial problem, and there are so many different attitudes taken in different parts of the country," Joe Ditzel, chairman of the committee, explained, "that we recommend to leave that to local autonomy." Auto unionists were hardly exceptional in their reaction to married women jobholders. The UAW's adherence to the ideology of the family wage was in keeping with the position historically held by the American labor movement. Discrimination against married working women was, moreover, widely practiced and accepted during the 1930s. New Deal social policies also generally assumed women's economic dependence on men in promoting the traditional, male-headed family. The union's willingness to tolerate discrimination against married women workers reflects, therefore, the conservative character of the 1930s generally and the industrial union movement particularly with respect to gender.[45]

The 1930s were not wholly without movement for American women. As the passage of the Fair Labor Standards Act in 1938 indicates, the idea that women in the public sphere merited equal treatment with men gained ground. Reflecting both the changing view of women and the democratic principles of industrial unionism, the CIO endorsed the idea of equal treatment at least insofar as organizing was concerned. Like other CIO unions, the UAW defined its task in gender-neutral terms and chose to organize women as workers rather than as women, a class-based strategy not without benefits for working women. By treating women as equal members of the working class rather than as a special group with special needs, the CIO offered women the opportunity to play a larger and more independent role in the labor movement than did the AFL, which regarded women as powerless victims in need of paternalistic protection. And women's interest in the larger role was evident in the extent of women's activism during the thirties. In industries where women represented a larger share of the labor force than they did in the auto industry, they played even a greater role than did women in the UAW.[46]

45. *1940 Convention Proceedings*, p. 264. On the American labor movement and the ideology of the family wage, see Martha May, "Bread before Roses: American Workingmen, Labor Unions and the Family Wage," in Milkman, ed., *Women, Work, and Protest*, pp. 1–21; May, "The Historical Problem of the Family Wage: The Ford Motor Company and the Five Dollar Day," *Feminist Studies* 8 (Summer 1982): 399–424. On discrimination against married women workers and New Deal policy in the 1930s, see Kessler-Harris, *Out to Work*, pp. 250–72; Lois Scharf, *To Work and to Wed* (Westport, Conn., 1980), pp. 43–65.

46. For women's experience of other CIO unions in the 1930s, see Strom, "Challenging 'Woman's Place' "; Strom, " 'We're No Kitty Foyles': Organizing Office Workers for

The equality of status accorded women by organized labor in the 1930s, however, was limited. In the absence of an analysis of the sources and implications of gender hierarchy at work and in the family—that is, without feminism—women's right to equal treatment tended to render women invisible. No group in American society in the 1930s offered a critique of gender ideology and woman's place. Neither feminist organizations nor the Communist Party and other leftist groups encouraged working-class women—or men—to integrate gender into an analysis of class relations. Male unionists, therefore, did not regard their treatment of women as either discriminatory or contradictory to the principles of industrial unionism. Rather, they perceived their actions as expressions of class interests against the interests of their employers. That women's particular gender interests were sacrificed in the process was of little or no concern given the larger context of the conflict. The new industrial unions might have offered women workers the ideological and political resources for challenging inequality. Since industrial unionism dictated an inclusive organizing strategy and implicitly opposed the differentiation of workers on the basis of ascriptive traits, it not only provided women with the practical bread-and-butter benefits of trade-union membership but also offered a rationale for attacking sex discrimination. In the 1930s, however, this facet of the democratic promise of industrial unionism was not realized. The UAW may have organized women, but its defense of the sexual division of labor and its acceptance of conventional ideology about woman's proper place only confirmed the unequal status of women in the auto industry and the union.[47]

Women were neither oblivious to nor acquiescent in the evidence of sexual inequality. The response of the woman in Local 212 who lost her job is unknown, but women at the Dodge Main works in Hamtramck, Michigan, complained to the Local 3 executive board about

the Congress of Industrial Organizations, 1937–50," in Milkman, ed., *Women, Work, and Protest*, pp. 206–34; Dolores E. Janiewski, *Sisterhood Denied* (Philadelphia, 1985); Vicki Ruiz, *Cannery Women, Cannery Lives* (Albuquerque, 1987); Milkman, *Gender at Work*, pp. 33–48; Ronald Schatz, "Union Pioneers: The Founders of Local Unions at General Electric and Westinghouse, 1933–1937," *Journal of American History* 66 (December 1979): 586–602; Nina Asher, "Dorothy Jacobs Bellanca: Women Clothing Workers and the Runaway Shops," in Joan Jensen and Sue Davidson, eds., *A Needle, a Bobbin, a Strike* (Philadelphia, 1984), pp. 195–226.

47. Scharf, *To Work and to Wed*, pp. 134–38; Robert Shaffer, "Women and the Communist Party, USA, 1930–1940," *Socialist Review* 9 (May–June 1979): 73–119; Strom, "Challenging 'Woman's Place.'"

the similar treatment accorded them. Complying with union policy forbidding the employment of women in the press room if they were to receive lower wages than men similarly employed, the plant management transferred the women to other jobs in the factory. The women, however, did not want to change job assignments and charged the local with callous disregard for the fate of female members, such as themselves, who fell between the cracks of the collective-bargaining system with respect to the sexual division of labor. There is additional evidence not only that male local leaders ignored the interests of women, especially those in all-female departments and those represented by women, but that women protested such practices. For example, when layoffs in other Dodge Main departments compromised the jobs of women in the department in which Evelyn Scanlon was steward, she lambasted the Local 3 executive board, contending, "The girls are getting no representation." Since women could replace only other women with less seniority under the collective-bargaining agreement's provision for separate seniority lists for women and men, women were competing for a limited number of jobs; and the local plant committee chairman evinced no sympathy for their employment crisis.[48]

Although women did challenge the treatment or status accorded them, however, the protests were episodic or isolated incidents that did not serve to mobilize women on the local, regional, or national level of the UAW. The absence of concerted and sustained action by female auto unionists in the interest of gender equality in the 1930s reflects the inability of industrial unionism alone to transform gender consciousness radically. The isolation of women in the plants, the paucity of female leaders, the prevalence of negative attitudes toward women, and the disinterest of male unionists in promoting equality all help to account for the generally conservative attitudes and behavior of women before 1941. The women of Local 3, for example, protested the treatment accorded them but did not attack the larger problem of a sexual division of labor that required the labeling of all jobs as either male or female and that arbitrarily restricted women to a small number of lower-paying jobs. It is possible that the Local 3 women recognized the source of their distress but felt

48. Executive Board meeting minutes, October 14, 1937, UAW Local 3 (unprocessed) Collection, Box 1, Executive Board Meetings 1936–1937 Folder, ALUA; Executive Board meeting minutes, March 7, 1940, ibid., Regular Executive Board Meetings 1940 Folder.

powerless to change and therefore to confront it. Many women auto workers, however, were unaware of the arbitrary character of the sexual division of labor. Laura Hayward recalls that women in the plants accepted their lower wages without complaint. "In those days we didn't think of it," she observes. "Or I don't know, I didn't think of it. Of course, I never did a job that would be a man's job."[49]

Women who appreciated the dynamics of occupational segregation by sex also occasionally invoked the sexual division of labor as a defense against management's assignment to women of very heavy jobs. "What should be done to make women's jobs better, and what kind of jobs should and should not be given to women," for example, were topics listed in a pamphlet inviting women employed at Ternstedt to a union rally in March 1940. The vulnerability of women to maltreatment by employers also is shown in a remarkable statement by Pat Wiseman at the Women's Bureau Labor Advisory Committee meeting in 1940. The woman who in 1937 was irate about receiving less pay than a man for the same work told the committee, "It would [not] be advisable for us to fight for equal work and equal pay." She explained that after the UAW had won a wage increase from 52 cents to 70 cents an hour for female employees, GM discovered that two men could do the work of three women and, because the male rate was 90 cents an hour, it could realize a savings in labor costs as well. Implying that all women were less competent and efficient than men, Wiseman contended: "If we fight for equal pay, we can't do as much work as men. We are not built for it and I think there is the danger of eliminating ourselves."[50]

Lacking incentives, women in the UAW did not advance the principle of sexual equality in the 1930s. Their sense of themselves and unionism dictated that their class interests transcend their more particularistic concerns as women. Married women, therefore, countered criticism of their employment not by appealing to the union to protect their right to equal treatment but by emphasizing the injustice of an economic system that compelled wives and mothers to seek employment outside the home. Irene Young spoke against the married women workers' resolution at the 1940 convention "not

49. Hayward quoted in Meyerowitz, "Women in the UAW," p. 35.

50. "A Personal Invitation to Ternstedt Women Folk," pamphlet, n.d. [1940?], Walter Reuther Collection, Box 22, Folder 6; transcript, Women's Labor Advisory Committee meeting, June 1940, pp. 10–11, 18, RG 86/NA, Box 1714, June 4, 1940 Conference Folder.

because I am against the spirit of the resolution itself." Explaining that married women worked only because the wages paid their husbands were inadequate to support a family, she added, "I know most of the married women working in the plant would be darned glad to get out of it."[51]

As the only formally constituted interest group to emphasize the importance of integrating women into the UAW, the women's auxiliaries might have been the catalyst for the development of a women's movement within the union. Organized by the wives, sisters, and girlfriends of male auto workers during the 1936 and 1937 strikes, the auxiliaries provided vital services for the union, organizing and operating strike kitchens, providing child-care services to enable mothers to participate in strike activities, staffing picket lines, and assisting with organizing drives. In the course of these strikes, auxiliary members acquired a well-deserved reputation for militancy. During the Flint sit-down strike, the Women's Auxiliary confronted police in the violent Battle of the Running Bulls, participated in the seizure by workers of Chevrolet Plant No. 4, and, on February 3, 1937, marched eight hundred strong through the streets of Flint accompanied by their children, who carried signs reading "Our Daddies Fight for Us Little Tykes." At the famous Battle of the Overpass at the Ford River Rouge plant in May 1937, members of the Detroit Women's Auxiliary were grabbed, kicked in the stomach, knocked down, and trampled by Ford servicemen. The importance of their work during strikes earned the auxiliaries the respect and gratitude of the union leadership and rank and file. Although the extent of support was a source of conflict between auxiliary and union leaders, the UAW did fund the auxiliaries and generally approved of their goals and purposes.[52]

Auxiliary organizers sought to establish the "womenfolk" as a permanent and important part of the UAW. Although they were concerned chiefly with mobilizing the nonworking wives of men in the industry, they encouraged women auto workers to participate in

---

51. *1940 Convention Proceedings*, p. 264. The relationship between class interests and gender interests in American unions is analyzed in Asher, "Dorothy Jacobs Bellanca"; Alice Kessler-Harris, "Problems of Coalition-Building: Women and Trade Unions in the 1920s," in Milkman, ed., *Women, Work, and Protest*, pp. 110–38; and Milkman, "American Women and Industrial Unionism during World War II," in Margaret Randolph Higgonet et al., eds., *Behind the Lines* (New Haven, 1987), pp. 168–81.

52. Yeghissian, "Emergence of the Red Berets"; Nancy Zimmelman, "The UAW Women's Auxiliaries: Activities of Ford Workers' Families in Detroit, 1937–1949," unpublished master's thesis, Wayne State University, 1987; *UAW*, May 29, 1937.

the auxiliaries. In contrast to union men's unenthusiastic reception of women workers, the auxiliaries recognized and publicly celebrated women workers' commitment to unionism. Activists often contrasted the conservatism of nonworking women with the militancy of women in the auto plants. This theme figured prominently in a radio broadcast by the Detroit auxiliary appealing for support of auto workers' wives in the UAW's strike against Chrysler in 1939:

> FIRST WOMAN: I worked for a while in a parts plant, and let me tell you, there's all the difference between heaven and hell—especially for the girls—when there's a union in the shop. . . . It's the union that makes the boss play fair.

> SECOND WOMAN: Any woman who has worked in Detroit knows that. The trouble is lots of girls never had a job in a factory. They lived at home till they got married, or they clerked or worked in an office. Of course, that's work, too, but it's not like working in an auto plant. Now some of them are married to fellows in the different Chrysler plants and they don't see this business the way a factory girl would.

Public statements such as these promoted and enhanced the image of women auto workers in the UAW.[53]

Auxiliary organizers were critical of the male leadership's insensitivity regarding the needs and concerns of women auto workers. Writing to thank Mary Anderson for agreeing to speak at the first National Conference of UAW Women's Auxiliaries, Helen Goldmann, chair of the union's Women's Auxiliary Committee, reported that the UAW educational director had promised "to educate the union on the importance of women's work." "Believe me," Goldmann caustically remarked, "we think they can use it." The auxiliaries also raised the issue of sexual discrimination in the auto industry. Asserting that "the women are a permanent factor in unionism," Fania Fish predicted in the April 1937 issue of the Flint auxiliary's monthly magazine, "When the slogan EQUAL PAY FOR EQUAL WORK spreads to every industry, every union, still more women will join the ranks of the organized, fighting side by side with the men workers for higher wages, less hours and better working conditions." The Cleveland Women's Auxiliary demonstrated its interest in reaching women in the shops by sponsoring a talk by Mary Anderson in

53. *UAW*, November 29, 1939.

August 1939. Decrying the discrimination against married women workers as a violation of women's rights, Anderson warned that the practice invited discrimination against all women regardless of marital status. The willingness of the auxiliaries to address these controversial problems contrasted sharply with the union leadership's own quiescence.[54]

Many women auto workers appreciated the auxiliaries' efforts. The Flint auxiliary, for example, included a sizable contingent of working women; and three of the five lieutenants of the Women's Emergency Brigade were auto workers. Women workers often felt more comfortable working with those of their own sex during strikes than with male unionists. The auxiliaries, moreover, enabled women to play a more active role than was usually possible in the male-dominated strike committees. After recognition was won, women plant workers formed the active core of several local auxiliaries. The enthusiasm of women auto workers for the auxiliaries verified the intents and purposes of those few, mostly female, organizers who recruited women in the plants for the UAW and attested to women's felt need for separate institutional space within the union. Like the Women's Trade Union League in the first quarter of the twentieth century, the women's auxiliaries served as a vital link between working women and organized labor. By providing an arena in which women workers could demonstrate their commitment to trade unionism and by raising issues of special concern to women in the plants, the women's auxiliaries performed a valuable and important service in behalf of gender equity.[55]

But despite the significance of their efforts, auxiliaries were neither the most effective nor the most appropriate advocates for women in auto plants. Because their chief constituents were nonworking wives, the auxiliaries devoted their principal attention to social and cultural problems outside the plants. Some auxiliaries limited their role to raising funds and directing social events. Others, most notably the Flint and Detroit auxiliaries, engaged in political action, participating in election campaigns and joining protests against the high

54. Goldmann to Anderson, March 10, 1939, RG 86/NA, Box 867, Auto Workers Folder; Meyerowitz, "Women in the UAW," pp. 74, 116–17; Fania Fish, "Women at Work," Auto Women Advance 10 (April 1937): 10, Joe Brown Collection, Box 33, Women's Auxiliaries Folder; UAW, August 2, 1939, and August 16, 1939.

55. Only recently have the women's auxiliaries of the American labor movement begun to receive attention from scholars. For the 1930s, see Julia Kirk Blackwelder, Women of the Depression (College Station, Tex., 1984), pp. 130–51.

cost of meat and housing. Although women auto workers also were concerned about the cost of living and the availability of social services, they defined their relationship to the UAW in terms of their position in the plants rather than in the community. Wage rates, working conditions, and shop-floor issues, however, were not within the purview of the women's auxiliaries. The auxiliaries, moreover, may have acted as militant defenders of their class, but by definition and inclination they did not challenge conventional views of woman's proper place. Like the union they aided, the auxiliaries endorsed the notion of gender hierarchy.[56]

As the name suggests, the women's auxiliaries assisted the UAW, but in a subsidiary or subordinate capacity. The association between auxiliary members and women auto workers, therefore, enabled the UAW to assign its female members a supportive rather than an active role in union affairs. A provision in Local 154's constitution illustrates how readily union men overlooked the crucial distinction between female unionists and women auxiliary members. The local, which represented the eleven thousand employees of the Hudson Motor Car Company in Detroit, indicated its concern for its two thousand female members by designating the office of fourth vice president for a woman "who shall have charge of women's affairs." She was directed, however, to "work in conjunction with the auxiliary"; in fact, the position more often than not was held by the president of the local auxiliary. By encouraging women workers to participate in the auxiliaries, the UAW abdicated its responsibility to these workers. Although the close association between the auxiliaries and women auto workers was to a certain extent mutually beneficial, it tended to confirm rather than challenge the marginal status of women in the auto industry and the UAW.[57]

Katherine Wilk's petition for the appointment of a woman to the UAW executive board at the 1937 convention suggests that some women auto workers resented the union's assumption that their interests were synonymous with those of the nonworking wives who composed the Women's Auxiliary. The tenuous position of women in

---

56. Yeghissian, "Emergence of the Red Berets"; Zimmelman, "The UAW Women's Auxiliaries." Marjorie Penn Lasky examines the limited potential of the labor movement's women's auxiliaries to transform gender consciousness in "'Where I Was a Person': The Ladies' Auxiliary in the 1934 Minneapolis Teamsters' Strikes," in Milkman, ed., *Women, Work, and Protest*, pp. 181–205.

57. *UAW*, February 26, 1938, December 17, 1938, and April 24, 1940.

the union and the plants muted this conflict during the late 1930s. As the absolute and relative number of women in the industry increased after 1941, the women began to mobilize in defense of their status as full-fledged members of the UAW. At the 1944 convention, Ruth Biggen, a Local 208 delegate, delivered the charge of discrimination more explicitly than Katherine Wilk had seven years earlier. "We as unionists feel our place is in the union and not in the Auxiliary," she asserted. "We want to and have been working with the men in the shops in our local unions, and we feel our place is in the union." That Biggen made her statement during discussion of a resolution instructing the International Executive Board to help local unions "eliminate [contract] clauses discriminating to women and [add] clauses protecting women workers" indicates the impact that World War II had on gender relations in the auto industry and the UAW. As their proportion of the UAW's membership climbed to 25 percent, women workers gained the confidence not only to demand fair and equal treatment from the union but to mount a challenge to sexual inequality in the auto industry as well.[58]

58. *Proceedings of the Ninth Convention of the United Automobile, Aircraft and Agricultural Implements Workers of America, September 11–17, 1944*, p. 120.

CHAPTER TWO

Women and the UAW-CIO during World War II

In December 1941 Kathleen Lowrie, a United States Women's Bureau field officer, reported to Mary Anderson, director of the bureau, that women auto workers were "a small but important minority with problems of their own [in the plants]" and stressed "the importance of the women in the union developing more confidence." Four years later, in November 1945, two hundred women carrying signs reading "Stop Discrimination Because of Sex" and "The Hand That Rocks the Cradle Can Build Tractors, Too" picketed outside the employment office of the Ford Motor Company's Highland Park plant in Detroit. The demonstration, organized by the Local 400 Women's Committee and supported by the local membership and leadership, protested the wholesale layoff of women workers and the employment of men with little or no seniority in the plant. The contrast between the vulnerability and timidity of the women Lowrie met in 1941 and the dramatic protest action by women auto unionists in November 1945 indicates the extent to which gender relations within the auto industry and the UAW changed during World War II.[1]

The entrance of 200,000 women into auto plants during the war

---

1. Lowrie to Anderson, March 6, 1942, Women's Bureau Papers, Record Group 86, Box 1416, Region V Early 1941–June 1943 Folder, National Archives, Washington, D.C. (hereafter cited as RG 86/NA); *New York Times*, November 9, 1945; *Detroit News*, November 8, 1945.

created an upheaval in the sexual division of labor. The integration of women into jobs formerly held by men and their placement in jobs newly created as a consequence of conversion to defense production made the once rigid boundaries between women's and men's work ambiguous and exposed the arbitrary character of occupational segregation by sex. In disputes over management's wartime wage, job-classification, and seniority policies, the male-dominated and male-oriented UAW sought to stabilize and recodify the sexual division of labor in anticipation of the postwar period, when women would surrender their jobs in the industry to returning servicemen.

At the same time, however, the influx of women into the work force prompted efforts to integrate them into the union. By encouraging women to seek local union office and participate in union affairs, the UAW not only strengthened their commitment to trade unionism but enabled them to gain valuable and much-needed political experience. These newly acquired skills and self-confidence, together with experience in the plants, provided women unionists with the resources to mount a collective challenge to sexual discrimination in employment practices in the last eighteen months of the war. Demanding a role in shaping the union's agenda and forcing male unionists to address the question of women's place in the industry, UAW women made certain that reconversion would not be as smooth a process as once was anticipated.

Although the federal government launched its defense program in 1940, the conversion of the auto industry to military production proceeded slowly and erratically. Enjoying substantial profits for the first time in several years, auto manufacturers insisted on simultaneous production of automobiles and defense material. Some companies opened and retooled plants that had been closed during the depression, but most refused to place existing facilities at the disposal of the defense effort. To fill military orders, the federal government underwrote the cost of construction for new plants, which were then turned over to the auto industry for the execution of defense contracts. While factories such as the Chrysler army-tank arsenal in Warren, Michigan, and the Ford bomber plant in Ypsilanti, Michigan, were being built, the industry increased its output of passenger cars.

The failure of the auto industry to develop and execute conversion plans frustrated government officials in charge of defense planning.

The competition between auto makers and the defense effort for machine tools and materials compelled William S. Knudsen, former president of General Motors and co-director with Sidney Hillman of the Office of Production Management (OPM), in April 1941 to order a 20 percent cut in auto production scheduled for August 1, 1941, to July 31, 1942. Leon Henderson, director of the Office of Price Administration and Civilian Supply, took stronger action toward industry conversion on July 20, 1941, ordering a 50 percent reduction in auto production for the 1941–1942 model year. Knudsen and auto executives, however, were able to delay implementation of Henderson's order until November 1. On the eve of Pearl Harbor, auto companies were still focusing their energies on the design and manufacture of new automobiles.[2]

The refusal of the auto industry to put its facilities at the disposal of the national defense program disturbed UAW leaders as well as government officials such as Henderson. The location of the new government-financed factories in towns outside Detroit both discouraged and prevented auto workers from transferring to defense jobs. The industry's dilatory approach to conversion of plants still engaged in auto production, moreover, prompted predictions of a protracted period of unemployment for industry wage earners while vital materials were diverted to defense plants and the industry was forced to begin the lengthy process of conversion. Convinced that the industry was using only half its potential production capacity, Walter Reuther, head of the UAW's General Motors Department, proposed a plan in the winter of 1940–1941 which he claimed would enable the auto industry to meet President Roosevelt's call for five hundred planes a day. Asserting that "the plane . . . is only an automobile with wings," Reuther called on the auto industry to pool its excess capacity for conversion to aircraft production. Supervised by an industrial council composed of representatives from government, business, and labor, conversion could be completed in six months rather than the one or two years projected by auto manufacturers, Reuther contended. The Reuther Plan won support within

2. For the story of the auto industry during the defense period, see Barton Bernstein, "The Automobile Industry and the Coming of the Second World War," *Southwestern Social Science Quarterly* 47 (June 1966): 22–33. See also Alan Clive, *State of War* (Ann Arbor, Mich., 1979), pp. 18–26; Nelson Lichtenstein, *Labor's War at Home* (Cambridge, England, 1982), pp. 39–40.

the Roosevelt administration, but auto executives balked at its provision for labor's participation in management of the industry.[3]

Denied a role in defense planning, the UAW devised strategies to protect auto workers during the protracted conversion process. Delegates to the UAW convention held in August 1941 adopted a resolution opposing "any attempt to train women to take the place of men on skilled jobs until such time as all the unemployed men have been put back to work." Reflecting the fear that the introduction of women on men's jobs would depress wage standards, the resolution also stated that women should receive equal pay with men should it become necessary to employ them on work also being performed by men. Both claims were defensive, intended as a warning to employers that the UAW would counter any effort by them to deny men jobs and reduce wages. The attempts of two local unions in 1941 to prevent the employment of women on defense production served notice to auto manufacturers that the UAW meant to act on its verbal commitment.[4]

As early as the winter of 1941, conflict over defense employment developed between UAW Locals 174 and 9 and two auto companies: Kelsey Hayes Wheel Company in Detroit and Bendix Corporation in South Bend, Indiana. In January the Local 174 bargaining committee pressed Kelsey Hayes to promise that women would be employed only on "light work" at the defense plant the company was building in Plymouth on the western outskirts of Detroit. Management, however, was evasive about its plans for the plant. In April a Kelsey Hayes representative did say the company was not likely to employ women at the new plant while men were available but added, "If there is a shortage of men maybe there will be all girls out there the same as in the last war." Tensions mounted in September, when Kelsey Hayes began to place women on jobs in the completed defense plant, transferring some female employees from the automotive plant as well as hiring other women. No men were displaced in the process, but, as the local union president later told Caroline Manning of the United States Women's Bureau, the men saw "women edging in on all the jobs." Believing the company would deny unemployed men jobs and

3. Lichtenstein, *Labor's War at Home*, pp. 85–89; Victor G. Reuther, *The Brothers Reuther* (Boston, 1979), pp. 225–34.

4. *Proceedings of the Sixth Convention of the International Union, United Automobile Workers of America, August 4–15, 1941* (hereafter cited as *1941 Convention Proceedings*), p. 37.

take advantage of the 15-cent differential between men's and women's hourly rates to reduce labor expenses, the UAW filed a strike notice on October 15, demanding "the removal of all girl employees from machine work" that in the local's view was "a man's job." Kelsey Hayes promised not to place any more women in defense jobs until the grievance was settled, but management on October 27 hired two women for the midnight shift, confirming workers' suspicions and prompting a walkout by the men.[5]

In a period of still-considerable male unemployment, the UAW local sought not the application of the equal-pay principle but the exclusion of women from most jobs. The local president tried to convince Manning that the strike originated as an effort to raise wage standards in the plant yet admitted that "the presence of the women greatly aggravated the situation and . . . of course the men could not afford to lose their jobs." The settlement of the thirty-six-hour strike, a victory for the union, provided for the removal of women from all screw-machine and profiling operations, confined women to a small number of jobs to be classified as "female work," and stipulated that henceforth "female employees at no time will exceed 25 per cent of the total [workforce]." Chiefly concerned with proscribing women's access to most jobs in the plant, the union had no objection to the agreement's provision for unequal wage rates for women and men in a few jobs with the same titles. According to the rate structure set forth in the settlement, women employed as subassemblers, light-drill-press operators, small-parts filers, and milling-machine operators all received 88 cents an hour, while men in these jobs received an hourly wage, respectively, of $1.01, $1.03, $1.01, and $1.05.[6]

UAW Local 9 in South Bend used a similar strategy to restrict Bendix Corporation's employment of women. On September 4, 1941, the local took a strike vote to protest the placement of women in aircraft-parts inspection, a new defense operation similar, it claimed, to work long performed by higher-paid male auto-parts inspectors in

5. Minutes of January 29, 1941 meeting, UAW Local 78 [174] Collection, Box 1, Folder 3, Walter P. Reuther Library, Archives of Labor and Urban Affairs, Detroit, Michigan (hereafter cited as ALUA); minutes of April 16, 1941 meeting, ibid., Folder 5; Manning Report, Summary of Conditions Which Led to the Strike, November 17, 1941, RG 86/NA, Box 1416, Region V Early 1941–June 1943 Folder; *Detroit News*, October 28, 1941, and October 29, 1941.

6. Kelsey Hayes Production Rates, November 5, 1941, RG 86/NA, Box 1416, Region V Early 1941–June 1943 Folder; Manning Report, November 17, 1941, ibid., Manning to James Wishart, November 17, 1941, ibid.

the plant. The union later concluded an agreement with Bendix which endorsed the customary practice of segregating women in particular departments, classifying jobs according to the sex of the operator, and paying women an hourly rate 25 cents less than that paid men in the same or similar jobs. The contract, however, also contained a feature that limited the future employment of women except in already demarcated "female" departments. Union leaders pressed for this provision when management refused to equalize the wages of women and men in defense jobs; seeking to protect men's jobs and wage standards, Local 9 conceded women's lower rates and compelled management to obtain the local's permission before hiring more women.[7]

The defensive reaction of male auto unionists to the employment of women attracted national attention. "The issue, raised in its present form for the first time since defense production got underway," commented *Business Week* on the strike at Kelsey Hayes, "promises to become one of the most dangerous and troublesome ones Washington will have to meet." More concerned about the precedent such agreements set for discrimination against women than for delays in defense production, Caroline Manning assailed them as "contrary to the usual democratic policies of the C.I.O." and asked UAW leaders to assist her "in making a square deal possible for women workers." UAW regional director George Young, however, offered Manning little consolation, vowing "to safeguard the rates of pay for women as well as for men" while maintaining that "it would be an advantage to the girls" if collective bargaining agreements included sex-based job classifications and separate seniority lists for men and women. Manning gave the regional director little credit for his revelation to her of long-standing inequities in men's and women's wages at Kelsey Hayes, noting that he had admitted when pressed that "he had not acted upon such violations" in the past. Leery of Young's attitude toward women workers, Manning concluded, "I do not feel sure what compromises he might make [to protect men]."[8]

Notwithstanding the correctness of such concerns, the sexual composition of the auto labor force in the defense period owed more to

7. *United Auto Worker* (*UAW*), September 15, 1941; decision of the National Board in case of Bendix Aviation and UAW Local 9, July 26, 1943, *War Labor Reports* (*WLR*) 10 (1944): 45–46.

8. *Business Week*, November 8, 1941, p. 59; Manning to Wishart, November 17, 1941, RG 86/NA, Box 1416, Region V Early 1941–June 1943 Folder; Manning to Mary Anderson, November 17, 1941, ibid.; Manning to Anderson and Bertha Neinburg, November 25, 1941, ibid.

managerial imperative than to union opposition. Employers generally had little interest in integrating women into defense work as long
as the labor surplus created by conversion unemployment existed.
Exercising their preference for a male labor force, employers refused
to recall or train women for defense jobs. Women's proportion of the
auto labor force steadily declined between 1939 and 1941 as substantially greater numbers of men found work in the plants. When the
tempo of conversion accelerated after the federal government's issu-
ance of curtailment orders in the spring and summer of 1941, the
number of female auto workers decreased, from 31,600 in April to
28,300 in October, while the number of male auto workers increased,
from 554,400 to 554,700. Before the events at Kelsey Hayes and
Bendix demonstrated union opposition to the employment of
women, Caroline Manning reported that auto firms in Detroit "have
no intention of transferring women to defense work or training them
for defense until the man supply is exhausted." She charged that the
practice of replacing female employees with men "has colored the
attitude of all Detroit," noting that "public sentiment generally is not
favorable to the women."[9]

Women auto workers who were denied access to defense jobs
claimed protection under the OPM Six-Point Transfer Agreement.
Concurred in by the UAW and the industry in September 1941, the
agreement was designed to protect the seniority rights of auto
workers in transfers, layoffs, and recalls. It allowed laid-off auto
workers to take defense jobs with new employers while continuing
to accumulate seniority with their original employers, which, in turn,
could recall former employees for defense work with one week's
notice. The agreement also stipulated that firms were to transfer
employees to defense work in line with seniority and to give preference in hiring to workers from local industry. Women, however,
discovered that the OPM policy offered them little protection from
discrimination. Separate seniority lists, for example, enabled employers to recall men ahead of women regardless of the latter's
higher-seniority status. Some employers stated flatly that women
were unsuited to defense jobs.[10]

Regarding women as interlopers, the UAW paid scant attention to

9. Bureau of Labor Statistics (BLS), *Handbook of Labor Statistics, 1947* (Washington,
D.C., 1947), p. 18; Manning to Anderson and Neinburg, October 20, 1941, RG 86/NA,
Box 1416, Region V Early 1941–June 1943 Folder.

10. *UAW*, September 15, 1941, and October 1, 1941.

the concerns of female auto workers. In the early fall of 1941 the UAW organized Defense Employment Committees in the Michigan cities of Detroit, Lansing, Saginaw, Pontiac, and Flint to monitor company compliance with the OPM agreement. Consisting of officers from the various local unions, the committees had no female representatives. In October fifty women from several Detroit-area locals met to discuss the special problems women were confronting as a result of conversion layoffs and to select a delegation to alert the international to the importance of protecting the rights of women under the OPM agreement. Contending that the all-male body was "entirely disregarding the needs of the women," the female unionists demanded the appointment of a woman to the Detroit Defense Employment Committee. George Addes, the union's defense employment coordinator, rejected their petition and warned them "not to make an issue at this time of women's rights." Asserting that the position of women auto workers was "too precarious" at the time, Addes explained that male unionists were "jealous of their jobs" and that employers were "not too favorable" when it came to hiring women for defense work.[11]

The full conversion of the auto industry to defense production after the Japanese attack on Pearl Harbor further attenuated the position of women auto workers. Asked to produce 20 percent of all American war material, the industry curtailed production of civilian motor vehicles "for the duration," the last car rolling off the assembly line on February 10, 1942. While companies retooled plants for the sudden changeover to the production of aircraft, tanks, and ordnance, auto workers were laid off in massive numbers. Having risen from 447,000 in October 1939 to 583,000 in October 1941, the number of production workers in auto plants nationwide fell to 429,000 in April 1942. Once employment began to pick up during the conversion period, the rate of reemployment of prewar women workers lagged far behind that of men. Until the male labor force was reabsorbed, auto companies had little interest in hiring women for defense jobs.[12]

The obstacles that five hundred female employees of the Fisher Body plant in Lansing, Michigan, confronted in obtaining defense

11. Manning interviews with union officers of Ternstedt Local 174, September 29, 1941, RG 86/NA, Box 1416, Region V Early 1941–June 1943 Folder; Manning to Neinburg, October 15, 1941, ibid.

12. BLS, *Handbook of Labor Statistics, 1947,* p. 18.

jobs after they had been laid off in February 1942 were typical of the experience of prewar women workers during the conversion period. Because auto companies in Lansing claimed there were no jobs available for women, the United States Employment Service (USES) office gave preference to men in its defense-work training program despite the seniority and industrial experience of the displaced women. Adding insult to injury, when Reo Motor Car Company hired four hundred women for defense jobs in June, only ninety-five were former Fisher Body workers; the remainder were women who had been employed as waitresses, shop clerks, and secretaries. In rejecting the job applications of women laid off from the Fisher Body plant, Reo informed them that its contract with the UAW local forbade the hiring of married women. Further investigation, however, revealed that many of Reo's new women workers were married. When several women confronted Reo with its apparent violation of the OPM Six-Point Transfer Agreement, the company asserted that it was not required to comply with the voluntary agreement.[13]

Former Fisher Body workers found a sympathetic listener in Victor Reuther, director of the UAW's War Policy Division. Earlier in the conversion period, when thousands of male auto workers were on indefinite layoff, Reuther had seen little reason to promote the employment of women on defense work. In response to a query by a Local 75 officer in March 1942 as to what could be done to prevent a company from retaining married female employees, Reuther explained that although no national legislation prohibited the employment of married women, married women were employed in some plants organized by the UAW, whereas local agreements denied them jobs in others. "It appears this matter is left solely to the disgression of the local management and the union concerned," Reuther reported. As the prewar male labor force was recalled for defense work beginning in the late spring and early summer of 1942 and the federal government was urging the recruitment of women to meet the nation's wartime needs, the UAW, its anxiety over male unemployment diminishing, started to intercede in behalf of women auto workers displaced during conversion.[14]

13. Edward Cushman to Ernest Kanzler, July 8, 1942, UAW War Policy Division Collection, Box 18, Edward Cushman Folder, ALUA; Clara Shipski and Myrtle Hewitt to John Gibson, September 21, 1942, ibid., Box 16, Women's Auxiliaries Folder.

14. Walter Miller to Walter Reuther, March 29, 1942, and Victor Reuther to Miller, April 10, 1942, ibid., Box 29, Local 75 Folder. The War Policy Division was established in 1942 to devise and implement the union's wartime programs and policies.

Victor Reuther sought to defend the right of the former Fisher Body employees to secure defense jobs. Notified by one of the unemployed women that Reo was using arbitrary standards such as weight, age, economic need, marital status, and "pulchritude" to deny jobs to women auto workers, Reuther and Edward Cushman, assistant director of the Michigan USES, confronted Byron Fields, director of industrial relations for Reo. Fields confessed that Reo had no ban on the employment of married women but conceded that "from time to time this excuse has been used to weed out some of the many applicants at the employment office." Unimpressed by Fields's admission, Reuther and Cushman recommended that he meet with the women, "since their activity is reflecting against the company in the community." In a letter to the deputy labor consultant for the War Production Board (WPB), Reuther condemned the refusal of Lansing-area auto firms to comply with the OPM agreement and to hire laid-off women auto workers before hiring women with no industrial experience. "The UAW has talked long and loudly about such matters," Reuther wrote to J. L. Thurston. "I know that you will appreciate the difficulties our organization will have in cooperating with the Government's program to recruit new women workers for war work, with other qualified workers such as these Fisher women still idle and without income."[15]

Although important, the UAW's intervention in the Lansing case did not indicate a change of heart on the part of male unionists regarding women in the industry. Reuther stepped in to defend the

15. Cushman to Kanzler, July 8, 1942, War Policy Division, Box 18, Cushman Folder; Reuther to Thurston, July 3, 1942, ibid., Box 15, WPB–Automotive Division, May–August 1942 Folder. Writing in response to Reuther's letter, Thurston outlined the WPB's program for the induction of women into the labor market. "An integral part . . . will be an attempt to educate all employers in critical labor market areas in the necessity for hiring all types of women—single, married, those with previous experience, and those without previous experience." Thurston added that the program would stress "the necessity for employing women with industrial experience." Thurston to Reuther, July 19, 1942, War Policy Division Collection, Box 15, WPB–Automotive Division, May–August 1942 Folder. Under pressure from the WPB and the UAW, the Nash Kelvinator and Olds Motor Works plants in Lansing agreed to hire the unemployed Fisher Body women. Clara Shipski, however, was denied employment because, the UAW regional office told Kathleen Lowrie, she "had been a particularly active organizer and Nash had refused to take her." Shipski was hired eventually; she was one of the two CIO representatives on the Lansing War Manpower Committee in 1943. Lowrie to Mary Anderson, November 24, 1942, RG 86/NA, Box 1416, Region V Early 1941–June 1943 Folder; CIO Representatives on Area War Manpower Committees, War Policy Division Collection, Box 13, WMC-Detroit, September–November 1943 Folder.

rights of experienced women workers over those of new female employees. The UAW, however, made little effort to protect the seniority rights of women who were not recalled to defense jobs that were being filled by new male hires. A study by the union's Research Department indicated that in June 1941 over one hundred Michigan auto plants employed 14,675 women; one year later only 11,806 women were working in the same factories. "In other words," the report concluded, "women with seniority are not yet back to work." Mae McKernan, a shop steward in Local 51, reported to the UAW convention in August 1942 that companies were replacing "hundreds and hundreds of women laid off who have seniority" with men having no history of employment in a plant. "If they train men, they can train women," McKernan stated. Urging male unionists to remember that "We are employees and women members paying our dues, the same as everybody else," McKernan remarked, "we are getting tired of [you] saying, 'Well, that's a woman's problem.' "[16]

The failure of the UAW to address seriously the question of the recall rights of prewar women workers soon became a moot issue. The rapid expansion of the industry and the conscription of male workers into the military effectively eliminated the greatest obstacle to female employment in defense production. In October 1942, 69,700 women were employed in auto plants. Not only had the absolute number of women increased since April, but their proportion of the automotive labor force had risen from 5 percent to 12 percent. By April 1943, 121,300 women worked in the industry; and when their numbers peaked at 203,300 in November, women represented 26 percent of the auto labor force.[17]

The influx of women into auto plants was part of a national trend hailed by both contemporaries and historians as the first significant advance in the history of women since the passage of the Nineteenth Amendment in 1920. Nearly half of the 11 million women employed in the United States in 1940 worked in low-paid, low-status clerical, sales, and service jobs. Similarly, the 20 percent who worked in manufacturing were concentrated in a few low-paid industries, such as textiles and clothing. World War II substantially improved the

16. Summary of Results of Survey of Female Employment as of July 1, 1942, UAW Research Department Collection, Box 32, Folder 9, ALUA; *Proceedings of the Seventh Convention of the United Automobile, Aircraft, and Agricultural Implement Workers of America, August 3–9, 1942* (hereafter cited as *1942 Convention Proceedings*), pp. 362–63.

17. BLS, *Handbook of Labor Statistics*, p. 18.

economic status of women as the demand for labor to meet the nation's wartime needs exceeded the available supply of male labor and opened occupations formerly closed to women. At the peak of women's wartime employment, in 1944, the percentage of the female labor force in clerical, sales, and service jobs had declined to 36 percent, while the proportion employed in manufacturing had increased to 34 percent. Although the entrance of over 3 million women into manufacturing represented a significant 140 percent increase over the figure for 1940, the 460 percent increase in the number of women employed in production in the "war industries"—metals, chemicals, and rubber—which had employed few women before the war, was even more dramatic. Of equal importance, the war offered many women upward occupational mobility. Although 49 percent of the women employed in war industries in March 1944 had not worked before the war, 27 percent had shifted from other occupations, attracted by higher wages, better working conditions, and the opportunity to learn new skills.[18]

Initially, women were employed in jobs long established within the auto industry as "women's work." Although a survey conducted by the USES in the spring of 1942 indicated that women could successfully perform 80 percent of the production jobs in the industry's defense plants, a study completed by the UAW's Research Department several months later found that women were working in only 28 percent of the industry's job classifications. Principally employed as assemblers, inspectors, filers, packers, and drill, punch-press, and sewing-machine operators, they were performing jobs customarily assigned to women. In contrast, few women were employed as riveters; solderers; broaching-machine operators; burring-, buffing-, grinding-, and polishing-machine operators; milling-machine operators; lathe operators; spot welders; core cleaners; core makers; or tool-crib attendants. Those were jobs generally held only by men before the war.[19]

The influx of women after 1942 demolished some of the barriers to their greater integration into the industry's occupational structure. The trend was evident in the presence of women in plants that before the war had employed men almost exclusively. The number of

18. Mary Elizabeth Pidgeon, *Changes in Women's Employment during the War*, Special Bulletin No. 20, Women's Bureau (Washington D.C., 1944), pp. 9, 12, 15.

19. *UAW Research Report* 2 (September 1, 1942): 1.

women in production at Ford's Highland Park plant soared from 300 in 1942 to 4,500 one year later. There were no female wage earners at Ford's massive River Rouge complex or at GM's Cadillac plant in Detroit in the spring of 1942; in March 1943, 5,000 women were employed at River Rouge and 4,400 at Cadillac. As those cultural icons Rosie the Riveter and Winnie the Welder suggest, women gained access to jobs once regarded as male preserves. Restricted to sewing auto upholstery before the war, women employed after 1942 at the Ford Highland Park plant, for example, were riveting and welding bomber wings. Not all the new positions were glamorous. Ray Vess, a union committeeman in the Pontiac Motors foundry, recalled that women were placed there in jobs "that a woman was never known to do before," such as core making and truck driving. Regardless of assignment, women war workers challenged assumptions about female capabilities in industry. "You had women getting jobs on intricate machines that never did anything but carry a baby around and a bucket of soup," explained John McDaniel, a Local 190 leader at the Packard plant in Detroit. "So there was not actually any set criteria about what a woman could do except in the minds of the company."[20]

The war, however, did not erase the boundaries separating women's and men's work as much as redraw them. Although women did hold untraditional jobs in war plants, many worked on operations that were the same as or similar to those performed by women in peacetime. Job segregation by sex persisted, women being unevenly distributed through the occupational structure in auto plants. A Bureau of Labor Statistics study of 180 Detroit-area auto plants in July 1943 found that although 42,157 women—22 percent of the production labor force—were in forty-two of seventy-two machining job classifications, most of them clustered in a few occupational groups; 17 percent of the women were Class C inspectors, and another 34 percent were distributed among four classifications: Class B floor assembly, Class C drill-press operation, Class C bench assembly,

20. UAW Research Department Questionnaire on Employment, July 1943, Research Department Collection, Box 11, Folders 8–11; Vess interview, October 12, 1961, p. 18, UAW Oral History Project, Institute of Labor and Industrial Relations, University of Michigan and Wayne State University, ALUA; McDaniel interview, May 26, 1961, ibid. Leila Rupp, in *Mobilizing Women for War* (Princeton, N.J., 1978), pp. 93–98, 142–53, examines the "glamorization" of war work in the media campaigns that were mounted to recruit women for defense jobs.

and Class C burring. By contrast, only 11 percent of the men in machining occupations were employed in the same five classifications. In the classifications in which they were concentrated, moreover, women outnumbered men. Just 25 percent of Class B inspectors were women, but three of every five Class C inspectors were female.[21]

Management used the same rationale for concentrating women in certain kinds of jobs as it had before the war. "It was realized that womanpower differs from manpower as oil fuel differs from coal," the industry's trade journal stated, "and an understanding of the characteristics of the energy involved was needed for obtaining best results." References invariably were made to women's superior ability in operations requiring manual dexterity or attention to detail. "Why should men, who from childhood on never so much as sewed on buttons," observed one plant manager, "be expected to handle delicate instruments better than women who have plied embroidery needles, knitting needles, and darning needles all their lives?" Stressing the different abilities of women and men, employers emphasized the suitability of women for certain kinds of work. "To understand these things does not mean to exclude women from the jobs for which they are peculiarly adapted, and where they can help win the war," the author of an article in the October 1943 issue of *Automotive War Production* commented. "It merely means using them as women, and not as men."[22]

Management also stressed the lesser physical strength of women in developing its plans for the utilization of labor during the war. Employers found that the installation of conveyors, chain hoists, and load lifters enabled women to equal, if not exceed, the production rates of men in jobs that formerly were performed only by male employees. "Take the twelve women who recently invaded that hitherto exclusively masculine province, the automotive foundry," commented one observer. "Supplemented by weight-lifting mechanisms, these feminine moulders not only quickly reached a production output of from 80 to 100 moulds—just under the average for

21. BLS, Division of Wage Analysis, Regional Office 8-A (Detroit), "Metalworking Establishments: Detroit, Michigan Labor Market Area, July 1943," December 3, 1943, Research Department Collection, Box 28, Folder 26.
22. "Provisions in Plants for Physical Differences Enable Women to Handle Variety of War Jobs," *Automotive War Production* 2 (September 1943): 7; "Engineers of Womanpower," *Automotive War Production* 2 (October 1943): 4–5.

men—but produced less scrap than the men." The necessity of employing women also offered the opportunity to improve production
processes at government expense. Despite the improved quantity
and quality of production, however, management cited the mechanization and simplification of certain operations as justification for
separately classifying the work done by women and men in jobs with
the same titles and establishing wage differentials based on sex.[23]

When management placed women in jobs that formerly were performed only by men but that did not require any modifications in the
way they were done, it used the language of sex typing to redefine
the operations as "women's work." Reporting that, with the same
training provided male workers, women "are proving adept at operating complex types of milling machines, presses and lathes," an
industry observer commented that "[women's] deft fingers are showing themselves particularly adaptable to burring, polishing, and lap-
ping and buffing on lathes, at handfinishing machined parts, at spot
welding, soldering, [and] spray painting." One report on women
employed as airplane crankshaft inspectors concluded with exuber-
ant lyricism: "These young women have eyes and fingers that coordi-
nate at incredible speed, brain cells that register results infallibly.
They are the daughters of nimble fingered ancestors who spun and
wove, embroidered and made fine lace." Another article described
the manufacture of bomb sights and automatic pilots as extremely
"delicate" work and asserted, "Instruments like those used to be
made by patient male artisans who devoted their lives to precision
work." "Typical housewives, those mistresses of cleanliness," the
report enthused, "turn them out now in wholesale batches for the
night bombing planes which ride over Hitler's industrial towns."[24]

As the attempt to exclude women from defense jobs became
an untenable strategy for maintaining wage standards, the UAW
pressed vigorously for application of the principle of equal pay for
equal work. Some companies, including Ford, Studebaker, and Vul-
tee, willingly incorporated an equal-pay clause into collective-bargaining agreements. The technological changes and dramatic shift in

23. "Provisions in Plants"; "Women Work for Victory," *Automotive War Production* 1
(November 1942): 4.
24. "Women Work for Victory"; "Engineers of Womanpower," p. 5. So enthusiastic
was the author of the second article that he ingenuously proclaimed that "the automotive industry has gone a long step in opening the doors of new opportunity to
women."

the composition of the labor force that attended the conversion process in the auto industry, however, made the once-rigid boundaries separating women's and men's work ambiguous and created uncertainty in many minds as to the correct application of the principle.

Auto unionists, for example, sensed that management's arguments for wage differentials between women and men in the same jobs were specious. But they seemed unable to reconcile their own commitment to a sexual division of labor with their growing concerns about the system's arbitrary character. At the UAW convention in August 1942, the president of Local 856 complained that, despite a contractual provision for equal pay, Goodyear Aircraft in Akron, Ohio, was paying women building wheel-brake assemblies less than men doing the same work because the women were unable to lift the completed hundred-pound assemblies from the bench. Critical of the "weasel words and loopholes" in the equal-pay-for-equal-work policy, the delegate wondered if "in this convention somewhere there is intelligence enough to circumvent this particular odious clause." An exchange between Victor Reuther and John Anderson, president of Amalgamated Local 155 in Detroit, further demonstrated the need for clarification of the union's equal-pay policy. Reporting that companies were refusing to establish equal rates for women and men in the same jobs because state law required that women, but not men, receive two fifteen-minute rest periods in each eight-hour shift, Anderson asked whether he nevertheless should insist on the establishment of equal hourly rates. "I don't know, John," Reuther replied lamely; "you will have to figure that one out yourself."[25]

The classification of newly created defense jobs that closely resembled prewar operations to which both sexes had been assigned but for which sex-differentiated wage scales had been established further confounded interpreters of the equal-pay principle. The UAW tended to argue that if a man ever had performed a job, it was ipso facto a "male" job and women now employed in it should receive the higher "male" rate negotiated before conversion. Employers feminized disputed operations and accorded them the lower "female" rate, claiming that the process of conversion had simplified the tasks once assigned to men, making them more like those done by women before the war. Both sides were somewhat disingenuous, since neither would admit the flimsy and esoteric basis for many prewar

25. *1942 Convention Proceedings*, pp. 359–61.

differentials. It was, however, increasingly difficult to differentiate between operations performed by men and women. Even management was uncertain, stressing women's special suitability for "delicate war jobs" while announcing that "women were being trained in skills that previously were considered exclusively in man's domain." One baffled foreman at GM's Delco Remy plant in Anderson, Indiana, referred an equal-pay grievance on an aircraft-part assembly job to higher management because both sexes had performed and were performing the operations associated with the job. "I am unable to determine which is to be done by men and which to be done by women," he confessed. In this confused and confusing environment, disputes over job classification and wage determination proliferated.[26]

The endorsement by the National War Labor Board (NWLB) of the equal-pay-for-equal-work principle promised to resolve the conflict between organized labor and industry over wartime wage policies. The decision of the NWLB in the landmark case brought by the UAW and the United Electrical Workers (UE) against GM established the equal-pay principle as board policy on September 26, 1942. The board also disallowed slight disparities in job content as justification for wage differentials. Directing GM and the unions to include in their contracts a clause stating that "wage rates for women shall be the same as for men where they do work of comparable quantity and quality in comparable operations," the NWLB rejected GM's claim that the necessity of employing male helpers to assist women on certain operations warranted its paying women less than men and asserted, "Wage-setting on such a basis is not compatible with the principle of equal pay for equal work." By ordering GM to establish wage rates for women and men on the basis of comparable quality and quantity of output rather than differences in the physical characteristics of the operations, the NWLB not only removed the opprobrium from the term *job dilution* but also called into question the legitimacy of sex-based job classifications and the pervasive devaluing of women's work.[27]

The NWLB decision in the GM case marked a milestone in the history of women's rights. In a letter to Walter Reuther, Mary Ander-

26. "Women Work for Victory"; "Engineers of Womanpower," p. 4; minutes of Management–Local 662 meeting, November 11, 1942, Neal Edwards Collection, Box 3, September–November Meetings Minutes Folder, ALUA.
27. Opinion of the Board in the GM case, *WLR* 3 (1943): 355–56.

son observed that the decision "not only represents [the NWLB's] first official recognition of the same pay policy for women as men, but marks the most significant advance by the Federal Government to implement this principle." The action by the NWLB in the GM case also was important because it defined the equal-pay principle broadly to encompass the concept of comparability, thus opening the door to a general equalization of wage rates by means of job-evaluation formulas. The prospects for improving the status of women and women's work in industry did not escape Anderson. Congratulating the UAW for its victory in the case, the Women's Bureau director hailed the union for its effort "to win recognition of the broad principle that 'the worker is worthy of his hire.' "[28]

Although the NWLB intended its equal-pay policy to fulfill its mandate to settle labor disputes, the ambiguous boundaries between women's and men's prewar and wartime work continued to make the determination of job classifications and wage rates exceedingly difficult in many instances; and conflict persisted in the auto industry and elsewhere. An NWLB case involving Bendix and UAW Local 9 demonstrates the dynamics of wartime discord over the sexual division of labor in industry. As war production intensified in 1942, Bendix sought to revise the agreement that restricted both the hiring and placement of women at its South Bend plant. The company now wanted the freedom to hire more women without the consent of the local, to place them in departments of the plant designated as for men only, and to pay them the lower rate accorded women in the same jobs in "female departments." Fearing a wholesale reduction in wage rates, the local, before it would agree to eliminate the contract clause restricting the employment of women, demanded that women placed in male departments in jobs also performed by men receive the higher male rate. Bendix refused to equalize wages, maintaining that implicit in the prewar agreement to classify the work of women and men separately was the assumption that the two sexes performed different and unequal work. Now to pay some women higher wages simply because they would be performing jobs elsewhere in the plant, the company asserted, would violate not only the contract but long-standing principles of wage determination.

Local 9 then placed itself in the unusual position of discrediting the

28. Anderson to Reuther, September 23, 1942, UAW General Motors Department Collection, Series I, Box 1, Correspondence UAW and GM, August 12–October 13, 1942 Folder, ALUA.

sexual division of labor in the plant. Arguing that there were no "female classifications" per se, the local insisted that wage rates should be determined on the basis of the content of the job, not the sex of the operator, and that even women employed in "female jobs" in "female departments" should receive the same pay as men and women similarly employed elsewhere in the plant. Bendix rejected this demand, claiming that to raise the wage rates of so many women would place the company at a competitive disadvantage in the industry. Management called the union's bluff by proposing an independent plantwide evaluation of the disputed jobs to eliminate sex labels and differentials. Confronted with the prospect of wage increases for some women and wage reductions for many men, Local 9 balked, withdrawing its demand for wage equalization and calling instead for a 10-cent differential between men and women in the same jobs. Bendix countered with an offer to increase the hourly rates of women in those jobs by 8 cents.

Unable to compromise, both sides invited NWLB arbitration of the dispute. In his decision, the board-appointed arbitrator, Harry Shulman, declared, "The differential between male and female rates was in origin and in its continuance based on nothing else but sex." Shulman agreed in principle with the company proposal for systematic job evaluation but rejected it as both impractical in wartime and offensive to the union. Stating "were this differential not agreed upon and were it not of long standing there would be little doubt that it should be completely eliminated," Shulman reduced but did not erase it. He granted the union's demand in pegging the hourly rate for women in the disputed classifications 10 cents below that already negotiated for men. He also removed the restriction on the company's freedom to employ women.[29]

Although the Bendix decision was notable for its justification for sex discrimination in compensation, the NWLB's settlement of the ongoing dispute between the UAW and GM was more significant because it provided a sophisticated rationale and method for maintaining the sexual division of labor in industry. In accordance with the NWLB's September 1942 decision, the national contract of October 1942 between the UAW and GM included an equal-pay clause. But at GM plants in Bay City and Flint, Michigan, and Melrose Park, Il-

29. Decision of the National Board in the Bendix case, September 20, 1943, *WLR* 11 (1944): 669–77.

linois, disputes arose over the correct application of this policy. At issue was the principle of wage determination for new jobs such as aircraft inspection, which were created during conversion to defense production. The union contended that the jobs were comparable to those previously and currently performed by men and that the women holding them should receive the higher male rate of pay. GM, on the other hand, insisted that the jobs in question were similar to those women had performed in the prewar era and that women holding them should be paid the negotiated "women's" rate.[30]

When negotiations failed to resolve the controversy, the UAW requested arbitration by the NWLB. William Simkin admitted in a decision issued on July 31, 1943, that "exact and certain allocation of a specific operation to a given type is by no means easy." Acknowledging the validity of both the company and the union points of view, Simkin remarked, "This sort of argument can be endless, particularly when there is a thirty-five cent per hour difference in the rates and when even in peacetime there was little difference, if any, between the most difficult female jobs and the least difficult male jobs." The solution, stated the arbitrator, "is to wipe out the sex designation of the . . . jobs and establish . . . rates for various types of work which reflect only the type of work performed." Simkin's solution, however, merely reinstated the sexual division of labor under a different guise. Despite his acknowledgment of the overlap between many "women's" jobs and "men's" jobs, Simkin substituted the terms *light* and *heavy* for the controversial "female" and "male" job labels and established a 10-cent wage differential between the two categories. The action reduced the hourly rate differential between male and female inspectors, for example, from 35 to 10 cents but retained in principle the system of sex-based job classifications. "Rates of each classification," Edwin Witte of the Regional War Labor Board later explained, "imply whether the employees are men or women."[31]

The Bendix and GM decisions reflect the NWLB's retreat from the broadly defined position on equal pay that the board had adopted in the fall of 1942. In May 1943 William Davis, chair of the NWLB,

30. UAW brief, n.d. [June 11, 1943], Walter P. Reuther Collection, Box 28, Folder 4, ALUA; summary brief submitted by Buick Motor Division–Melrose Park, June 14, 1943, ibid., Folder 5; summary brief submitted by Buick Motor Division–Flint, June 17, 1943, ibid., Folder 6.

31. Arbitrator's decision on women's rates in the GM case, July 31, 1943, ibid., Folder 5; decision of Regional Board XI, October 9, 1943, WLR 11 (1944): 745.

criticized the unions' use of the equal-pay-for-equal-work policy pro-mulgated by the board to increase wages in job classifications to which only women had been assigned in the past, asserting: "The rates for such jobs, especially when developed by collective bargain-ing[,] are presumed to be correct in relation to other jobs in the plant. . . . Their determination should not be related to the equal-pay for equal work question." In the Rotary Cut Box Shook Industry case, Wayne Morse further ruled that the equal-pay doctrine "is not to be invoked to abolish wage differences between jobs which have histor-ically been performed by women almost entirely and jobs which have been recognized in the industry as jobs limited for the most part to men." The board was not unmindful of the extent to which wages in women's jobs were artificially low. In a case involving UAW Local 743 and the Bendix Aviation plant in Owosso, Michigan, for example, George Bowles ruled that the same-titled jobs held by women and men were different enough to warrant wage differentials but ques-tioned their scope. "That all females are paid the same rate," he noted, "would indicate that the evaluations tend strongly toward a uniformity of rates not wholly measured by precise differences in job content." The slippery and inconsistent character of the sexual divi-sion of labor also undermined NWLB attempts to render clear and unambiguous decisions. The board, however, like other federal agencies during World War II, chose not to lead a revolt against long-standing and deeply rooted ideas about women's place in American industry.[32]

Together with the process of conversion and the increased employ-ment of women, NWLB rulings disturbed the UAW's equanimity with respect to the sexual division of labor. In combination, they com-pelled the union to make its case for higher wages for the growing share of its membership that was female by acknowledging the ex-tent to which the distinction between women's and men's work had been and still was arbitrary and irrelevant. The union was placed in the novel position of proving that women's jobs were the same as men's jobs despite the prewar practice, in which the UAW had con-

32. National War Labor Board (NWLB), *The Termination Report of the National War Labor Board*, vol. 1 (Washington, D.C., 1947), pp. 293–96; decision of the National Board in Rotary Cut Box case, *WLR* 12 (1944): 605–9; arbitrator's decision in Bendix Aviation Owosso case, November 15, 1943, copy in Research Department Collection, Box 32, Folder 15; Eleanor Straub, "U.S. Government Policy toward Civilian Women during World War II," *Prologue* 5 (1973): 240–54.

curred, of distinguishing among jobs on the basis of sex. T. A. John-stone of the UAW's GM Department, for example, criticized the position taken by William Davis on wage rates for so-called women's jobs. "Historically, a differential in women's rates was established on the basis of sex alone," Johnstone explained to George Taylor, then vice-chairman of the NWLB, "and none of the factors which would tend to equalize rates were given consideration by management." In its exception to Simkin's decision in the GM case, the UAW insisted that no discrimination should be made between "light" and "heavy" operations, disagreeing that the work performed by women and men in same-titled jobs was dissimilar enough to warrant wage differentials and noting that within any job or rate classification there were tasks that ranged in level of difficulty. This was a considerable advance over the UAW's position before and during the period of conversion, when it had sought to preserve wage standards by restricting women to a small number of jobs and excluding them from the larger number of male jobs. The new perspective suggested a revision of the union's rather limited notion of equal pay for equal work to include the idea of equal pay for comparable work or work of comparable value, a concept better able to address the problem of occupational segregation by sex in the auto industry.[33]

The UAW's reaction to Simkin's decision, however, indicated both the progress the union had made toward recognizing the problem of occupational segregation by sex and the distance it had yet to travel. "With such great numbers of women employed, displacing men for military service," the UAW contended, "it is essential that the wage-structure built up through years of laborious effort be maintained for the preservation of morale, on the part of the men so displaced." The foundation of that wage structure, however, was a sexual division of labor. Still thinking in customary terms, the union challenged the light-heavy distinction introduced by Simkin and reasserted what it believed was the more fundamental distinction. "Where new operations are introduced having no previous classification," the UAW argued, "such operations should, wherever it is comparable to that

33. Johnstone to Taylor, June 8, 1943, Walter Reuther Collection, Box 28, Folder 4; UAW exception to arbitrator's decision in GM case, August 18, 1943, ibid. The process whereby the union came to acknowledge the arbitrary character of the sexual division of labor is illustrated in the minutes of meetings between Local 599 and the Buick Motor Division in Flint during May 1943 as both sides debated application of the NWLB's equal-pay order. UAW Local 599 Collection (unprocessed), Box 3, Women's Rates Folder, ALUA.

performed by men, be classified and rated accordingly." In the union's view, women employed in "male" jobs should receive the "male" rate and those employed in "female" jobs should receive the "female" rate. By continuing to describe the wage and occupational structure in the auto industry in gender-specific terms, however, the UAW undermined its position on equal pay and the sexual division of labor because it played into the hands of employers that also asserted the importance of difference in establishing lower rates for women regardless of occupation. Industry members of the Regional War Labor Board, for example, objected to Simkin's decision because it used a standard of comparability in narrowing the differential between women and men in same-titled jobs. "There is different work being done by women than that being done by men," they maintained. By talking in terms of men's jobs that women could do and women's jobs that men did not do, the UAW confirmed rather than challenged management's position. The equivocal position held by the UAW would bedevil its efforts late in and after the war to challenge occupational segregation by sex and eliminate sexual discrimination.[34]

In the end, then, both the UAW and the NWLB fell short of delivering on the promise of the equal pay principle. NWLB orders and the UAW's efforts to achieve equal pay for women in jobs the union defined as "men's" did benefit female workers. In General Order No. 16, issued on November 24, 1942, the NWLB ensured implementation of the equal-pay policy by exempting voluntary upward adjustments of women's wages from the federal government's wartime wage freeze. Together with the stimulus provided by cost-plus defense contracts, the board's endorsement of the equal-pay-for-equal-work principle increased the paychecks of thousands of women workers during the war. Between November 1942 and January 1944 alone, 2,250 voluntary wage adjustments affecting 59,500 women workers were reported to the Wage Stabilization Board. Similarly, the gap between men's and women's wages in the automobile industry narrowed during World War II, with women's share of men's straight-time average hourly earnings increasing from 67 percent in 1940 to 79 percent in 1943. Women did not, however, gain the advantage that a

34. UAW exception, August 18, 1943, Walter Reuther Collection, Box 28, Folder 4; decision of Regional Board, October 9, 1943, WLR 11 (1946): 746.

revision of the organization of work might have offered them in terms of both wage equity and wider access to jobs in industry.[35]

The UAW's interest in ensuring that women's employment in men's jobs be limited to the period of the war emergency was also evident in its wartime seniority policies. Separate seniority lists for women and men, a well-established practice in the auto industry in peacetime, were the primary means adopted by the union to limit women's access to postwar jobs. "We wish to be foresighted and save ourselfs a lot of grief later on," explained Harold Thompson, an international representative, in July 1942. "If [women] now become entrenched within our seniority system, how then will we be able to regulate this when this war work is all over?" Acknowledging the "difficulties" that might arise from increased female employment, George Addes, the UAW's secretary-treasurer, assured Thompson, "Insofar as we are concerned it is permissible to maintain separate seniority lists for women [if the lists would] prove beneficial." After the NWLB ordered the elimination of separate seniority lists in its settlement of several equal-pay cases, the International Executive Board (IEB) adopted a resolution in February 1944 opposing the establishment of separate seniority lists in plants where single lists were already in effect. The IEB, however, indicated its own ambivalence by also resolving that where separate seniority lists had been estblished before the war, the decision to abolish or continue the practice was a matter for local option.[36]

The IEB expressed no opposition to the more blatantly discriminatory practice of providing only temporary seniority for women employed in "men's" jobs. A procedure followed by many locals, including those in all GM plants, this arrangement stipulated that length of service on war jobs was to have no practical value in computing seniority in the reconversion period unless the worker had a peacetime job to which the time could be applied. Prewar

35. General Order No. 16, *WLR* 4 (1943): xxviii; NWLB, *Termination Report*, vol. 1, p. 297; Annual Averages for Male and Female Wage Earners in Automobile Industry 1929–1943, Research Department Collection, Box 28, Folder 27.

36. Thompson to Addes, July 2, 1942, and Addes to Thompson, July 9, 1942, George F. Addes Collection, Box 94, Folder 7, ALUA; *Ammunition* 2 (March 1944): 13. The most prominent NWLB decision was in a case involving the UAW and Chrysler. In the case involving Bendix in Owosso, the judges also ordered the elimination of separate seniority lists based on sex. *WLR* 10 (1944): 551, 559, 567; arbitrator's decision in Bendix Aviation Owosso case, November 15, 1943, copy in Research Department Collection, Box 32, Folder 15; Jonas Silver and Everett Kassalow, "Seniority in the Automobile Industry," BLS investigation, April 1944, p. 26, War Policy Division, Box 22, Seniority in Detroit UAW Locals Folder.

women workers who transferred from "female" classified jobs to jobs formerly reserved for men, therefore, accumulated seniority in their old jobs; at the end of the war, they were presumably to resume their peacetime jobs. Women who were hired into jobs classified as "male" accrued seniority only for "the duration." Since the bulk of the war-time female labor force had not been employed in auto plants before the war, the practical effect of this arrangement was to deprive women of reemployment rights after reconversion.[37]

The UAW was not alone in its defense of the sexual division of labor in industry. Craft unions were much more exclusionary. The International Association of Machinists, Molders and Foundry Workers, Iron Shipbuilders and Helpers, the Ironworkers, and the Carpenters and Joiners finally changed their policy of not admitting women to membership after Pearl Harbor, but the International Brotherhood of Boilermakers refused to do so until the fall of 1942. Even after the international altered its policy, Boilermaker locals in the Puget Sound, Washington, defense area persisted in denying women admission. Hoping to prevent the erosion of job standards and the loss of employment for their prewar male memberships, AFL and CIO unions as a group generally sought to recodify the sexual division of labor for the duration of the war. Not all unions adopted wholly conservative stances, however. The UAW began at least to rethink its approach to wage determination. The UE went even further, guarding against wage cutting by challenging the very basis for wage discrimination by sex. In an NWLB case against General Electric and Westinghouse, the UE charged management with sys-tematically undervaluing the work performed by women. Endorsed by the NWLB in its 1945 decision, the UE's position essentially ad-vanced the same argument as does our contemporary concept of equal pay for comparable worth. But the UE's campaign ultimately failed. Its own position, moreover, was limited in certain important respects. The union, for example, did not also advocate sex-blind job assignments. World War II, therefore, was important in establishing precedent for reconsideration of wage disparities specifically and occupational segregation by sex generally, but it was not the time for meaningful or permanent change in the status of women in the labor market.[38]

37. Silver and Kassalow, "Seniority in the Automobile Industry," pp. 25–27.
38. Philip Foner, *Women and the American Labor Movement from World War I to the Present* (New York, 1980), pp. 361–62; Karen Beck Skold, "The Job He Left Behind: American Women in the Shipyards during World War II," in Carol Berkin and Clara

Women with prewar experience in the auto industry and in the UAW approached the issues raised by the war emergency from a different perspective than did male unionists. Although they strongly agreed that women who replaced men during the war should receive the same rate previously paid male employees, female activists alerted union leaders to the potential that the war offered for contravening the marginal and unequal status of women in the auto industry. "Except that there is a division as to what's heavy and what's light, there's no difference in men's and women's jobs," Irene Young stated at a February 1942 conference. "They just decide what are women's jobs and what are men's jobs. Men get all the way from ten to twenty cents more on the same jobs," she remarked. During discussion of the union's equal-pay policy at the 1942 convention, Young reminded the male delegates: "We women who have been in industry ten or fifteen years have battled for an awfully long time. In those places where the women can see that they are doing exactly the same jobs that the men are, there always has been a feeling among the women that they have not been getting a square deal in this thing, and I think if we are ever going to get it, now is the time."[39]

Women criticized the limited character of the union's commitment to equal pay. "So many of the men take the attitude of displeasure— and opposition against us," declared Neva Colter, recording secretary of Local 680, in June 1942. "It isn't right I know, especially in a union," she said, "however the men have always sought for higher wages, with little effort to get women any advantage along this line whatsoever." Louella Robinson contended that male unionists were as responsible as management for the persistence of wage inequities. "The first thing I feel we have to do is to convince the men in our union that the women are really worth what the men get," she said. "It seems to me most men feel that women are a little inferior to them and cannot quite produce the work they do." Young went a step further, charging that men were more interested in preserving their

---

Lovett, eds., *Women, War, and Revolution* (New York, 1980), pp. 55–75; Amy Kessel-man, "Hidden Resistance: Women Shipyard Workers after World War II," in Christine Bose, Roslyn Feldberg, and Natalie Sokoloff, eds., *Hidden Aspects of Women's Work* (New York, 1987), pp. 283–98; Karen Anderson, *Wartime Women* (Westport, Conn., 1981), pp. 23–74; Ruth Milkman, *Gender at Work* (Urbana, 1987), pp. 77–83; Nancy Gabin, "The Issue of the Eighties: Comparable Worth and the Labor Movement," *Indiana Academy of the Social Sciences Proceedings, 1988* 23 (February 1989): 51–58.

39. Transcript of Women's Conference, February 7, 1942, War Policy Division Collection, Box 2. Conferences Folder; *1942 Convention Proceedings*, p. 357.

dominant position in the labor market than in obtaining wage parity for women. "In the past where women have been brought in on jobs where the rates are equal to those given the men," she observed, "you had a feeling among the men that the women were taking their work away from them. The feeling that . . . the men wanted to have the women kicked out of the shop . . . has been manifested at every convention I have attended." Warning that intergender conflict weakened the union, Young advocated the use of a job-evaluation formula as the most effective means of establishing equitable wage rates. "Let's try to get away from this stuff of trying to figure out how many pounds and how many cases as compared with a man. Let's set it up on the basis of what it is worth, and no matter who works on it, we will get the money."[40]

Few male unionists evinced interest in the issues that women raised at this time. At the close of the 1942 convention, Sam Sage of Local 742 in Detroit warned that the union's unwillingness to challenge the sexual division of labor would cost it the support and loyalty of women in the industry. "I believe we sold the fair ladies an empty sack," Sage said, "and sold ourselves a kick in the pants for future dates." Sage's admonition was not heeded. Established early in the war period as women were entering the industry in large numbers for the first time, the union's policies regarding wages, job classifications, and seniority were largely products of conflict between male workers and management. Neither group consulted the proportionately smaller number of women who had worked in auto plants before the war and had attained leadership positions in the locals.[41]

Although the results obtained were meager, the attempt by women to integrate the concerns of female workers into the union's agenda was in itself an important precedent. Never having mobilized collec-

40. Colter to Research Department, June 25, 1942, Research Department Collection, Box 32, Folder 12; *1942 Convention Proceedings*, pp. 357, 360. Colter made her comments in a letter attached to the Research Department questionnaire regarding female employment in plants under contract with the UAW. "If the women get any consideration in regard to equal wages, etc.," she said, "it will be because you make it your business to see that we do." Colter implored the Research Department to "appreciate my confidence in you and treat this letter as such. . . . I'm not trying to be underhanded, but I am trying to get help which my own local doesn't seem to provide." Colter to Research Department, June 25, 1942, Research Department Collection, Box 32, Folder 12.

41. *1942 Convention Proceedings*, p. 375.

tive action on an interlocal basis before, women activists, with the assistance and encouragement of Caroline Manning and Kathleen Lowrie of the Women's Bureau, launched their first campaign in the fall of 1941 to demand that the union leadership protect the right of laid-off female auto workers to reemployment on defense jobs. Their persistence resulted in the decision of the IEB to convene a women's conference, the first of its kind in the history of the UAW. Held in Detroit on February 7, 1942, the conference, although ostensibly called to discuss the problem of unemployment in the auto industry during the conversion period, became a forum for debate on a much wider range of issues, including equal pay for equal work, sex-based job classifications, and the need for women in policy-making positions. Meeting to share their concerns about conditions in the plants and to protest the treatment accorded them by employers and male unionists, the seventy women from UAW locals in the Michigan cities of Detroit, Pontiac, Lansing, Flint, Saginaw, and Bay City established a basis for future action in behalf of women's rights.[42]

The tone and content of discussion during the conference demonstrated how frustrated the women were at the indifference of the union leadership. George Addes, who served as conference chairman, had rebuffed several participants a few months earlier, and his defensiveness at the conference was evident from the outset. Stating in his introductory remarks, "I think everyone recognizes that there is a tendency . . . on the part of the male employees [to] feel that women ought not to be absorbed until the male help is absorbed," Addes urged the delegates "not to debate that tendency at this meeting." Tempers flared, however, at the start of the afternoon session. "Since this is a woman's conference," asserted Martha Strong of Local 174, "I think it would be very fitting at this time to choose a woman chairman for the afternoon session." Stating that he would "gladly entertain the motion," an insulted Addes retorted, "I'm not too much interested in chairing this meeting . . . because I have a lot of other work I could attend to." The delegates decided to retain Addes as chair, not because they disagreed in principle with Strong's proposal but "because our problem which is concerned with the

42. Kathleen Lowrie to Mary Anderson, March 6, 1942, RG 86/NA, Box 1416, Region V Early 1941–June 1943 Folder; transcript of Women's Conference, February 7, 1942, War Policy Division Collection, Box 2, Conferences Folder.

women needs to be [dealt with] by the International and [our decisions] should be carried out by the International."[43]

The participants indicated that they were unwilling to continue allowing men to define their interests. Conflict erupted a second time at the conference when Addes announced that the IEB was no longer committed to the view that the all-male defense-employment committees "could handle the problems of the women as well." Hoping to mollify the women, Addes blundered, proposing that just one woman be added to each committee, since "you don't have the problems the men have." Madeleine Carroll charged that the UAW was insensitive to women's concerns. "We have helped the men, we have been in the organization as long as the men, [and we] want the same kind of representation as the men," she protested. Another delegate demanded the creation of an all-female labor committee that would meet with representatives from business and government to formulate policy relative to the employment of women in defense work. Denying that "we don't do anything for women in industry," Addes offered a compromise arrangement whereby three women would be named to the Detroit committee and one woman would be placed on each of the other five city committees. The delegates accepted the compromise and elected Mae McKernan, Irene Young, and Ruby Long to the Detroit committee and Pauline Young, Edna Montgomery, Patricia Williams, Helen Moore, and Laura Fedor, respectively, to the Pontiac, Saginaw, Bay City, Lansing and Ypsilanti defense-employment committees.[44]

In the months following the February conference, women activists sought unsuccessfully within the union to raise issues of concern to them and their constituents. Rebuffed or ignored in forums such as the annual convention and largely absent from local and regional bargaining committees, they devised strategies to amplify their voice and influence in the union. Recognizing the potential that the anticipated increase in female employment in the plants offered for strengthening women's position in the union, women leaders em-

43. Transcript of Women's Conference, February 7, 1942, War Policy Division Collection, Box 2, Conferences Folder.

44. Ibid. Kathleen Lowrie, who represented the Women's Bureau at the conference, reported to Caroline Manning, "It was a fine conference, very democratic, and intelligent as to content, and very lively." Lowrie to Manning, February 25, 1942, RG 86/NA, Box 1416, Region V Early 1941–June 1943 Folder.

phasized the need to organize the new women workers and to teach them about the goals and purposes of trade unionism. To this end, they exploited the union's interest in such issues as the preservation of wage standards. Women new to the industry "will come from bakeries, beauty shops, restaurants and all other kinds of employment where the rates are very, very low," Irene Young warned delegates to the 1942 convention. "Once you get these women at forty or forty-five cents higher pay than they have been used to they will think it is a lot." The tactic, together with the increasing number of women in the plants, was effective. In October women from several Detroit locals met with Victor Reuther, Mary Ann Loeser of the Research Department, and William Levitt, director of the Education Department, to discuss "what might be done to strengthen the union's position among the many thousands of women now being hired . . . to whom the Union has little significance." At the suggestion of the women, the directors of Regions 1 and 1A (Detroit area) called a conference "to discuss and clarify UAW policy in relation to these new problems [resulting from] the increasing numbers of women who are finding employment in UAW plants."[45]

The conference, held in Detroit on January 31, 1943, was described by Kathleen Lowrie as "a real milestone in Michigan history." In contrast to the February 1942 conference, it was attended by men as well as women. Urged to send executive board members as well as shop stewards, fifty-two Detroit area locals dispatched 326 delegates, 155 of whom were male officers. "At the first conference last February, the women delegates made their position clear," observed Lowrie in a letter to Mary Anderson, "but it didn't get to the local officers as forcibly as it will this time." Five committees, each consisting of six to ten female delegates and one male international representative, wrote resolutions at the conference which were then discussed and voted on by the conference as a whole. Resolutions protesting discrimination against black women, demanding increased hiring of women from the area, and advocating extension of Lanham Act funding for child-care facilities were approved by the delegates. Asserting that "length of service should govern between men and

45. *1942 Convention Proceedings*, p. 357; Victor Reuther to George Addes, October 16, 1942, War Policy Division Collection, Box 17, George Addes–September 1941 to October 1942 Folder; Co-Directors of Regions 1 and 1A to the Presidents of All Local Unions in the Detroit Area, November 3, 1942, UAW War Policy Division–Women's Bureau Collection, Box 2, Folder 11, ALUA.

women as to who gets the job after the war," the collective-bargaining panel opposed the practice of offering only temporary seniority to women in "men's" jobs and demanded the abolition of separate seniority lists based on sex. The panel also proposed that job surveys be conducted in the plants to demonstrate the degree of comparability between women's and men's jobs and urged the international to insist that wage rates be determined on the basis of the operation rather than the sex of the operator. "Seething with important information" on these matters, the delegates adopted both resolutions after lengthy debate.[46]

Of the five committees, the one devoted to the organization and education of women was concerned with "the most live subject" at the conference. In devising its resolution, this group took into consideration a debate that had arisen after the February 1942 meeting among women activists, many of whom also attended the second conference. Acutely aware that the prospects for change were contingent on their own efforts, women had discussed whether to establish an extralocal women's council to lobby for union action on particular issues or to exert influence by seeking appointment to policy-making committees and running for local offices in addition to that of steward in all-female departments. The committee opted for direct representation and an informal associational network. Emphasizing the need for greater female participation in union affairs "to maintain standards while the men are away," the committee proposed that the IEB appoint a woman as assistant educational director with responsibility for "women's activities," that locals establish women's committees to spearhead organizational and educational campaigns, and that the UAW encourage women to seek elective office in the locals.[47]

In urging UAW men to organize and educate wartime workers, women activists hoped to serve the interests of female solidarity as much as union solidarity. The rapid and massive influx of women

46. List of Delegates to Women's Conference, January 31, 1943, Emil Mazey Collection, Box 13, Folder 6, ALUA; Lowrie to Anderson, November 24, 1942, and February 11, 1943, RG 86/NA, Box 1416, Region V Early 1941–June 1943 Folder; *UAW*, February 15, 1943. Under the 1940 Lanham Act, which provided federal funds to aid war-boom communities, the government helped build and operate child-care centers during World War II. For a description and analysis of this program, see Karen Anderson, *Wartime Women*, pp. 122–53; William Chafe, *The American Woman* (London, 1972), pp. 161–72.

47. Lowrie to Anderson, November 24, 1942, and February 11, 1943, RG 86/NA, Box 1416, Region V Early 1941–June 1943 Folder; *UAW*, February 15, 1943.

into the plants unsettled relations among women as well as between the sexes. The equal pay issue, for example, caused conflict between women with prewar experience in the plants and those new to the auto industry. Alice Cox, an activist who had worked in GM's Delco Remy plant in Anderson, Indiana, before the war, was bitter when women working there accepted management's offer of a flat 10-cent-an-hour increase rather than insisting on equal pay on jobs also performed by men. Able to convince only six of the women who attended the ratification meeting to vote against the 10-cent raise, Cox reported: "The women at the meeting were mostly new to the industry. All they could see was the ten cents right then." When a majority of the women employed at the Chevrolet Commercial Body plant in Indianapolis similarly acceded to management's offer to raise their hourly rate of 82 cents to 96 cents rather than demanding the $1.09 rate paid to men in the same jobs, women who had worked in the plant before the war told a United States Women's Bureau representative that they were "out of heart." Distressed by the disinterest among younger women in the issue of equal pay for equal work, they were reluctant to continue pressing for equal pay.[48]

The integration of black women into the labor force in auto plants also undermined female solidarity. According to a UAW survey of plants under contract with the union, less than .5 percent of all women employed in production in the spring of 1942 were black; and of the 115 black women working in the industry, 100 were employed in the Glenn Martin plant in Baltimore, Maryland. One year later another UAW survey found 5,000 black women employed in the industry, a number that rose as the war continued. The same survey, however, also revealed that many of the new workers were either in janitorial and maintenance jobs or in laborer positions, all of these among the heaviest, dirtiest, and lowest-paid occupations in defense plants. To avoid integrating production jobs, firms such as Murray Body in Detroit trained black women for defense jobs and then fired them for spurious reasons during the probationary period before employees were eligible to join the union and gain its protection. Many employers simply refused to place black women in jobs for which they had received defense training, such as welding and riveting, or in assembly-line and machine jobs requiring little or no

48. Local Union 662 Schedule, May 1944, RG 86/NA, Box 1703, Union Schedules Folder; May Bagwell to Mary Anderson, March 18, 1944, ibid.

experience. Some made no pretense of their prejudice. A job-placement official at the Ford bomber plant in Willow Run, Michigan, for example, denied Donna Rolland transfer to an inspection job for which she had received training because "the whole trouble is that Niggers are trying to move ahead too fast." Other managers and employers cited interracial tensions as justification for their discriminatory hiring and placement practices. Although a smokescreen for their own racist attitudes, the argument spoke to the very real problem of white workers' resistance to racial integration. "Once we accept Negro women into the shops even during this crisis," Evelyn Scanlon, a Local 3 shop steward, warned the participants at the February 1942 UAW women's conference, "we will always have them. When they come into the shops to work you know what that means. They'll be working along side of us, they'll be using the same rest rooms." During and after conversion, white workers indicated their refusal to work with blacks by participating in "hate strikes." Not all whites shared such views, however. Warning that racial conflict threatened unionism, Martha Strong, a Local 174 officer in the Ternstedt plant in Detroit, for example, challenged Scanlon, charging: "People fight against us Southern whites. We are on the same basis as Negroes." But interracial tensions could not be ignored, and they impinged on the efforts of female activists to mobilize a collective challenge to sexual discrimination.[49]

In 1943 the UAW began to address the questions and problems that women had raised in the preceding months. Confronted with the rapid and massive influx of women into the plants, the male leadership no longer could relegate issues of special concern to women workers to the periphery of the union's agenda. Organizing the new workers was not the union's most pressing concern now. The UAW had signed contracts before Pearl Harbor with the auto firms employing the bulk of the wartime labor force, and few workers availed themselves of the escape clause in the maintenance-of-union-mem-

49. Results of 1942 Research Department survey, Research Department, Box 32, Folder 9; reports from 1943 Research Department survey, ibid., Folders 8–11; discharge at Murray Body, n.d., UAW War Policy Division Collection, Box 29, Local Union 2 Folder; Donna Rolland complaint, August 24, 1943, ibid., Local Union 50 Folder; August Meier and Elliott Rudwick, *Black Detroit and the Rise of the UAW* (Oxford, 1979), pp. 125–34, 165–72; transcript of Women's Conference, February 7, 1942, War Policy Division Collection, Box 2, Conferences Folder. For the experience of black women during World War II, see Karen Anderson, "Last Hired, First Fired: Black Women Workers during World War II," *Journal of American History* 69 (June 1982): 82–97; Jacqueline Jones, *Labor of Love, Labor of Sorrow* (New York, 1985), pp. 238–53.

bership formula that the UAW, like other unions, received in return for its pledge not to strike during the war. The integration into the union of the new members, half of whom were female, posed the greatest challenge for the union. The UAW undoubtedly would have developed some kind of wartime program for the benefit of women without the prodding of its female members, but the women with prewar experience in the industry and the union who took the initiative in 1942 to pose questions, suggest policy, and establish a basis for mobilization ineluctably shaped the character of that program.[50]

The increase in the number of married women workers in the plants created a constituency with concerns that the UAW never before had addressed. Before the war, the union generally had not objected to the industry's common practice of simply discharging female employees who became pregnant. The local union women's committee at a Detroit-area Ford plant organized an important campaign in the spring of 1943 to protest this practice. Contending that women were concealing their pregnancies to avoid dismissal and incurring miscarriages and other injuries as a consequence, the committee successfully persuaded plant management to permit pregnant employees to work as long as they wished and to return to work as soon as they felt able. In February 1944 the IEB adopted a formal policy defending the rights of pregnant workers and issued a model maternity clause for inclusion in contracts. Stipulating that a woman could work through the seventh month of her term and ought not have to work at any job requiring heavy lifting or continuous standing, the clause also provided that a woman's seniority would accumulate during the period of her maternity leave of absence and that she could return to work whenever she felt able.[51]

50. Emerging from a series of decisions by the NWLB, the maintenance-of-union-membership formula provided that workers who were union members at the time a contract was signed were required to remain dues-paying members until they left their jobs or the contract came up for renewal. Workers hired after that date were allowed to withdraw from the union during the first fifteen days of their employment. Joel Seidman, *American Labor from Defense to Reconversion* (Chicago, 1953), pp. 94–108.

By June 1941 the Big Three auto companies had all recognized the UAW as bargaining agent for their plant workers. On the eve of Pearl Harbor, the union claimed 500,000 dues-paying members, approximately 10 percent of whom were women. Wartime conditions, including maintenance-of-membership clauses, made the UAW the nation's first million-member union. Subtracting the figure for prewar female membership from the union's claim of 280,000 women members by 1945, I find that women composed half of the union's total new membership.

51. Ernest Goodman to George Addes, August 7, 1943, Research Department Collection, Box 32, Folder 21; Model Maternity Clause, February 24, 1944, Mazey Collec-

Just as the demand for labor eased conventional disapprobation of the employment of married women in traditionally male occupations, so too did the concern with absenteeism among defense workers justify the use of public funds to establish day-care centers. The UAW publicly advocated the government's wartime funding of day-care facilities for the children of working mothers, lobbying for extensions of Lanham Act funding and encouraging locals to pressure community boards of education to apply for Lanham Act funds to finance nursery schools and canteens.[52] The international also acted to quell resistance to its policy regarding child care. Claiming that "there are no arms around a child like its mother's" and that nursery schools were "a capitalistic sop to the laboring classes," the members of the Warren, Michigan, school board, many of whom were officers in UAW locals, adamantly opposed the institution of a government-funded day-care center in their community. Further investigation revealed that the school board's overriding fear was that if child care were institutionalized, women would remain in the plants after the war and deprive returning veterans of jobs in the auto industry. Dismayed by the lack of sympathy for working mothers and sister unionists, Victor Reuther pressured the board members to change their policy. In contrast to the intransigence of the UAW men in Warren, unionists in other locals, especially those with a contingent of active women, voluntarily established child-care committees to promote the principle and inform women of the availability of such services.[53]

The UAW also demonstrated concern for women by instituting a novel and widely acclaimed system of union counselors in the plants. In 1942 defense contractors began hiring women to serve as counselors to their new female employees. Concerned to reduce absenteeism and labor turnover, employers instructed the counselors to ease women's transition into the plants and make referrals to community

tion, Box 14, Folder 8; interview with Josephine Gomon, December 22, 1959, p. 33, UAW Oral History Project.

52. Catherine Gelles to All Detroit Local Union Presidents, December 29, 1942, and R. J. Thomas to All Executive Board Members, International Representatives, and Local Union Presidents, November 18, 1943, in War Policy Division–Women's Bureau Collection, Box 1, Folder 16.

53. Caroline Burlingame to Mildred Jeffrey, February 10, 1944, War Policy Division–Women's Bureau Collection, Box 5, Folder 8; Victor Reuther to Irving Little, February 22, 1944, ibid.; Jeffrey to John Gibson, March 7, 1944, ibid., Box 2, Folder 2; Ben May to Gibson, March 14, 1944, ibid., Box 5, Folder 8.

services. Although generally sympathetic to workers and appreciated by many, women's counselors also were the target of labor criticism. Unionists complained that counselors deflected legitimate grievances over occupational health hazards, shielding management from responsibility for providing safe and sanitary working conditions, while they solicited employee problems for which they had no solutions, deceptively placing the onus for inaction on the union.[54] When the War Production Board's Office of Labor Production (OLP) in August 1943 offered the UAW assistance in training women workers to help union members with out-of-plant problems not within the purview of the grievance machinery, such as housing shortages, transportation difficulties, shopping problems, and child care arrangements, the union was happy to accept. The War Policy Division recommended to the IEB in November 1943 that the UAW take advantage of this offering and issued its own proposal in the winter of 1944. Noting that the OLP was interested in the program "from the angle of war production," the War Policy Division stated:

> The union's interest . . . is broader. It is our responsibility to reach out to these new workers and help them with these problems that are burdening their lives, not only so that we can help in cutting down absenteeism and turnover, but so that we can demonstrate to these new workers that the union can effectively help them. To thousands of our new members who have merely inherited the improved working conditions in our plants without realizing the union's role in the advantages they are enjoying, this may be the first practical means of demonstrating to them how a union functions or that the union, being their organization, can be used to represent and help them on many fronts.

The division also emphasized the importance of the union counseling service as a means of counteracting management's use of its own

---

54. Manpower Division–Worker Supply Committee, "Report of Subcommittee on New Workers," April 29, 1943, Automotive Council for War Production Papers, Manpower . . . New Workers Subcommittee Folder, Detroit Public Library, Detroit, Michigan (hereafter cited as ACWP/DPL); UAW-CIO, *Proceedings of the First Annual Education Conference* (Detroit, 1944), pp. 93–94; "To Cure the Disease Called Company Counselors," *Ammunition* 2 (August 1944): 19. For an important example of the antiunion bias of women's counselors, see Jeanne Nunn to Josephine Gomon, May 28, 1943, Josephine Gomon Papers, Box 1, Correspondence May 1943 Folder, Michigan Historical Collections, Bentley Library, Ann Arbor; Jo Gomon to Children, April 10, 1944, ibid., Correspondence April 1944 Folder.

counselors "to inculcate anti-union attitudes among women workers."[55]

Introduced in several Detroit locals in February 1944, the union counseling program succeeded to an extent not anticipated by its proponents. Although theoretically the counselors were only supposed to provide information about community services, in practice they functioned as unofficial stewards. Women workers approached them with problems that they felt uncomfortable bringing to the attention of male union representatives. Edith Brysse, a Local 154 counselor, for example, explained the contract to a pregnant women who feared dismissal but "was too embarrassed about her condition to ask advise from the male steward." "She was glad to have a woman union counsellor advise her," Brysse observed. Other counselors dealt with complaints ranging from sexual harassment to the poor quality of sanitary napkins in plant restrooms. Recognizing the value of the program, local union officers themselves asked counselors to perform a variety of duties. "We have a lot of calls from the stewards to come into [the departments] to talk to women about different problems that women are shy or ashamed to talk over with their male stewards," Brysse reported. Through their activities, the counselors demonstrated to women workers that the union was a sympathetic ally rather than an impersonal bureaucracy.[56]

55. WPB-OLP, "Problems of Women War Workers in Detroit," August 20, 1943, War Policy Division–Women's Bureau Collection, Box 1, Folder 2; WPD Projected Program, November 1943, p. 7, War Policy Division Collection, Box 27, WPD April 1942–December 1943 Folder; Training Course for Women War Workers, n.d. [September 1943?], War Policy Division–Women's Bureau Collection, Box 4, Folder 9; UAW Proposals for Union Counseling System, n.d. [1944], ibid.; UAW-CIO Union Counseling System, n.d. [July 1944], War Policy Division Collection, Box 27, War Policy–Women's Bureau October 1942–October 1944 Folder. The OLP also proposed that the UAW and management consider solutions to in-plant problems "impairing women's health" as "production ideas" rather than as grievances and that the counselors rather than shop stewards handle them. Charging that grievance procedures were too slow, the OLP observed, "Speed in adjusting a work bench, adjusting a weight, *etcetera*, may make the difference between continuous performance and an absentee." The UAW, however, rejected this suggestion, insisting that the program should not "cut across the lines of collective bargaining or interfere with the steward system in any way. The union counselors will be made familiar with union procedures [and] will be instructed to encourage workers to go to stewards with any in-plant problems." OLP, August 20, 1943 Report, War Policy Division–Women's Bureau Collection, Box 1, Folder 2; UAW Proposals, n.d. [1944], ibid., Box 4, Folder 9.

56. Counsellors' Report Slips, Local 154, February 1944–June 1944, War Policy Division–Women's Bureau Collection, Box 4, Folder 9. Although the union counselors were available to help male and female workers, the assumption shared by all involved

Printed materials augmented the UAW's effort to convince women of the benefits of unionism. Drawing attention to its support for equal pay for equal work, maternity leaves, child-care facilities, and in-plant counselors, the UAW urged women to consider union dues an investment rather than a form of taxation. A pamphlet titled *Sister, You Need the Union!* informed women that "only the unions are fighting for full postwar employment which will assure you and your man of jobs if you want them" and that the CIO "is the only big group in the nation fully supporting Lanham Act appropriations." *It's Your Union, Sister*, a pamphlet issued by the education department of Local 600, explained that equal pay for equal work, safe working conditions, and the confidence that "you will not be pushed out of your jobs at the whim of company policy" were consequences of the UAW's success in winning wage increases, grievance procedures, and seniority systems. "The union is not so much a business as a social institution," the pamphlet asserted. "The purpose of a business is to make profits. The purpose of a union is to improve the well-being of its members. . . . That's why it takes an interest in community projects, such as child care centers, to make sure that when the mother is in the shop, her children are well provided for in day nurseries, under the best trained supervision."[57]

Fearing that the introduction of great numbers of women with little or no union experience might undermine the strength of the UAW, the male leadership for the first time actively encouraged women to participate in union affairs. Some of these messages were rather stern and self-serving. "You are directly responsible for keeping up the standards established in our industry by which you have benefited," a pamphlet instructing women to seek election to local union office dictated. "You are responsible for keeping the union strong and bettering working conditions." Others, however, praised women's wartime achievements and encouraged rather than lectured. "In every industry women are holding their own with men in the effi-

---

was that women were the principal concern. Bea Madson, for example, explained at a Local 400 meeting that the counselor would assist committeemen who were confronted with a variety of problems. "Most of these problems," Madson stated, "come from a sister carrying two jobs, working at home and in the shop." Plantwide meeting minutes, June 4, 1944, UAW Local 400 Collection, Box 65, Folder 11, ALUA.

57. *Sister, You Need the Union!*, UAW Education Department pamphlet, n.d. [1943], War Policy Division Collection, Box 18, Education Department November 1943–November 1944 Folder; *It's Your Union, Sister*, Local 600 Education Department pamphlet, n.d. [1944], War Policy Division–Women's Bureau Collection, Box 5, Folder 15.

cient performance of their jobs," asserted one pamphlet. "They are commanding complete self-respect because their dignity as human beings is becoming recognized. By their accomplishments they are destroying the old superstition that women are inferior to men." The union, another pamphlet stated, was an arena where women could assert their new identity. "The union offers you the greatest opportunity of your life—the opportunity to express your personality, to speak at meetings, to keep in step with the rhythm of our changing times." Stressing the mutually reinforcing relationship between women and the union, the appeal concluded: "At meetings you will get to know many people, you will learn about their shop problems and therefore more about your own. . . . By being active in the union you improve yourself. As you improve yourself you will be able to contribute more to the union. And the stronger and better the union becomes, the more it can do for all of us."[58]

Some regarded the negative ideas that many men had about women generally and about women's ability to lead particularly as a great deterrent to female participation and threat to union security. After reading accounts of a speech made by UAW president R. J. Thomas in which Thomas complained that the union's new female members "think of us—if they think at all—as radicals and trouble-makers" and worried that "the pretty little things in pink pants" would destroy the UAW, Barney Hopkins, financial secretary of Local 3, criticized Thomas for jeopardizing the union. Such statements, Hopkins informed Thomas, not only were untrue but did not "help the cause of educating women war workers into labor unions" and "only aggravate our purpose." "There has been very little effort made to bring into and develop leadership among the thousands of splendid women who have come into the plants," complained William Levitt, director of the UAW Education Department in 1944. "There are almost as many excuses for not bringing women into leadership of locals as there are women working in the plants." To counter such tendencies, the union also issued directives to male unionists. "Union sisters are the shock troops brought in to replace the thousands of hard-hitting union men being withdrawn from the locals every day by . . . the draft," read one appeal. "They must and can shoulder many of the union-building, war-winning burdens of the homefront. . . . Alert locals will lose no time taking advantage of this

58. *Sister, You Need the Union!; It's Your Union, Sister.*

new reservoir of union builders, realizing that just as the women need the union, the union needs the women, too."[59]

Such appeals may have helped, but there were more fundamental causes of the great increase in the number of women in leadership positions in the UAW during World War II. The draft left a power vacuum in the locals which offered women new opportunities for leadership on local executive boards. The increase in the number of women employed in the plants, moreover, not only created a constituency for women seeking the office of shop steward or shop committeewoman but compelled many male union leaders to recognize women for the first time. Jack Zeller, a Local 490 officer, attributed the increase in the number of female chief stewards in his local from one to six to "the reality of the girls becoming the majority in the departments." Before the war, Zeller admitted, women were regarded as a minority and "naturally they were not advanced," but since then, men had discovered that women "were interested in real trade unionism . . . [and they] got a lot of consideration." In 73 percent of the locals surveyed by the UAW's Education Department in August 1944 women were active as shop stewards, and in 60 percent of the locals women served as members of local union executive boards. Reflecting in part the persistence of negative attitudes toward the leadership abilities of women unionists, a smaller percentage of the locals surveyed, 37 percent, had women on plant bargaining and negotiating committees. That figure nevertheless represented a significant achievement for women, given their limited participation in this capacity before the war. Although precise figures are unavailable, the UAW estimated at the end of the war that three hundred women were officers in local unions and that at least one thousand women served on various committees in local unions.[60]

The attendance of women at the union's annual conventions was another indication of the increasingly important role played by women in the UAW during the war. Convention delegates were elected by local members rather than appointed by the leadership, and election was generally contingent on an individual's holding some other elective office in the local. The number of female delegates tripled between 1941 and 1942 and then doubled from 1942 to

59. *UAW*, November 1, 1943; Hopkins to Thomas, November 9, 1943, R. J. Thomas Collection, Box 9, Folder 7, ALUA; *UAW*, March 1, 1944; *Ammunition* 1 (April 1943): 11.

60. UAW-CIO, *Proceedings of the First Annual Education Conference*, pp. 129–30; *Ammunition* 2 (December 1944): 21; Mildred Jeffrey to Frieda Miller, November 19, 1946, RG 86/NA, Box 867, Auto Workers Folder.

1943; the last wartime convention, held in September 1944, included 105 women delegates. Although the proportion of women among all convention delegates rose modestly, from 2.6 percent in 1942 to 5 percent in 1944, an increasing number of local unions sent women to the conventions. In 1941 only 13 locals had women in their delegations. In 1943, 60 of the 533 local delegations included women; and in 1944, 69 of the 641 delegations contained at least one woman.[61]

Wartime conditions enabled women with prewar experience in the industry and the union to move up in the ranks of local union leadership. The career of Caroline Davis is one of the most notable examples of this trend. When the Excel Corporation plant in Elkhart, Indiana, was organized in 1941, Davis, an employee since 1934, was elected to the bargaining committee of Local 764. Elected vice-president of the local in 1943, she ascended to the presidency when the president was drafted four months into his one-year term. A skillful and successful negotiator, Davis was elected president in her own right in 1944 at the age of thirty-one. Local members, 80 percent of whom were men, reelected Davis president by overwhelming majorities four times more, until she received an appointment to the staff of the international union in 1948. Other women who were union activists before the war were elected to higher posts at the local level. For example, in late 1942 Mae McKernan became the first woman worker to be elected to the Detroit Industrial Union Council, a group composed of representatives from area unions affiliated with the CIO. At the Kelsey Hayes plant in Plymouth, where in October 1941 men struck against the employment of women, Gertrude Kelly, a founding member of Local 174 and a shop steward, played an important role in 1942 in winning equal pay for women in jobs also performed by men and was elected to the plant bargaining committee in 1943. Kelly also ran unsuccessfully for election to the Detroit city council in 1943. Although less dramatic than Davis's experience, the achievements of women such as McKernan and Kelly were equally important in increasing the visibility of women within the UAW.[62]

61. Figures for female attendance at the conventions were derived by counting the number of women's names on delegate rolls for the 1941, 1942, 1943, and 1944 UAW conventions. *1941 Convention Proceedings; 1942 Convention Proceedings; Proceedings of the Eighth Convention of the United Automobile, Aircraft, and Agricultural Implement Workers of America, October 4–10, 1943* (hereafter cited as *1943 Convention Proceedings*); *Proceedings of the Ninth Convention of the United Automobile, Aircraft, and Agricultural Implement Workers of America, September 11–17, 1944* (hereafter cited as *1944 Convention Proceedings*).

62. "Two Aces King High," *Ammunition* 5 (March 1947): 2–7; *Pittsburgh Courier,*

Women new to the industry also availed themselves of the new opportunities for leadership. Grace Blackett, whose father was a founder of Local 190 in the Packard plant in Detroit, worked at the Ford bomber plant in Willow Run for two years. Her union activities enabled her to obtain a regional staff appointment, making her the second female international representative in UAW history. Blackett's tireless efforts in behalf of women employed in UAW plants in Chicago earned her the respect of many, including Martha Ziegler of the United States Women's Bureau, who called Blackett one of the two "outstanding women union representatives in the area."[63]

The activism of black women also attests to the importance of the war in opening new space for women in the UAW. The effort of black women first to gain access to defense jobs and then to attain the same jobs held by white women earned them a reputation for assertiveness and militancy. Even employers recognized the commitment of black women. Reporting that some black women had applied to as many as thirty plants before finally being hired, an official of the Automotive Council for War Production, the industry's own wartime organization, averred that they "have been more willing than Negro men to try to break down barriers to Negro employment." Black women fought to secure their job prospects on their own and with the encouragement and assistance of groups such as the Double Victory clubs and the NAACP which promoted fair-employment practices in defense industries. Acting to end "hate strikes" and quell rank-and-file resistance to integration, local and national UAW leaders also defended the right of black men and women to work in production jobs, even at the expense of white members' support. UAW leaders at the Briggs Mack Avenue plant in Detroit, for example, told a group of white women who had struck to protest the placement of black women on the same jobs that they would be fired

November 20, 1948, clipping in UAW Public Relations Department–Frank Winn Collection, Box 14, Women's Bureau–War Policy Division Folder, ALUA; Kathleen Lowrie to Mary Anderson, January 18, 1943, RG 86/NA, Box 1416, Region V Early 1941–June 1943 Folder; *1942 Convention Proceedings*, p. 359; Nominees for National Women's Conference Committee, n.d. [Fall 1944], War Policy Division–Women's Bureau Collection, Box 5, Folder 13.

63. Nominees for National Women's Conference Committee, War Policy Division–Women's Bureau Collection, Box 5, Folder 13; Ziegler to Frieda Miller, March 1, 1945, RG 86/NA, Box 1395, Ziegler January to June 1945 Folder. The first female international representative was Patricia Wiseman. The second woman cited by Ziegler was Alice Smith of the United Electrical Workers (CIO).

without union opposition if they did not end their work stoppage. The women were "bitter" and "mad," recalled Local 212 leader Jess Ferrazza, and, after returning to work, "just would not talk to us." Not all white women opposed the entrance of black women into the plants. Donna Rolland, for example, told the hostile placement official at the Willow Run bomber plant that not only had she not encountered any resistance from white workers, even from the "hill-billies" the manager accused of harboring such disruptive sentiments, but that all the white women with whom she worked had "offered to sign a petition to the effect that they enjoyed working with me and would like for me to get on Inspection." The willingness of auto unionists to defend the rights of black women to defense jobs helped make these women strong supporters of the UAW and led some to seek leadership positions themselves.[64]

Although they acquired the taste and reputation for militance while confronting racism, black female activists also achieved prominence as women's advocates during the war. Support from white women in the union helped offset some of the bitterness engendered by the hate strikes. And even those white women who resisted racial integration could change their hearts and minds. Wanita Allen, a black woman who worked in the foundry at Ford's River Rouge complex, recalls that after a Local 600 committeeman, who also was black, refused to endorse a work stoppage by white women in the foundry over the introduction of Allen and other black women, the white women were angry, but "they eventually got over it. . . . After we worked awhile and got used to each other, then we'd laugh about [it]." As they forged bonds as fellow workers, union sisters, or personal friends, black and white women focused on what they shared on account of sex, a common ground for female activism. Lillian Hatcher, a riveter at the Briggs aircraft plant in Detroit, first became active in the union when she protested the transfer to the midnight shift of a group of female employees, white and black, all of whom had children. Elected to the executive board of Local 742 in 1943, Hatcher organized the local's first women's conference in February

64. Laura Vitray to Mr. Cronin and Mr. Hadley, January 17, 1944, ACWP/DPL, Manpower Committees . . . New Workers Subcommittee–Women Folder; Meier and Rudwick, *Black Detroit and the Rise of the UAW*, pp. 136–38, 147–54, 166–67; interview with William Oliver, March 5, 1963, pp. 2–3, UAW Oral History Project; interview with Jess Ferrazza, May 26, 1961, pp. 18–20, ibid.; interview with John K. McDaniel, May 26, 1961, p. 26, ibid.; Donna Rolland complaint, August 24, 1943, War Policy Division Collection, Box 29, Folder 50.

1944. Hatcher and other black women unionists in this way became important members of the growing network of female activists who pressed the issue of sexual equality.[65]

Female unionists used their greater voice and influence to represent the interests of their co-workers in the plants. The efforts of Jennie Taylor to mobilize women in Local 154 epitomized the changes brought about by the war. In the late thirties the local, which represented the workers at the Hudson Motor Car Company in Detroit, designated the office of fourth vice-president for a woman who was to have responsibility for "women's affairs," but the position usually was held by the president of the local women's auxiliary. Elected to the post in March 1943, Taylor, a power-machine operator, used the position to organize a women's committee and agitate for local action on such issues as child care and equal pay for equal work. Taylor's high profile in the local was reflected in her election to the bargaining committee in November 1943; the only woman among the five candidates chosen for the committee, Taylor was the third-highest vote getter. A prominent figure in the expanding network of women activists in the UAW, Taylor typified the "new woman" of the 1940s. No longer diffident or deferential, women unionists took responsibility for defining their own interests as workers and UAW members. In so doing, they contravened the marginal status the locals had accorded women and issues of concern to them in the prewar period.[66]

UAW women were part of a general surge in female activism in labor unions during World War II. Total union membership increased by 65 percent between 1940 and 1945. Reflecting the tremendous changes in the composition of the labor force in basic industries, women's share of union membership grew more substantially, from 9.4 percent in 1940 to 21.8 percent in the last year of the war. Scholars have documented the vitality and importance of women's participa-

65. Miriam Frank, Marilyn Ziebarth, and Connie Field, *The Life and Times of Rosie the Riveter* (Emeryville, Calif., 1982), pp. 57–58; interview with Wanita Allen, pp. 16–17, *Life and Times of Rosie the Riveter* film transcript, Tamiment Institute Library, New York University, New York, New York; interview with Lillian Hatcher, pp. 16–19, 47, The Twentieth Century Trade Union Woman: Vehicle for Social Change Oral History Project, Institute of Labor and Industrial Relations, University of Michigan, Ann Arbor; *Detroit News*, February 4, 1944.

66. Nominees for National Women's Conference Committee, War Policy Division–Women's Bureau Collection, Box 5, Folder 13; General Assembly Minute Book, October 24, 1941–December 22, 1944, UAW Local 154 Collection, Series I, Box 2, ALUA.

tion in union activities during World War II. As their numbers grew from 800,000 to 3 million, more women than ever before also became union activists and leaders. In the UE, the best-documented union besides the UAW for this period, women increased their share of the membership from 15 percent to 40 percent. With women such a large proportion of its membership, the UE, like the UAW, actively encouraged women to participate in union affairs and promoted women as leaders. Partly because of the greater presence of women, the UE granted women even greater access to power than did the UAW; more than one-third of the UE's full-time organizers were female, and in 1944 Ruth Young became the first woman on the UE executive board. Although it was not always easy to combine loyalty to the union with concern for women's special interests, female activists also raised gender issues to a greater extent than unionists had before the war. In varying degrees, women in unions experienced a new sense of empowerment during World War II.[67]

Their increased numbers gave women activists in the UAW the confidence to press more assertively for recognition from the international leadership. Reviving the idea of forming an extralocal women's council, they debated through the fall of 1943 the merits of a demand for the establishment of a women's department at the international level. Pat Sexton, a UAW member and plant steward at the time, recalls that opinion was divided regarding this bold proposal. "Some," she notes, "thought it would increase the segregation of women, limit rather than broaden the attention given them, and pacify their demand for general representation. Supporters thought that women needed a staff to perform an advocate's role in the union." The women introduced the idea at the 1943 UAW convention during an acrimonious debate over a resolution proposing the establishment of a minorities department to be headed by a black unionist. Victor Reuther contended in opposition: "If there is a special post for Negroes, then in all justice there should be a post at large for the Catholics, the women, the Jews, and the Poles and all the rest. That is not in keeping with democracy or true trade unionism." Emma Mur-

---

67. Gladys Dickason, "Women in Labor Unions," *Annals of the American Academy of Political and Social Science* 251 (May 1947): 71. On women's activism in unions during World War II, see Melissa Hield, "'Union Minded': Women in the Texas ILGWU, 1933–50," *Frontiers* 4 (Summer 1979): 59–70; Vicki Ruiz, *Cannery Women, Cannery Lives* (Albuquerque, 1987); Milkman, *Gender at Work*, pp. 84–98; Marc Miller, "Working Women and World War II," *New England Quarterly* 53 (March 1980): 42–61.

phy, an activist in Dodge Local 3, retorted, "What in the hell is wrong with a woman board member?" Speaking also in behalf of the women who had organized and attended the February 1942 and January 1943 conferences, Murphy reported that "we haven't heard a damn word" from the directors of Regions 1 and 1A, who had promised to seek the appointment of a woman to the Education Department. "The women are very definitely a minority group and we very definitely have problems," Murphy asserted. "Yes, we have them piled four miles high and we do not get the representation on these problems we deserve." A majority of the delegates, however, agreed with Reuther.[68]

In February 1944 women submitted a proposal to the IEB for the establishment of a women's department to serve both as a symbol of the UAW's commitment to women and as an institutionalized advocate of women's interests. Headed by a woman from the Detroit area, the department was to "give special attention, study and advice on organizing and solving the problems of the women in the shops." To augment the work of the department, the women also demanded that each of the sixteen regional UAW offices employ at least one woman organizer to work among the women in the region, with the cooperation of the Women's Department. The women outlined a program for the proposed department designed to link the problems experienced by the female membership outside and inside the plants. Asserting that "the woman union member will become more active and better integrated into the union life of her local when she has been released from a few of the many antiquated methods of homemaking," women activists argued that "the problems of child care, laundry, feeding, and shopping must become the property of the union." They claimed that with this program the union would demonstrate the benefits of unionism to women, strengthening their commitment to the UAW and promoting self-assertive activism. They contended that union action against sexual discrimination in wages and seniority agreements would be of similarly mutual benefit to the UAW and working women. Unequal pay and unequal sen-

68. Patricia Sexton, "A Feminist Union Perspective," in B. J. Widick, ed., *Auto Work and Its Discontents* (Baltimore, 1976), pp. 27–28; *Proceedings of the First Annual Education Conference*, pp. 98–99; Elizabeth Hawes, *Why Women Cry or, Wenches with Wrenches* (New York, 1943), p. 211; interview with Lillian Hatcher, pp. 50–51, The Twentieth Century Trade Union Woman Oral History Project; *1943 Convention Proceedings*, pp. 373, 384.

iority rights were not only unjust, they asserted, but served to inhibit intergender solidarity within the ranks and to make women suspicious of or hostile toward the UAW and trade unionism.[69]

Attesting to the new power of women in the union, the IEB granted their request. In April 1944 R. J. Thomas, president of the UAW, announced the establishment of a Women's Bureau as a department of the War Policy Division. Instructed to "develop recommended policy and program affecting our women members," the bureau, Thomas explained, "will give special consideration to seniority, safety standards, maternity leave practices, and other problems relating to the employment of women." The bureau was also assigned the task of developing "techniques for interesting women in general union activities and in developing their sense of union citizenship." Out-of-plant problems such as child care, shopping, and transportation were to be the province of the union counseling program, which was to be jointly administered by the Women's Bureau and the War Policy Division.[70]

Mildred Jeffrey served as the first director of the Women's Bureau. A graduate of the University of Minnesota and the Bryn Mawr Department of Social Economy and Social Research, Jeffrey worked as an organizer for the Amalgamated Clothing Workers and the CIO's Textile Workers Organizing Committee in the 1930s. In 1940 she and her husband, who also was active in the labor movement, took jobs in the Roosevelt administration. Employed by the War Production Board in the press and public relations department, Jeffrey met Roy Reuther, who subsequently lived with the couple in Falls Church, Virginia. Her husband's decision to move to Detroit to take a job in the Ford River Rouge plant coincided with the decision of the UAW to establish the Women's Bureau. On the recommendation of his brother Roy, Victor Reuther offered Jeffrey the directorship.[71]

During the spring of 1944 the Women's Bureau focused its attention on projects designed to increase women's participation in union affairs. It assisted local unions in developing programs of interest to women and establishing women's committees, and it cooperated

69. Women's Department Proposal, February 3, 1944, RG 86/NA, Box 901, Union Conference–Union Contract February 21, 1944, Folder.

70. Thomas to All Regional Directors and Local Union Presidents, April 22, 1944, War Policy Division–Women's Bureau Collection, Box 5, Folder 10.

71. Interview with Mildred Jeffrey, April 13, 1976, pp. 1–49, The Twentieth Century Trade Union Woman Oral History Project; Gabin interview with Mildred Jeffrey, August 1, 1983.

with the War Policy Division in extending the union counseling program to sixteen Detroit locals. In June the bureau sponsored a visit to Fort Knox, Kentucky, by 137 women from sixty-eight locals in Michigan, Ohio, Illinois, Indiana, Wisconsin, Missouri, and Tennessee. Inspired by a similar trip by union men to Camp Atterbury in Indiana, the intent of the project was both to provide women the opportunity to see in action the equipment they produced in the plants and to demonstrate to the soldiers the contributions made to war production by women and the UAW. Although the trip's ostensible purpose was "to promote better understanding between UAW-CIO women on the production front and the men in the Armed Forces," Jeffrey observed in retrospect that it "accomplished a great deal in giving the women participants a much greater sense of their recognition by the International union and of their duties and responsibilities as full-fledged union members."[72]

By the summer of 1944 the postwar employment prospects of women auto workers caused a shift in the focus of the bureau. Reporting in August that employment in 447 war plants had declined by 16 percent as a result of cutbacks in defense production, the union's Research Department indicated that women were being laid off in numbers disproportionate to men. Although they composed 42.2 percent of the work force in aircraft-parts plants, for example, women constituted 60.2 percent of those laid off. Women had made up 39.2 percent of the work force in plants producing aircraft engines, but they constituted 86 percent of those laid off. Confirming suspicions that employers intended to exclude women from the plants and that male unionists would not conscientiously monitor layoff and recall procedures, the bureau received many reports from women that they were being laid off without regard to their seniority. In cooperation with activist women in the union, the bureau began to alert the UAW to the importance of protecting women's right to postwar employment in the auto industry.[73]

The first obstacle women confronted in demanding that the UAW protect their seniority rights in layoffs and recalls was the widespread

72. Women's Bureau Report to the IEB, May 1, 1944, War Policy Division Collection, Box 27, War Policy Women's Bureau September 1942–September 1944 Folder; List of Delegates to Fort Knox Trip, Report on UAW-CIO Women's Delegation to Fort Knox, June 29, 1944, War Policy Division–Women's Bureau Collection, Box 3, Folder 8; Mildred Jeffrey to IEB, August 1, 1944, ibid.
73. *Research Report* 4 (August 1944): 1–2.

notion that women workers would voluntarily leave their wartime jobs when peace was declared. The comment made by James Burswald of Local 329 in response to a Women's Bureau survey of local union policies toward women was characteristic of the attitude of many male unionists. "Our first interest is in interesting male members in Union activity," he remarked, "since women very likely will not be employed in our shop after the war." A concerned Research Department representative told Kathleen Lowrie in July that men assumed that women were "working only for patriotic reasons and [are] desirous of returning home." "The hope seems to be," she added, "that as many as possible of the 'new' women workers will unobtrusively slip back into the home."[74]

Men soon learned that they were indulging in wishful thinking. To the surprise of many union men, 85.5 percent of female UAW members surveyed by the Research Department in the summer of 1944 stated that they wanted to keep their jobs in the auto industry after the war. "The results of the survey prove conclusively," the department reported, "that most of the current gossip that women will return to the home after the war is without foundation and that no postwar plan is realistic if it assumes that a majority of women will not work after the war." In response to the survey, R. J. Thomas asserted, "The interests of women and of all other groups in our economy would be best served by the UAW-CIO program of jobs for all, with maximum utilization of our nation's machinery, labor power and natural resources." Thomas, however, ignored the question of women's place in the postwar automotive labor force. Critical of the union leadership's refusal to acknowledge the fact that women would not acquiesce in the loss of their jobs, C. G. Edelin, president of Local 51, presciently warned, "If a long-range policy covering female workers cannot be worked out before peace is declared abroad . . . we may find ourselves in some very warm water."[75]

74. Local 329 Report, War Policy Division–Women's Bureau Collection, Box 5, Folder 10; Lowrie to Frieda Miller, July 15, 1944, RG 86/NA, Box 1416, Lowrie 1943 to Date Folder.

75. *Research Report* 4 (March 1944): 3; C. G. Edelin to IEB, February 7, 1944, UAW Local 51 Collection, Box 28, Folder 9, ALUA. Women auto workers echoed the sentiments of their counterparts in other basic industries. A United States Women's Bureau survey found that 84 percent of the women employed in manufacturing during the war planned to continue working in the same industry after the war. Also, 98.5 percent of the single women responding to the UAW survey and 100 percent of those who were widows said they wanted to keep their jobs. To the surprise even of the Research Department, 68.7 percent of those who were married also said they wanted

At the annual convention held in September 1944, eighty female delegates indicated that women intended to resist the discriminatory treatment accorded them by both employers and male unionists. To facilitate the reconversion process, they warned, "pressure may be brought by some managements to break down seniority protection of women workers." They asserted, "Women workers must receive fair and just treatment in seniority rights." Noting that a majority of female union members wanted to remain in the industry after the war, the women asked the male delegates to "reaffirm the democratic principle that all members should be guaranteed the fullest protection of their union membership without discrimination based on sex or marital status." Emma Murphy demanded the abolition of separate seniority lists for women and men and urged the international leadership to "fight in every way possible to see . . . that there are jobs . . . for all of our good union sisters who wish to remain in the automobile industry."[76]

At the request of the IEB, the Research Department compiled a list of forty-one union contracts containing discriminatory seniority agreements. Indicating that the list represented just the tip of an iceberg, the department singled out as the worst offenders the contracts negotiated by three local unions. The contract covering the employees of Federal Mogul Corporation not only provided for separate, noninterchangeable seniority lists for women and men but also stipulated that women hired after July 1, 1942, "shall be placed on a special seniority list . . . and their tenure of employment shall be limited to the duration of the war, or as soon thereafter as they can be replaced by former male employees or other male applicants." Local 822's contract with H. A. Douglas Manufacturing Company required the replacement of women employed on jobs defined as "men's" by men "as soon as the labor supply becomes adequate without regard to seniority." At United Steel and Wire, men were allowed to replace women holding "men's jobs" regardless of the latter's greater seniority, but women were not permitted "to bump a man employee off a man's job." In a memorandum attached to the report, R. J. Thomas explained to regional directors and local union presidents that the disproportionate number of women among those recently laid off

---

to remain in the plants. U.S. Women's Bureau, *Women Workers in Ten War Production Areas and Their Postwar Employment Plans*, Bulletin No. 209 (Washington, D.C., 1946), p. 42; *Research Report* 4 (March 1944): 3.

76. *1944 Convention Proceedings*, pp. 120–21.

was attributable to separate seniority lists, and he instructed them to eliminate such clauses from their contracts. The union president, however, did not specify any penalty for failure to comply with the order. He also failed to issue a statement regarding the importance of enforcing contract clauses that did provide for equal seniority in transfers and layoffs. As female employment in the plants continued to decline, women became frustrated with the dilatory response of the international to their demands for a sex-blind reconversion policy.[77]

Women voiced their concerns loudly and clearly at a conference held in Detroit on December 8–9, 1944. Attended by 149 women in ninety-nine locals, from all states except New York and California, the conference was intended principally "to formulate plans to protect . . . women workers who entered war plants from being considered 'expendable homefront soldiers' after the war." Although the women designated in-plant problems such as child care, lunch and rest periods, and local union counseling programs as areas of special interest, they attached greater and more immediate importance to a resolution protesting discriminatory behavior by both management and the union regarding women's seniority status. Condemning management for denying women their seniority rights in transfers, layoffs, and recalls and for an "unceasing psychological drive to harass women out of the plants," the women asserted, "The union has a serious responsibility in eliminating any practices or policies over which they have control and which in any way may contribute to unfair or unjust treatment of women." They urged the IEB to denounce publicly "the malicious attempts of some managements to weaken the seniority structure and to pit one group of workers against another." Criticizing local union stewards, committeemen, and members of bargaining committees who did not adhere to contract provisions that protected women's right to fair and equal treatment, the delegates recommended an end to discriminatory contract clauses, separate job classifications and rates, and separate seniority lists.[78]

77. Thomas to Officers and Regional Directors, November 13, 1944, and Clauses Pertaining to Seniority of Women, both in Mazey Collection, Box 13, Folder 5.
78. *Detroit News*, December 8, 1944; R. J. Thomas Report to the IEB, January 22, 1945, War Policy Division Collection, Box 27, Women's Bureau November 1944–January 1945 Folder. Planning for the conference began in the summer of 1944. Mildred Jeffrey was assisted by the National Women's Conference Committee, a group

The women at the conference also addressed the issue of veterans' seniority and job rights. The delegates to the 1944 UAW convention had adopted a resolution criticizing the Selective Service Administration's advocacy of "superseniority" for veterans. The resolution contended that the policy would undermine the hard-won principle of seniority and stated that veterans should be granted seniority equal to the time spent in military service but that they should not be allowed to "bump" a nonveteran with greater seniority. Expressing the view of most women in the union, Emma Murphy asserted at the convention, "We realize that many of the jobs held by women today are jobs that were vacated by our boys who are now in the armed forces, and I, for one, certainly don't propose to have our sisters keep jobs that belong to our boys when they return from the Army." A few women at the conference pressed for an affirmative-action policy to ensure the preservation of the gains made by women during the war. "If they can make special provisions for returning veterans, union officials, [and] shop stewards," asserted Florence Walton, a Local 330 shop steward, "there should be some provision made for women and Negroes now in industry." To a certain extent the issue divided women who had worked in auto plants before the war and those new to the industry. In response to the "newcomers," who feared they would be discharged, prewar women workers cited as proof of the importance of maintaining the seniority structure management's attempts to force women to quit by transferring them to undesirable jobs. A majority of the delegates, however, preferred not to ask for "special consideration or privilege." Demanding only that their seniority rights be respected, they vowed that they did not want "to prevent returning servicemen from getting jobs."[79]

---

consisting of nine women who had been nominated by their regional directors. Composed of some of the most vigorous proponents of women's rights in the union, the committee included Jennie Taylor, Lillian Hatcher, Gertrude Kelly, Fern Halchack, Grace Blackett, Lynne Monroe, Phoebe Blair, Mabel Johnson, and Irma Finkle. Meeting in Detroit on November 17 and 18, the committee unanimously elected Blackett as chair of the group and established an agenda for the conference. The delegates to the conference urged the UAW to increase the size of the committee and establish it as a permanent National Women's Committee. Although Thomas recommended that the IEB grant the women's request, I have found no evidence indicating that the board approved the proposal. Thomas report to the IEB, January 22, 1945, ibid.

79. *1944 Convention Proceedings*, pp. 81–90, 120; *Michigan Chronicle*, December 16, 1944, clipping in Research Department Collection, Box 32, Folder 17; *New York Times*, December 10, 1944; Seniority Resolution, Thomas Report to the IEB, January 22, 1945, War Policy Division Collection, Box 27, Women's Bureau November 1944–January 1945 Folder.

During the last seven months of the war, women leaders devised strategies to ensure that women would have access to postwar jobs in the auto industry. In response to managerial attacks on women's ability to perform peacetime jobs, they stressed the impact of the war on the sexual division of labor. "I think it is necessary and important that we emphasize and reemphasize the job that has been done by women when a crisis is at hand," Grace Blackett stated at a United States Women's Bureau conference of women trade unionists in April 1945. "The more that that is emphasized now, the more that we can use it when the post-war period comes and we begin to get the back seat again, which we are going to get—we might as well face the facts." Reporting that auto companies were claiming that a particular job was not a "woman's job" as justification for laying off female employees, Mildred Jeffrey observed, "The experience in breaking down jobs during the war period is one which we must save and use further."[80]

Although the national women's conference had called the attention of men in the UAW to the issue of postwar job security for women auto workers, female unionists recognized that the initiative in challenging the violation of their rights as union members lay with women themselves. Writing to the organizer of the Local 45 Women's Committee, Jeffrey explained that women had "to show management, the general public and our own union leaders that women want to work and are going to fight for that right." "Unless women demonstrate now that they are not going to take discrimination lying down," she warned, "we are going to be in a much weaker position to combat it later on." Many women who had attended the conference tried to mobilize their co-workers by informing them of their rights as dues-paying members of the UAW. Stressing that length of service was an indisputable and specific standard governing layoff and recall procedures, activists urged women to make use of the grievance machinery when that contractually guaranteed right was violated. In addition to stressing that women could individually and legitimately resist dismissal, organizers alerted them to the necessity for collective action. Management's argument that women were unsuited for jobs on peacetime production, they asserted, was an unsubstantiated claim devised to demoralize wartime women workers,

80. Transcript, Official Report of Proceedings, Conference of Women Representatives of Labor Unions in War and Postwar Adjustments of Women Workers, April 19, 1945, pp. 14, 65, RG 86/NA, Box 899, Conference Folder.

facilitate their voluntary exodus from the industry, and forestall both individual and collective resistance.[81]

The efforts of women unionists to raise the issue of women's right to postwar employment in the auto plants demonstrated the extent to which the war changed the character of gender relations in the UAW. Taking advantage of wartime conditions, women were able to integrate issues of concern to women into the union's agenda and to establish a presence for women in the ranks of both local leadership and the international bureaucracy. Although the UAW's conservative and discriminatory wage and seniority policies had been established early in the war period, the impact of female activism was evident by the end of the war. Announcing that the IEB had issued a policy recommending the elimination of job classifications by sex, Mildred Jeffrey observed, "It took the women's conference really to get that on official policy in the union."[82] Achievements of this sort spurred women to mobilize resistance to the attempt to expel women from auto plants during reconversion and to mount a campaign within the union to extend equal rights and opportunity to women auto workers.

81. Jeffrey to Ruth Adlard, July 5, 1945, War Policy Division–Women's Bureau Collection, Box 1, Folder 1.

82. Transcript, Official Report of Proceedings, Conference of Women Representatives of Labor Unions, p. 65, RG 86/NA, Box 899, Conference Folder.

LISTEN, BROTHERS!

We're Union Members, Too—and We Intend to Stay That Way

Despite the efforts of the Ford Motor Company to turn women workers in the Highland Park plant against the union by carrying through a policy of discrimination, we intend to stick with our union and fight!

The company is laying off women union members in violation of seniority. It isn't just a problem of the women, either. It's a union issue that concerns men, too. If the company is allowed to ignore the seniority provisions to do a job on one group—what's to prevent them from doing a job on you? Once the precedent is set what course will you follow if your group is singled out next? Will veterans be pitted against non-veterans? Foreign-born against American-born? It's all the same! It's the old Ford Game! Don't be sucked in by company tricks!

LOOK, SISTER!

The Cartoon May Be Funny, But What's Happening to Us Isn't!

On April 20, the Ford Motor Company gave 103 women in the Bomber Wing Press Shop, slips reading: "Discharged, due to physical inability to perform job to which their seniority entitles them." The job in question is box car loading.

Under our new Interchangeable Occupational Seniority Agreement, known as Appendix A, workers can bump the employee with the least seniority, first in the occupational group, then in the labor pool.

In violation of the spirit and intent of the agreement the company interprets sections of the agreement to discriminate against groups of employees—in this instance, the women, in the future the men. The Company hypocritically implies that it is forced to interpret these sections in a discriminatory way. Our answer is:

WE WANT FAIR PLAY, NOT TECHNICALITIES!

When women with 2½ and 3 years seniority are laid off while probationary employees are still working in the plant there is foul play afoot no matter how many excuses are offered.

MAYBE YOU THINK YOU ARE GOING TO VACATION ON YOUR UNEMPLOYMENT COMPENSATION!

Well, the Company is fighting the claims of the women already laid off. Their legal staff is advising the Labor

Relations office how best to word the lay-off slips to avoid payment of benefits.

So there you are—not content with ignoring our seniority rights, the Company is out to chisel on our hard earned unemployment checks.

The first step in fighting these company tricks is to get together—to learn the facts, and to plan the fight! Let nothing stop you from attending the meeting Sunday! OUR JOBS ARE AT STAKE!

Issued by WOMEN'S COMMITTEE OF LOCAL 400, UAW-CIO

Pat McLean, chairman; Celia Paransky, vice-chairman; Caroline Garvey, secretary; Beatrice Madson, Lynne Moore, Janet Varrone, Gussie Oliver, Mary Vartanian, Sally Elias, Victoria Frederichs, Elvira Bivens, Beth Stuart, Dorothy Madson, Rose Shotenfelt, Hazel Hughes, Elizabeth Boehlin, Juanita Cunningham, and Tillie Martin.

PLANTWIDE MEETING
FOR WOMEN —EXECUTIVE BOARD MEMBERS ARE INVITED

Sunday, May 6   2:30 PM
Northeastern High School   E. Warren at Grandy

1. Local 400 Women's Committee flyer, May 1945. The Archives of Labor and Urban Affairs, Wayne State University.

2. Picket line at Ford Motor Company plant in Highland Park, Michigan, November 1945. National Archives and Records Administration.

3. Women upholsterers at the Desoto plant in Warren, Michigan, c. 1950. The Archives of Labor and Urban Affairs, Wayne State University.

4. Women wiring the dashboard at Plymouth plant, 1953. The Archives of Labor and Urban Affairs, Wayne State University.

5. Region 1-1A Women's Committee conference, Detroit, November 1955.
The Archives of Labor and Urban Affairs, Wayne State University.

6. UAW Women's Department staff: Caroline Davis, Gwendolyn Thompson, and Mary Francis, c. 1955. Archives of Labor and Urban Affairs, Wayne State University.

7. Women working on the body drop of Chrysler assembly line, 1965. Archives of Labor and Urban Affairs, Wayne State University.

8. Woman working under the hood on an assembly line, 1971. Archives of
Labor and Urban Affairs, Wayne State University.

9. UAW Women's Conference, Black Lake, Michigan, 1972. UAW *Solidarity*.

10. UAW Women's Conference, Black Lake, Michigan, 1975. UAW *Solidarity*.

CHAPTER THREE

"They Have Placed a Penalty on Womanhood": Women's Reconversion Experience, 1945–1947

Employed during World War II as a riveter at the Ford Motor Company's huge River Rouge complex in Dearborn, Michigan, Gwendolyn Thompson was laid off from her job in June 1945. She, like other discharged defense workers, wanted to return to the comparatively well-paid jobs in the auto industry, and she reported promptly to her employment recall in the winter of 1946. Thompson was accustomed to hard work, but she found her new job unusually heavy and difficult. As a leader of the Local 600 Women's Committee, Thompson recognized her experience as just another attempt by plant management to harass female employees out of their jobs. Nevertheless, she told Mildred Jeffrey, director of the UAW Women's Bureau, that she was seriously considering quitting. Jeffrey pleaded with Thompson not to surrender and to "hang on," both for her own sake and for that of other women who needed her leadership to assert their own rights and interests. Thompson took Jeffrey's advice, called the company's bluff, and retained her right to postwar employment at the River Rouge plant. She also sought the first of several offices she would hold in Local 600 and extended her activities in behalf of women.[1]

1. Kathleen Lowrie to Frieda Miller, March 13, 1946, U.S. Women's Bureau Papers, Record Group 86, Box 1416, Lowrie Folder, National Archives, Washington, D.C. (hereafter cited as RG 86/NA); interview with Mildred Jeffrey, p. 52, The Twentieth Century Trade Union Woman: Vehicle for Social Change Oral History Project, Institute of Labor and Industrial Relations, University of Michigan, Ann Arbor.

Although exceptional in some respects, Thompson shared the experience of thousands of female defense workers. Some women voluntarily left their jobs, and some who had accumulated little seniority were among the first to be laid off. But many women who were laid off had seniority equal to or greater than that of men who were retained on their jobs or of new male workers with no history of employment in auto plants. Women who were unwilling to relinquish the benefits of industrial employment and who expected that the seniority they had accumulated during the war would enable them to remain in the plants after reconversion found that discriminatory practices in transfers, layoffs, and recalls violated and abrogated their seniority rights.

The efforts of female auto unionists such as Thompson to contest attempts to exclude them from the postwar automotive labor force mobilized the women's movement that had emerged in the UAW during the war. Ranging from the filing of individual grievances to picket lines outside plant employment offices and local union halls, women's protests were the culmination of wartime developments and compelled UAW men to confront the meaning of the idea of equality that was implicit in the principle of industrial unionism. Although the strength of opposition to the continued presence of women in the industry, the rapidly diminishing number of women in the plants, and the absence of a feminist movement to lend additional legitimacy to the protest of female auto workers minimized the prospects for a successful challenge to sexual discrimination, the defense made by women of their right to postwar employment in the plants further changed the UAW's policies on issues of concern to female auto workers and laid the foundation for renewed activity by women in the years that followed reconversion.

The rapid reduction of the female labor force in the auto industry after World War II was in part an unavoidable consequence of the race to reconvert the industry to consumer production. In the first week following the surrender of Japan, half of the workers in plants under contract with the UAW were laid off; and layoffs of both men and women continued as the cancellation of war contracts eliminated many of the jobs held by workers during the war. Women represented a disproportionate number of those laid off in the industry. During the war, the Ford Motor Company employed nearly one quarter of the 200,000 women working in the auto industry, and women composed nearly 22 percent of the Ford work force. The proportion of women workers was even higher in some plants, such as the one in Highland Park, Michigan, where, at the peak of wartime employment in 1944, 43 percent of the 13,500 workers were women. By January 1946 only 4,900 women, representing just 4 percent of all Ford employees, were working in company plants. The absolute and relative number of women employed by General Motors also dropped after V-J Day. The 117,100 women employed in production in GM plants in November 1943 represented 32 percent of all GM workers. By November 1945, 31,670 women were working in these plants, where they accounted for 16 percent of the company's labor force.[2]

Most women laid off during reconversion were not recalled to jobs in auto plants. In November 1943 there were 203,300 women employed in auto plants, and they composed 26 percent of all production workers in the industry. By June 1945 their number had dropped to 132,400, and their proportion of the auto labor force to 20 percent. After falling to a postwar low of 366,200 in December 1945, the total number of production workers in the auto industry steadily increased; in June 1946 there were as many auto workers as there had been one year earlier. Women, however, represented just 8 percent of the automotive labor force in that month, a figure only one percentage point higher than that for 1939.[3]

The rapid and dramatic demobilization of the female automotive labor force indicated that management, having viewed the employment of women during the war as a temporary expedient, did not include women in its postwar plans. Managers had praised the performance of women during the war and had taken advantage of their presence to simplify production processes and reduce wages on jobs ordinarily performed by men. The integration of women into the traditionally male-dominated basic industries, however, had been facilitated by the notion that it was only for the duration of the war. As management devised plans for reconversion to automobile production, the renewed availability of a male labor supply precluded

2. James Wishart to George Addes, September 10, 1945, UAW Research Department Collection, Box 11, Folder 2, Walter P. Reuther Library, Archives of Labor and Urban Affairs, Wayne State University, Detroit, Michigan (hereafter cited as ALUA); *UAW Research Report* 6 (April 1946): 4; Report of John Carney to International Executive Board (IEB), November 7, 1945, George Addes Collection, Box 69A, Local Union 400 Folder, ALUA.

3. Bureau of Labor Statistics (BLS), *Handbook of Labor Statistics, 1947* (Washington, D.C., 1948), p. 18.

any serious examination of the possible economic benefits of employing women.

Auto companies justified their hiring policies by emphasizing the disjunction between the war and postwar periods. Managers who had lauded women for tackling "men's" jobs during the war now declared them unqualified for such work. "Reconversion meant that the wartime light assembly work involved in airplanes gave way to the heavy, tiring assembly work of cars," an industry spokesman stated in February 1946. "Women can't handle such tough work." Some companies officially revised their earlier favorable reports on the wartime experiment. "The factor of having so many women mixed in an industrial situation just didn't bring about satisfactory results," explained a director of the Ford Labor Relations Department. "From foreman all over the place to the highest—from the lowest to the highest level, so to speak—there was a sigh of relief when they could let women go," he recalled. "The general expression was, 'Thank God, that's over! And we'll pray that it never has to happen again.' "[4]

Jointly negotiated agreements providing women with seniority rights unequal to those of men not only facilitated and expedited the expulsion of women from the plants but protected management from liability for discrimination. Contracts that provided women hired during the war with only temporary, wartime seniority deprived women of any basis for protesting their dismissal. Separate seniority lists for women and men, a well-established feature of the industry's collective-bargaining agreements, operated to the disadvantage of prewar women workers as well as those hired after 1941, since they denied women the right to displace male employees with less seniority.

Agreements providing for departmental or occupational group seniority could nullify a provision for a single seniority list for employees of both sexes. Under these contracts, women employed in predominantly or exclusively female departments or job categories were not permitted to "bump" men on jobs elsewhere in a plant. As a result of these provisions, when military contracts were canceled, women employed in defense work lost their jobs. The experience of women employed at the Ford Highland Park plant illustrates the

4. New York Times, February 19, 1946; interview with H. S. Ablewhite, May 16, 1951, p. 28, Oral History Project, Ford Motor Company Archives, Dearborn, Michigan (hereafter cited as FMCA).

onerous consequences of such agreements for female employees. In March 1945 Local 400 attempted to negotiate with management a plantwide interchangeable occupational group seniority agreement that would have permitted women who were unable to perform a job in their occupational group to "bump" an employee with less seniority on an appropriate job in another group. Refusing to accept the local's plan, management had it revised to restrict seniority to the occupational group or to the labor pool. In a decision that the local union president later admitted as a "serious blunder," the membership voted to ratify the agreement. Following the agreement, management curtailed work in the bomber-wing-press shop and transferred 103 women with the least seniority of all employees in the occupational group to work loading boxcars, the only job in the labor pool to which their seniority entitled them. Since they were physically unable to perform the job, management discharged the women as "quits." As a result, the women not only were deprived of seniority but also could not qualify for unemployment compensation. In his decision on a policy grievance filed by the local on behalf of the 103 women, UAW-Ford umpire Harry Shulman explained that it was not within his power "to decree some wise solution for the difficult problems involved." "By the parties' own choice," he observed, "my power is limited to their contracts and to a determination of what those contracts require." Although the local protested that management had manipulated the seniority agreement in order to discharge both female and elderly or disabled male employees, Shulman, unable to read into the contract what was not there, decided that the protested practice was in accord with the local's seniority agreement and did not violate any agreement between the company and the union.[5]

To eliminate women from the plants, management also took advantage of contractual provisions limiting the period of time in which laid-off employees could exercise seniority rights in recalls. The UAW's contract with Ford, for example, permitted employees hired before June 20, 1941, to retain and exercise their accumulated seniority for a period of up to four years. Those hired after June 20, 1941, however, were entitled to a "break period" equal only to their ac-

5. Report of John Carney to IEB, November 7, 1945, Addes Collection, Box 69A, Local Union 400 Folder; Hazel Bradshaw to Harry Truman, August 27, 1945, RG 86/NA, Box 836, Michigan Folder; Report of the Women's Committee of Local 400 to the IEB, November 7, 1945, Addes Collection, Box 69A, Local Union 400 Folder; Ford Motor Company and UAW-CIO Umpire Opinion, A-211, November 30, 1945.

cumulated seniority; if they were not recalled within a period of time equal to their accrued seniority, they were removed from plant seniority lists. The significance of the two types of seniority becomes evident when it is noted that Ford, which had employed few women before the war, had begun hiring women for wartime production jobs beginning in 1942. A number of women laid off during reconversion had acquired three years of seniority, but most had accumulated less. The longer management delayed recalling women who had been laid off during the first months of reconversion, the slimmer their chance of returning to work. The Commerce Pattern Foundry and Machine Company of Detroit, to cite another example, was so intent on excluding its wartime female employees from the shop that it slowed production to delay the recall of women with seniority.[6]

Some employers used methods of discharging female workers which violated and abrogated their seniority rights. Although many collective-bargaining agreements provided for separate seniority lists for women and men, a provision for a single list was incorporated into a number of contracts during the early 1940s. The first contract negotiated between the UAW and Ford contained a provision granting female employees seniority rights equal to those of men, and in 1943 a single seniority list replaced a provision in the UAW's contract with Chrysler for separate seniority rosters. In response to pressure from women activists, other local unions during the war also renegotiated contracts to eliminate dual seniority lists. Management, however, ignored the rights provided women under such agreements, laying off women without regard to their seniority and retaining men with less seniority. Once the process of retooling for consumer production was completed, women often were not notified of recalls while men with less seniority or no history of employment in a plant were offered jobs.[7]

6. Richard Leonard to Mildred Jeffrey, March 7, 1946, UAW Ford Department Collection, Box 15, Miscellaneous Correspondence 1946 Folder, ALUA; Larry Yost to Walter Reuther, August 8, 1946, Walter P. Reuther Collection, Box 89, Folder 2, ALUA; *Ammunition* 5 (January 1947): 30–31. Although the provision for two types of seniority in the Ford-UAW contract would appear to be a clear case of discrimination against women, the fact that the contract did not stipulate the sex of the employee and that June 20, 1941, marks the ratification of the first contract indicate otherwise.

7. "Women in Unions in a Mid-West War Industry Area," unpublished U.S. Women's Bureau study, July 10, 1945, pp. 19–22, RG 86/NA, Box 1701, Union Study Folder. For an indication of the UAW's growing acceptance during the war of the idea of single seniority lists, see minutes of Special Meeting between Buick Shop Committee and Management, December 27, 1943, UAW Local 599 Collection (unprocessed), Box 3, Women's Rates Folder, ALUA; Timothy J. Daily to Walter Reuther, June 5, 1944, Mildred Jeffrey Collection, Box 19, Folder 13, ALUA.

Other methods of reducing the female labor force in auto plants similarly limited women's opportunity for postwar employment. Women who were processed as quits or were disqualified from jobs for disciplinary infractions, poor health, or a failure to meet production standards lost the right to exercise their seniority. Companies were then free to retain men with less seniority or hire those with no history of employment in the plant. Some employers, for example, used capricious and arbitrary standards to induce women to quit and to justify the dismissal of female employees. A woman told a *Detroit News* reporter: "Plant managements are awfully fussy about women workers now. It's all right for men to wear wrist watches and rings, but just let a woman worker show up on the job wearing them. Bingo—she's fired for violating regulations." Ford's River Rouge management subjected the women it recalled to stringent medical exams even though the women protested that their health had not substantially changed since they had first been hired and argued that the exams were a device to deny them postwar employment in the plant. Laid off from the River Rouge plant after V-J Day and recalled in January 1946, Louise Hamilton was unable to keep up with production after only one hour on the job and was disqualified from employment in the plant; what had occurred was out of keeping with the usual qualifying procedure and was the cause of much female protest in auto plants in this period. Women in other plants were disqualified for such dubious reasons as absenteeism or making scrap. After Local 140 protested the discharge of thirty-one women from the Dodge Truck plant in Detroit, for example, management recalled the women but subjected them to various kinds of harassment and then fired them all for "incompetence." "It's funny," remarked one of the discharged women, "I was all right during the war. What's wrong with my work now?"[8]

To accelerate the exodus of female employees, management sought to discredit the ability of women to perform production jobs in peacetime. A common practice involved placing women transfers or rehires on jobs they were physically unable to perform. "Every woman in the plant has been discriminated against," asserted two women employed in the Ford plant in Memphis, Tennessee. "When we are called back to work we are placed on the heaviest jobs." One

8. *Detroit News*, July 19, 1945; Yost to Reuther, August 8, 1946, Reuther Collection, Box 89, Folder 2; Louise Hamilton to William Oliver, November 5, 1946, Ford Department Collection, Box 8, Ford Local 600–Letters to and from Officers Folder; *Ammunition* 6 (March 1948): 32–35.

of the women reported that she was discharged because of her inability to hang car tops weighing ninety-seven pounds. "I picked up a side of the top and moved it about 5 feet and turned it over and pasted insulating in the top, but I was unable to then turn it straight up and walk about 10 feet and hang them in the ceiling. Lots of men cannot do it." Plant management ignored her request to be transferred to a window-washing job despite the fact that she had greater seniority than men employed on the job. The similar experience of women employed at the Ford Highland Park plant prompted Local 400 to file an appeal with the union-management umpire. Holding that management had violated the understanding between the company and the union regarding the recall of female employees, Harry Shulman explained, "The evidence shows that the aggrieved were placed on a job which a powerful Katinka could doubtless do but which was regarded as beyond the competence of women generally." Shulman concluded that the company's practice of placing women on jobs "which are known to be beyond the competence of the average woman" distorted the principle of the recall and had become "a means of disqualification rather than reemployment of women."[9]

The UAW Women's Bureau and the network of female activists that developed during the war spearheaded a campaign to protest discriminatory layoffs and recalls. Although they encouraged women to file grievances individually when their contractually guaranteed seniority rights were violated, the leaders emphasized the importance of collective action against discriminatory practices. "It's high time you got together with some of the other women you know and tried doing something about [unfair layoffs]," the bureau advised in July 1945. Urging women to form committees within the locals, the bureau suggested that they join forces interlocally and "plan your campaign in concrete terms and definite objectives." Collective action, women leaders believed, not only would make resistance to managerial practices more effective but also would direct the attention of male unionists to the issue of women's rights.[10]

The response of the Local 400 Women's Committee at the Ford Highland Park plant to the plight of the 103 women who were unfairly discharged and deprived of their seniority rights in April 1945

9. Jennie Lee Murphy and Millie Sowell to Thomas J. Starling, April 13, 1946, Ford Department Collection, Box 9, Local 903 Folder; Ford Motor Company–UAW Umpire Memorandum, M-1371, October 10, 1947.
10. *Ammunition* 3 (July 1945): 16.

demonstrated how determined women were to resist the loss of their wartime jobs. In response to their request for assistance, John Carney, the local union president, asked management to change the women's discharge slips to read "laid off" rather than "quit" so that they could be eligible for unemployment compensation and retain their seniority in the event of a recall. When management refused to comply with his request, Carney directed the union building chairman and committeeman to file grievances with management for the 103 women on the ground that men with less seniority than the women were working on jobs that women could perform.[11]

It soon became apparent that the women did not have the full support of their local leadership. The building chairman and committeeman refused to write up grievances for the women. Carney consequently performed the task himself, giving the reports to the committeeman for processing. But when Pat McLean, chair of the Women's Committee, inquired about the progress of the grievances, she was informed that the grievance reports had been stored in a committeeman's locker and that all 103 of them, in triplicate, had "mysteriously disappeared from the locker." This act of sabotage by the men enabled management to stand by its position; the head of labor relations in the plant refused to respond to the grievances until the union's triplicate copies had been presented.[12]

Angered by the resistance of the male leadership and its complicity with management, the Women's Committee called a plantwide meeting for May 6. In the flyer the women distributed at plant gates to advertise the meeting, they were careful to include an appeal to male workers. Condemning the efforts by management "to turn women workers in the Highland Park plant against the union by carrying through a policy of discrimination," the authors of the flyer promised that "we [women] intend to stick with our union and fight" and warned that management's violation of the seniority rights of the 103 women would set a precedent that could eventually threaten male employees as well. "The first step in fighting these company tricks," the organizers of the meeting explained to women, "is to get together—to learn the facts, and to plan the fight! Let nothing stop you from attending the meeting Sunday! OUR JOBS ARE AT STAKE!"

11. Report of the Women's Committee of Local 400 to the IEB, November 7, 1945, Addes Collection, Box 69A, Local Union 400 Folder.
12. Ibid.

When the meeting was held, the women devised an alternate strategy for registering their protest against management. With the approval and assistance of Richard Leonard, director of the UAW Ford Department, they filed a policy grievance against management with the UAW-Ford umpire.[13]

Experiences similar to those of women in Local 400 inspired five women from four other Detroit-area locals to request an appearance before the July IEB meeting in Minneapolis to address the problems confronting women in the plants. Consisting of Grace Blackett, Della Rymer of Local 653, Trilby Riopelle of Local 600, and two women from Local 190, the group represented the network of female union activists who had pressed since the fall of 1944 for an official statement of union principle and policy regarding the job rights of women auto workers. The women, who charged that the union was failing to defend its female membership, demanded that there be greater female representation on the international level and that the union deal more effectively with discrimination on the local level. The women also urged the IEB to act on the union's commitment to women workers and publicly voice its opposition to the precedent established by the National War Labor Board (NWLB) in its favorable ruling on an agreement between the Michigan Tool Company and the Mechanics Educational Society of America (MESA) which sanctioned the surrender by women workers of their seniority rights in return for four weeks' severance pay.[14]

When the women arrived in Minneapolis, the IEB, claiming it had not received their letter, refused to grant them an audience. The male members of the IEB were openly hostile to both the presence of the women and their objectives. Riopelle later recalled to a group of women: "Members of the board discussing the situation in bars and hotel lobbies invariably asked 'What can we do to get these women out of town?' 'What are they going to do anyhow?' And [they made] such remarks as 'Who is that cute little number from the Packard local [190]?'" Antagonized by a hostile comment by John Livingston, a UAW vice-president, Grace Blackett slapped the union official. After three days the women were finally permitted to speak with R. J. Thomas and Walter Reuther in Thomas's hotel room. Insulted and

13. Flyer, *Plantwide Meeting for Women*, and Report of the Women's Committee, November 7, 1945, ibid.
14. *Detroit Times*, July 19, 1945, clipping in UAW Public Relations Department–Frank Winn Collection, Box 14, Women Folder, ALUA.

angered by the treatment accorded them, the women charged the UAW "brass hats with pushing us around more than management ever thought of doing" and vowed to return home "to stage a revolution the union will never forget." "We are making the bullets now," Riopelle told a *Detroit Times* reporter, "and we will give the board members a blast that will blow them out of their shoes."[15]

In the weeks following the Minneapolis episode, the women mobilized support for an assault on the international by a series of meetings at Detroit-area locals. On July 25 women from nineteen locals met at the Local 190 hall to plan a program of action. Condemning management's efforts to lay off women without regard to their seniority and noting that the violation of the principle of seniority threatened all workers, Riopelle argued, "Some of us are a lot better trade unionists than some of the men." The women decided to nominate a female candidate for the directorship of Region 1C (Flint), a position that had been vacated by the resignation of Carl Swanson during the July IEB meeting. Fifty women from UAW locals in the Pontiac region attended a second protest meeting in Pontiac on July 29. Della Rymer told the group that if the union's Fair Practices Committee had not "placed a penalty on womanhood" and instead had considered sex a category worthy of antidiscriminatory action, "we wouldn't be fighting our own battles." The women not only approved the plan to nominate a woman for Swanson's position but also decided to send telegrams to Thomas, George Addes, and vice-president Richard Frankensteen demanding that single seniority lists be included in union-management contracts and requesting that Pontiac locals support this principle. Finally, the women decided to confer with William McAulay, the Pontiac regional director, to seek his assistance in obtaining justice from management. On August 5 at another meeting held at Dodge Local 3 in Hamtramck, thirty-seven women stressed the need for more women in international and local leadership positions and planned to present their grievances to the September IEB meeting.[16]

Granted an audience with the IEB, Grace Blackett and Lottie Crank presented the issues that women had raised in the preceding two

15. *Detroit Times*, July 19 and 21, 1945, clippings, ibid.; Gabin interview with Mildred Jeffrey, August 1, 1983.

16. *Detroit Times*, July 26 and 30, 1945, clippings in Public Relations Department Collection, Box 14, Women Folder, ALUA; *Wage Earner*, August 17, 1945, clipping in Vertical File, Women Members and Auxiliaries Folder, ALUA.

months. Crank, an officer in Local 581, reported that only 60 of the 460 women employed at the Fisher 1 plant in Flint during the war still had jobs in the factory. Condemning the contract's provision for only temporary, wartime seniority for women employed in "men's" jobs, Crank asked the IEB to revoke such agreements. "Women are being laid off," she asserted, "whose husbands are veterans of World War II, women who have children to support and who are entitled to those jobs by reason of their seniority." Blackett reported that local union officers were collaborating with management to discriminate against women in transfers and layoffs. Denouncing these "violations of trade union principles," she reminded the IEB that it bore "the responsibility of servicing the entire membership of the union."[17]

The protests made by women did have an effect on union policy. The IEB rejected the request that a woman be appointed to the staff of each regional office, and the women lost their campaign to elect a woman to the board. Their emphasis on the threat that violations of women's seniority posed to the principle of seniority, however, moved the IEB to action. In August 1945 the UAW submitted a statement to the Detroit War Labor Board protesting its ruling in the Michigan Tool Company and MESA case. In a letter to George Taylor, chair of the NWLB, Thomas explained that although the UAW was aware that it had no standing in the case, it nevertheless believed that it would be "unfortunate if the government in any way dilutes its own policy relating to nondiscrimination against women workers." In its statement on the case, the union expressed concern that the ruling would establish an undesirable precedent. "We believe it obvious," the UAW asserted, "that the company is seeking to reinstitute its pre-war discriminatory hiring policy against women and is using an ill-conceived device for the purpose." In a letter addressed to all local union presidents, regional directors, and international representatives, Thomas outlined the union's position on the MESA agreement and explained its implications for the UAW. "This action focuses the attention on one of the major problems facing local unions today," he declared, "that of zealously protecting seniority rights in the transfer, lay off and rehire of all members without prejudice because of race, creed, national origin, sex or marital sta-

17. Minutes of the IEB Meeting, September 10–18, 1945, pp. 13, 51–52, Addes Collection, Box 25, Folder 3.

tus." "In a sense," Thomas continued, "this is a test period in which we are being called upon to make a reality of our principles of equality of membership rights.[18]

After the September IEB meeting, Thomas, in a memorandum addressed to union officials, outlined steps that local unions should take to protect the rights of female plant workers. Noting that he had recently received "disturbing reports of situations in which equal and just seniority protection has been denied women members," Thomas warned, "If management is successful in disregarding seniority rights of women workers now, they will be in a stronger position to disregard seniority rights of other workers later on." He directed local unions to insist that management observe seniority lists in layoffs and recalls and to seek the assistance of regional directors "if management is unyielding in its opposition to women workers." Thomas also instructed locals "not [to] accept management's word that a job cannot be performed by a woman" and to "see that women have opportunities to try jobs to which they are entitled by virtue of their seniority."[19]

The UAW's monthly magazine disseminated international policy to the rank and file. "The catch phrase, a woman's place is in the kitchen," one article warned, "is a silly slander, and a cover slogan for tricky attacks on everyone's standard of living and everyone's political rights." "Women work because they have to, for the same reason most other people work." Another piece outlined the union's position regarding the seniority rights of veterans and women workers:

> Should veterans without seniority be given jobs over women who have seniority rights in UAW plants?
> Here is Jimmy Smith, he's just 22 and a veteran of two years in the Pacific. He's had miscellaneous jobs before he went into service—delivery jobs, drug and grocery store clerking, but no re-employment rights to a job he's interested in. He's hired at X auto plant, simply because

18. Minutes of the IEB Meeting, July 16–23, 1945, pp. 139–40, ibid., Box 24, Folder 11; Thomas to Taylor, August 6, 1945; Emil Mazey Collection, Box 13, Women's Division Folder, ALUA; Statement of the International Union, UAW-CIO, Protesting the Regional War Labor Board's Ruling, ibid.; Thomas to All Local Union Presidents et al., August 6, 1945, ibid.

19. Thomas to All Local Union Presidents, Regional Directors, and International Representatives, September 26, 1945, Ford Department Collection, Box 11, R. J. Thomas Incoming Folder.

he's a veteran. When he goes to work he cuts our Alice Jones who was next on the seniority list. With three and a half years in X plant Alice, who was laid off the day after V-J day, has exhausted her unemployment compensation and needs a job desperately . . . she's got two children to support.

Should Alice Jones be responsible for providing Jimmy Smith with a job? *The UAW says no.*[20]

Other articles celebrated the willingness of male unionists to defend the rights of women during reconversion. When Local 174 officers protested the refusal of the Commerce Pattern Foundry and Machine Company to recall women in line with seniority, management slowed production to take advantage of a clause in the contract limiting the period of time in which laid-off employees could exercise seniority. The local bargaining committee recognized that the strategy adopted by the company might set a precedent for future attacks on male employees. Demanding the extension of seniority rights to all employees for an additional year, the local threatened to strike in defense of the rights of members who had been laid off. Although the company claimed there were no jobs suitable for women, it agreed to recall five women on a trial basis. Placed on jobs in the foundry, the women called the company's bluff and exceeded production standards, forcing management to recall the other seventy-five women. Reminding readers of *Ammunition* that women at the Kelsey Hayes plant had conducted a sit-down strike in 1937 to win for male co-workers the same wage increase they had won for themselves, Local 174 officers explained, "Since they sat down for us, we've got to stand up for them." Another article hailed the efforts of Local 140 in behalf of thirty-one women laid off from the Dodge Truck plant in Detroit. After the local protested the layoff of the women despite their seniority, plant management recalled them. Subjected to various kinds of harassment, all the women were fired for "incompetence." Local 140 appealed the action to the Chrysler-UAW umpire and won an award of $55,000 in back pay for the women.[21]

The policies advanced by the international provided women in the union with a legitimate platform for contesting the violation of their rights as UAW members. Framed as a defense of the hard-won principle of seniority, women's demand for fair and equal treatment

20. *Ammunition* 4 (February 1946): 20; *Ammunition* 4 (August 1946): 22.
21. *Ammunition* 5 (January 1947): 30–31; *Ammunition* 6 (March 1948): 32–35.

during reconversion won the moral and active support of a proportion of the male leadership and membership. Andrew Montgomery,
a skilled tradesman and Local 653 officer, averred that the UAW's
official recognition of the right of women to postwar employment
based on seniority was "one of the big changes" brought about by the
war and reconversion. "Possibly a lot of people will not agree with
me on this," he admitted in 1961, referring to the persistent belief
that the union should oppose the employment of married women
when "some young fellow who is trying to raise a family maybe does
not have enough seniority to work in the plant." "You have got to
have your seniority rights in my opinion," Montgomery stated. "I
think that once we lose the seniority rights then we are done as an
organization." Ken Morris, a Local 212 officer until his election to the
IEB in 1955, recalled that local's battle with Briggs management during reconversion to secure the right of wartime female employees to
reemployment in line with their seniority. Briggs "had hired and
brought in all kinds of women into the plant during the war, and now
the company wanted to get rid of the women saying we wanted to go
back to our prewar status. This we could not agree with. They were
part of our membership and we felt that if they could work during the
war, they could work now, based on their seniority." Local leader Jess
Ferrazza added that some male members of Local 212 protested the
union's advocacy of sexual equality. "But it was a question of seniority at that time. The women had the seniority and could do the
job," Ferrazza asserted. "So there was nothing else that they could do
about it."[22]

Women laid off from the Ford Highland Park plant also benefited
by appealing to the men in their local to join them in defense of the
principle of seniority. The distress of women in the plant became
acute after V-J Day. Before the war the plant had employed 3,800
workers, of which 100 were women. The war-induced manpower
shortage had forced management to hire more women; in 1944, at the
peak of wartime employment, 5,800, or 43 percent of the 13,500
workers in the plant, were women. Although Ford, which intended
to reconvert the plant to tractor production after the war, anticipated
postwar employment of 13,000 at the plant, it did not intend to allow

22. Interview with Andrew Montgomery, July 31, 1961, pp. 16–17, UAW Oral
History Project, Institute of Labor and Industrial Relations, University of Michigan
and Wayne State University, ALUA; interview with Ken Morris, June 28, 1963, p. 40,
ibid.; interview with Jess Ferrazza, May 26, 1961, p. 22, ibid.

women to participate in the postwar expansion. By November 1945 only 300 women were still working at the Highland Park plant. Although women with up to twenty-seven years' seniority were being laid off, the company was hiring male workers with no background of employment in the plant on jobs women were capable of performing. On October 27 the membership of Local 400 voted unanimously to support "morally, actively, and financially" a picket line the Women's Committee wanted to set up outside the plant employment office. Carrying signs reading "Stop Discrimination Because of Sex" and "The Hand that Rocks the Cradle Can Build Tractors, Too," 150 women picketed on November 8 to protest management practices in layoffs and recalls.[23]

Local 400 subsequently made a determined effort to force the management at the Highland Park plant to recall women in line with seniority. Surveying the occupational structure in the plant, the local on several occasions submitted lists of jobs it deemed suitable for women with greater seniority than men currently employed. In August 1946 Ford negotiated a formal policy with the UAW calling for the rehiring of female employees. Agreeing to recall women with sufficient seniority, management nevertheless warned that if a woman failed to meet production standards, she would be processed as a "quit," would be removed from the recall list, and would lose seniority rights under the contract. In a separate memorandum, the Ford labor relations director advised plant building superintendents that "'soft jobs' are not to be picked out for these people." It instructed the superintendents, however, to handle the matter "carefully and tactfully . . . in order that the company may not be laid open to the charge of attempting in any manner to rid itself of female employees." The company persisted in placing the women it recalled on jobs they were physically unable to perform. Relaying a list of nine men newly hired for jobs women were capable of performing, a local committeeman asked Ken Bannon, president of Local 400, "Is there some way we can wake up the employment office?" Charging that the company was "attempting to circumvent the Women's Agreement," Bannon asserted in May 1947 that "this Local Union in

23. Reports of John Carney and Women's Committee to IEB, November 7, 1945, Addes Collection, Box 69A, Local Union 400 Folder; Layoffs in Representative UAW-CIO Plants–Detroit Area since the Surrender of Japan, Research Department Collection, Box 11, Postwar Employment 1945 Folder; *Detroit News*, November 8, 1945; *New York Times*, November 9, 1945.

no way condones the action of the Ford Motor Company in this matter."[24]

The efforts of Locals 174, 212, 400, and others attest to the presence and importance in the UAW of male allies, but not all men responded as favorably to women's requests for assistance in challenging the discriminatory treatment accorded them during reconversion. Despite the international's public stance and the changes brought about by the greater integration of women during the war, the issue of veterans' seniority and job rights and the prospect of a return to the high unemployment levels of the 1930s tended to reinforce the view still held by male unionists that women were a threat to wage standards and competitors for a limited number of jobs. Unwilling to relinquish their dominant position in the labor market, these men preferred not to recognize management's practices as unfair or discriminatory and often resisted efforts to ensure or widen women's access to jobs in the plants.

The response of the leadership of Local 600 to women's attempts to secure their jobs at the Ford River Rouge plant illustrates the negative attitude of many male auto workers after the war. In the months following V-J Day, women improperly laid off or not recalled to jobs in line with seniority were offered minimal assistance by local leaders. "In our mind," a Local 600 executive board member later explained bluntly, "there was no reasonable expectation of the women being called back because we were interested in the men being laid off." Complaints of discriminatory practices by foremen and labor relations staff members multiplied during the winter and spring of 1946, but women received no support from the local in protesting the disputed transfers, layoffs, and recalls. At a meeting on May 15 with William Grant, president of Local 600, and Leon Pody, a staff member of the UAW's Ford Department, a group of women requested that the union undertake a survey of jobs in the plant in order to determine what jobs women would be capable of performing. Because the

24. Clarence Donovan to Ken Bannon, September 19, 1946, Ford Department Collection, Box 6, Female Employees Folder; Bannon to Joseph Bailey, June 23, 1946, UAW Local 400 Collection, Box 85, Folder 19, ALUA; Manton Cummins to All Building Superintendents, August 30, 1946, ibid.; Bannon to Edward Greenwald, May 6, 1947, ibid.; Roy Hilts to Bannon, November 4, 1947, ibid. Other locals conducted departmental or plant surveys to find jobs for women with seniority. See, for example, Joseph Hattley's comments about Local 7 at the Chrysler plant at Kercheval and Jefferson in Detroit. Interview with Hattley, August 4 and 8, 1961, pp. 35–36, UAW Oral History Project.

contract provided that women who had worked in the plant during the war would remain on the recall list for a period of time equal only to their accrued seniority, the women were eager for prompt action. The local, however, made no effort in the weeks following the meeting to initiate the survey. Appearing before the executive board on June 13, Trilby Riopelle complained that women were not being "given a square deal" by the local union or the company and asserted, "Some of the officers of the local and some committeemen have expressed sentiments against having women in the plant." As if in retaliation, the executive board tabled Riopelle's request that it grant formal recognition to the Local 600 Women's Committee. The all-male executive board added insult to injury when it essentially denied the existence of the problem of sex discrimination by refusing to recognize the women's committee on the grounds that "the women should not have separate meetings as no other minority group in Local 600 [has] this privilege."[25]

In July the women's committee responded to a new series of layoffs in the motor building by threatening to establish a picket line in front of Local 600 headquarters. Meeting on July 24 with Grant, William Oliver, head of the union's Fair Practices and Anti-Discrimination Department, Mildred Jeffrey, and Harry Ross, a representative from the union's Ford Department, the women's committee protested that women with two to three years' seniority had been laid off on jobs in the motor building while men with no history of employment in the plant were being hired to fill the positions. The women argued that the union should have anticipated the problem of management discrimination against women before reconversion began rather than waiting until the women complained about the treatment accorded them and threatened to set up a picket line.[26]

In his report to Richard Leonard, director of the Ford Department, Oliver stated circumspectly that the threatened picket line "was rea-

25. Local Executive Board meeting minutes, November 27, 1945, and December 4, 11, 18, 1945, UAW Local 600 Collection, Box 1, Folder 10, ALUA; Local 600 Special Executive Board Meeting minutes, December 20, 1946, ibid., Box 2, Folder 1; Kathleen Lowrie to Frieda Miller, March 13, 1946, RG 86/NA, Box 1416, Lowrie 1943 to Date Folder; William Grant to Leon Pody, May 15, 1946, Ford Department Collection, Box 6, Female Employees Folder; Local Executive Board meeting minutes, June 13, 1946, UAW Local 600 Collection, Box 1, Folder 15; Local Executive Board meeting minutes, September 23, 1946, ibid., Box 1, Folder 15.
26. Report of Meeting on Women's Rehire Problem, July 24, 1946, Ford Department Collection, Box 16, Harry Ross Reports Folder.

son for grave concern, since previous experiences of yours and mine at Highland Park did not result in too favorable an attitude toward the union." Mildred Jeffrey had assured the anxious leaders of Local 600 after the July 24 meeting that there would be no picket line if action against discrimination were taken. Shortly thereafter, Leonard, in a letter to Manton Cummins, director of labor relations for the Ford Motor Company, condemned management practices in layoff and recall procedures and stated that he was instructing Local 600 to conduct a job survey and to make certain that women were recalled in line with their seniority as provided in the contract. This action defused the threat to establish a picket line. In October, however, women reported that Local 600 had not yet conducted the promised survey despite the fact that the company was hiring men for jobs that laid-off women could perform. At the peak of wartime employment, in November 1943, there were 7,209 women and 33,814 men working on production jobs at the River Rouge industrial complex. In October 1946 only 755 women were working in the plants, while the number of male employees had risen to 35,774.[27]

In contrast to the dilatory Local 600 leaders, men in other locals refused even to acknowledge as legitimate the complaints by women that their rights to postwar jobs were being violated. Marjorie McMahon's employer told her after V-J Day that she would not be recalled to work in line with her seniority because all the jobs were too heavy for women. The predominantly male membership and leadership of Local 87 not only repudiated the grievance filed by McMahon to protest the decision but also voted down a motion to approve the policy statement issued by R. J. Thomas recommending that women be afforded the opportunity "to try jobs to which they are entitled by virtue of their seniority." "This work was on a machine that I had worked on before and other women worked on . . . all during the high peak of employment," McMahon reported to the IEB. "I believe [this] is an injustice to the women members of U.A.W.-C.I.O. Local 87." Advising the officers of Local 900 not to challenge management's claim that jobs were unsuitable for women even if it were discovered that women were able to perform them, an international representa-

27. Oliver to Leonard, August 1, 1946, and Leonard to Cummins, July 31, 1946, Reuther Collection, Box 89, Folder 2; report of Meeting on Women's Rehire Problem, July 24, 1946, and Leonard to Thomas Thompson, October 3, 1946, Ford Department Collection, Box 6, Female Employees Folder; River Rouge Factory Counts, Accession No. 735, Boxes 2 and 4, FMCA.

tive asserted, "I don't think we should stick our chin out." Attitudes such as these in effect sanctioned management's discrimination against women.[28]

Other locals actively colluded with management to deny women postwar employment by entering into agreements that arbitrarily defined the sexual division of labor. Locals 670 and 125 nullifed the provision in their contracts for plantwide seniority irrespective of sex when they negotiated with management to limit the number of jobs to which wartime female employees could apply their seniority in layoffs and recalls. In the fall of 1945 Local 12 and the Spicer Manufacturing Division of the Dana Corporation, to cite another example, agreed that women would be placed in a small number of jobs, despite the fact that they had ably performed many others during the war. Following this agreement, four hundred female employees were offered the option of quitting voluntarily and waiving their seniority rights in exchange for severance pay. To facilitate the exodus of the women from the plant and to prevent resistance to the plan, management and the union warned the women that state labor laws, which had been suspended for the duration of the war, prohibited their employment on nearly all jobs. The Local 12 Women's Committee protested the agreements, charging that the list of "female" jobs was arbitrary and that the argument about state labor laws was a smokescreen for sexual discrimination; the committee demanded an objective survey of all jobs in the plant. When the survey revealed that women legally could perform a larger number of jobs, the Women's Committee insisted that women who had been laid off out of line with seniority be recalled to those jobs, regardless of whether they had signed the waiver. The men in the local, however, rightly feared that the proposed recall would displace hundreds of men with less seniority. Conflict over "the female problem" dragged on for months and was never fully resolved. "Every attempt has been made to solidify our ranks so we can determine the course of the union in arguing with the company," the regional director explained to Emil Mazey, the UAW secretary-treasurer; "however, because of our continued division in our own ranks, it has been impossible to say to the company that the union's position is this or that."[29]

28. McMahon to IEB, October 22, 1945, and Gerald Knoll to George Addes, November 5, 1945, Addes Collection, Box 74, Folder 5; report of meeting with Lincoln Plant Committee and Company on Women's Problem, July 26, 1946, Ford Department Collection, Box 16, Harry Ross Reports Folder.
29. Mildred Jeffrey and Roy Reuther to William Oliver, December 16, 1946, Addes

The reluctance and refusal of male unionists to enforce international policy and challenge management's practices during reconversion angered female activists. Charging that local officers were colluding with management to deprive women of their seniority rights, they appealed to the top leadership of the UAW to take stronger action in defense of women's right to postwar employment in the auto industry. In November 1945 John Carney asked the IEB to "meet the issue of discrimination against female members of our union fairly and squarely and set a policy for this problem." Referring to Local 400's onerous noninterchangeable occupational group seniority agreement, he suggested that "all Regional Directors and heads of departments be instructed to scrutinize all future proposed seniority agreements for trick clauses which will allow discrimination against any group because of sex, color or racial origin." Carney warned that the picket line established by the local women's committee was only "a forerunner of other demonstrations to come," and he asked the IEB "to consider the damage that can be done by the reprisals of 5,000 female employees of the Highland Park plant alone . . . [who] have a feeling that they have been double crossed by their union." Patricia McLean told board members that the women's committee intended to maintain the picket line "until our seniority rights are recognized." She noted that collusion between some local union officers and plant managers and the dilatory response of international officials to reports of discrimination and requests for assistance had made "many women feel as bitter towards the union as towards the company." Beatrice Madson concluded the group's presentation to the board with the comment: "The fight of the women is also the fight of the men."[30]

Their dissatisfaction with the response of the UAW to the plight of women workers having increased during the winter of 1945–1946,

Collection, Box VII, Folder 5; Appeals Committee Report, Alice Sowden vs. Local 125, March 22, 1946, ibid., Box 75, Folder 5; Spicer Labor Relations to Frank Rostetter, June 6, 1947, and Charles Ballard to Mazey, December 17, 1947, ibid., Box 71, Folder 13. The Local 12 Women's Committee asked the IEB to intervene in the case in January 1948. The IEB ordered the local bargaining committee to seek the reinstatement of the four hundred women in June 1948. As of November 1949, the women had not been recalled. It is not known whether they ever reclaimed their jobs. Barbara Welch and Louise McNaught to Mazey, January 14, 1948, ibid., Box 71, Folder 14; Mazey to Welch, June 29, 1948, Walter Murphy to Mazey, September 9, 1948, Ballard to Leonard Woodcock, April 1, 1949, and Woodcock to Randolph Grey, November 1, 1949, ibid., Box 71, Folder 13.

30. Minutes of the IEB Meeting, November 7–12, 1945, pp. 36–41, Addes Collection, Box 25, Folder 6.

women unionists voiced their anger at the UAW convention in March 1946. On the first day of the convention the delegates approved a resolution urging the passage of a full-employment act, federal legislation providing equal pay for equal work, and the institution of government-supported child-care centers. Despite this action, female delegates were suspicious of the international's motives in advocating federal and state action against discrimination. Pat McLean called the resolution an attempt "to pass the buck on to the United States Government rather than setting a policy within our own union." Reporting that the seniority rights of women at the Ford River Rouge plant were being abrogated in layoffs and recalls, Minnie Jones, a Local 600 delegate, condemned the callous belief of men in the local that women war workers belonged in the home and cited the example of war widows who had children and who needed to work in the auto plants, where the wages were higher than those in traditional women's jobs. Inez Walker, a Local 927 delegate, supported the resolution but asked: "What happened to all the wonderful resolutions we passed at the [December 1944] Women's Conference? They have never been executed. . . . I should like to see this resolution not only adopted but actually worked on and carried into effect."[31]

Following the floor discussion of the resolution, Edna McNamara of Local 651 and Sylvia Woods of Local 330 led the ad hoc Council of Women Delegates in drafting a second resolution, which demanded union action against sex discrimination. To enhance "the strength and solidarity of our Union as a whole," the resolution stated, the UAW should give "increased attention and aid . . . to the status of women workers." Seeking to codify the wartime gains made by women and to incorporate the lessons of reconversion into union policy and practice, the Council of Women Delegates asked the union to reaffirm its position against such employment practices as unequal pay for equal work and sexually discriminatory layoffs, recalls, and discharges. The resolution went further, instructing the UAW to expand its definition of discrimination based on sex and to declare publicly its opposition to the inclusion in contracts of separate seniority lists for women and men. Reminding male unionists that "the basic security for each and every Union worker is to be found in a

31. *Proceedings of the Tenth Convention of the UAW-CIO, March 23–31, 1946,* pp. 52–54 (hereafter cited as *1946 Convention Proceedings*).

Union contract" and that "full membership rights are pledged to every worker regardless of . . . sex or marital status," the women urged the UAW to fulfill the democratic promise of industrial union- ism and defend female members against discriminatory employment practices.[32]

The resolution, which was unanimously adopted by the Resolu- tions Committee and approved by the delegates in the closing min- utes of the convention, directed the international leadership to instruct regional directors to disapprove any contract that discrimi- nated against women. By making the IEB responsible for the imple- mentation of the resolution on women's rights, the Council of Women Delegates remedied a major weakness in the UAW's ap- proach to the problem of sexual discrimination. The reconversion crisis had revealed the extent of male opposition to the presence of women in the plants. By obstructing grievance procedures, ignoring violations of contract provisions that protected women's rights, and complying with agreements and practices that discriminated against women, male unionists had facilitated management efforts to exclude women from the postwar automotive labor force. The international leadership had demonstrated its own ambivalence by failing to do much more than inform the locals in writing of its preference for fair and equal treatment. Although the resolution did not stipulate any penalties for noncompliance by local unions, it eliminated ambiguity about the union's commitment to women auto workers and made the IEB responsible for implementing the agreed-upon policy.

The efforts of female auto unionists to secure the jobs of women workers challenge prevailing interpretations of American women in the 1940s. The dramatic advances made by women workers in the United States during the World War II years and the setbacks they experienced in the immediate aftermath of the war have been a subject of considerable historical interest. Stressing the extent to which the war failed to challenge basic assumptions about women's role in society, recent works dealing with the experience of women in the 1940s have attributed the withdrawal of women workers from basic industries during reconversion to the power of ideology about gender. Despite agreement about the limited and impermanent char- acter of change during the war, there is debate over the attitudes and behavior of women themselves. Some scholars depict women as

32. Ibid., pp. 328–29; *United Auto Worker*, March 1946.

unwilling victims of the resurgent emphasis on domesticity. Others, however, regard women as complicitous in the retreat to the home and conventional roles. The attitudes and behavior of women workers, these historians contend, conformed to the dictates of the decade's conservative consensus. According to this view, women workers continued to regard their primary role as that of wife and mother and perceived their employment in previously male-dominated industries as responsive to the needs of a war economy. Instead of defending their economic interests as workers, it is argued, women acquiesced in the loss of their wartime jobs during reconversion, choosing more conventional forms of employment in the postwar era. "Most women," one historian has stated, "failed to grasp whatever opportunity for advancement the war afforded."[33]

It is apparent that a proportion of the women employed in the auto industry during the war did not plan to seek continued employment in the plants in the postwar period. Some women had never intended to continue working after the war, and others were content to return to jobs in the traditionally female employment sectors. Many women, viewing their wartime experience in basic industry as temporary, saw no reason to protest when they were laid off. Flora Chavez, who worked as an aircraft assembler in southern California

33. Nationally, the proportion of women among all workers employed in basic industries fell from a wartime high of 25 percent in October 1944 to 13 percent in April 1947, a figure only four percentage points higher than that for 1939. Although the number of women in the labor force never fell to prewar levels and eventually exceeded wartime figures, the occupational distribution of women resembled that before 1941. Of the 17 million women working outside the home in 1950, 58 percent were employed in the clerical, retail, and service sectors; and the majority of the 19 percent employed in manufacturing worked in the textile and clothing industries. Mary Elizabeth Pidgeon, "Women Workers and Recent Economic Change," *Monthly Labor Review* 65 (December 1947): 666; U.S. Women's Bureau, *Women as Workers: A Statistical Guide* (Washington, D.C., 1953), p. 13. The view that women were unwilling victims is most vividly presented in the film *The Life and Times of Rosie the Riveter* and in Miriam Frank, Marilyn Ziebarth, and Connie Field, *The Life and Times of Rosie the Riveter* (Emeryville, Calif., 1982). See also Karen Anderson, *Wartime Women* (Westport, Conn., 1981), pp. 154–82; Leila Rupp, *Mobilizing Women for War* (Princeton, N.J., 1978), 175–81; Sheila Tobias and Lisa Anderson, "What Really Happened to Rosie the Riveter: Demobilization and the Female Labor Force, 1944–1947," *MSS Modular Publications*, module 9 (1973). For the argument that women did not protest the loss of their jobs because the war had not changed their own fundamentally conservative views and expectations, see D'Ann Campbell, *Women at War with America* (Cambridge, Mass., 1984), pp. 213–28; William Chafe, *The American Woman* (London, 1972), pp. 174–95; Alan Clive, "Women Workers in World War II: Michigan as a Test Case," *Labor History* 20 (Winter 1979): 44–72. The quotation is from Clive, "Women Workers in World War II," pp. 71–72.

during the war, explains that women expected to lose their jobs. "You didn't know you were being discriminated against," Chavez says. "That's just the way it was." Dorothy Haener, who worked in the Ford Willow Run bomber plant during the war and later served as a UAW international representative, recalls that as a young woman in the early 1940s, she, like many other women, considered every job temporary. She viewed her experience at Willow Run as no exception, although at the time she was aware that her job paid higher wages than the traditionally female jobs she had held prior to the war. "I really expected to do what everyone else, every woman who . . . grew up under the circumstances I did, with the conditions and the culture we had, [did]," she remarked. "I really expected to get married and not have to work anymore."[34]

Although the prevalence of these attitudes undoubtedly undermined the prospects for collective action and confirmed the view of employers and male unionists that women did not belong in auto plants after the war, many women wanted to keep their jobs in the industry. Women who did not have the option of choosing to work or not to work were eager to retain auto jobs because the wages they received were substantially greater than those received by women employed as secretaries, retail clerks, and domestic servants. Female store clerks in Detroit, for example, took home $24.85 per week while female auto workers received an average $40.35 per week. "You knew then, as a woman, that there was no chance of going out anyplace else and getting a job. If you didn't get back [in], why, there was just no place to go," explains Mildred Eusebio, an aircraft assembler during World War II at the Ford bomber plant at Willow Run and the Douglas aircraft plant in Los Angeles. "Of course there was the clothing factories," Eusebio admits, but "that was not my line at all." "Other women throughout America still have jobs," Minnie Jones chided the delegates to the 1946 UAW convention, "and certainly we are not going to work to organize the union and then go back to work for $15.00 a week."[35]

34. Interview with Flora Chavez, vol. 7, p. 54, Rosie the Riveter Revisited: Women and the World War II Work Experience Oral History Project, California State–Long Beach Foundation, Long Beach, California; interview with Dorothy Haener, 1976, pp. 17–18, Twentieth Century Trade Union Woman Oral History Project.

35. U.S. Women's Bureau, *Women Workers in Ten War Production Areas and Their Postwar Plans*, Bulletin No. 209 (Washington, D.C., 1946), p. 44; interview with Mildred Eusebio, vol. 2, p. 44, Rosie the Riveter Revisited Oral History Project; *1946 Convention Proceedings*, p. 52.

Black women as a group were especially eager to retain their jobs in the auto industry. World War II offered black women their first meaningful opportunity for upward occupational mobility. Thousands moved from low-paid, nonunion agricultural and service jobs to higher-paying, union-protected manufacturing jobs. The importance of this shift helps account for the prominent role played by black women in the UAW women's campaign for gender equality during reconversion. Women such as Edna McNamara, Sylvia Woods, Gwen Thompson, Louise Hamilton, and Lillian Hatcher were persistent and important critics of sexual discrimination. Black women certainly suffered double jeopardy during reconversion, facing discrimination on the basis of race as much as sex. The fact, however, that black men as a group fared better than did their female counterparts in securing a foothold in auto plants after the war attests to the significance of gender for the treatment accorded black women during and after reconversion. Sharing the stigma of gender with white women, they made common cause, racially integrating the network of female activists.[36]

The relationship between the attitudes and behavior of women who worked in basic industries such as auto manufacturing during the war simply was more subtle and elusive than historians have acknowledged. The onset of reconversion in basic industries occurred suddenly and without adequate planning. The confusion and chaos in the months following V-E Day and V-J Day made the coordination and monitoring of layoffs and recalls in plants with thousands and tens of thousands of employees a daunting and difficult task. Ray Berndt, president of Local 5 during reconversion, remembered the problem of reducing the number of employees at the Studebaker plant in South Bend, Indiana, from 22,000 to 8,000. "You [had] headaches over not being able to find employment for this many people," Berndt explained. Layoffs at the Ford Highland Park plant occurred "on such a scale," Pat McLean told the IEB, "that even trigger-quick

36. Karen Anderson, "Last Hired, First Fired: Black Women Workers during World War II," *Journal of American History* 69 (June 1982): 95–97; Jacqueline Jones, *Labor of Love, Labor of Sorrow* (New York, 1985), pp. 256–60; August Meier and Elliott Rudwick, *Black Detroit and the Rise of the UAW* (Oxford, 1979), pp. 213–14; Herbert Northrup, *The Negro in the Automobile Industry* (Philadelphia, 1968), p. 32. Race relations among union women were not universally harmonious. For another view, see Dolores Janiewski, "Seeking 'a New Day and a New Way': Black Women and Unions in the Southern Tobacco Industry," in Carol Groneman and Mary Beth Norton, eds., *To Toil the Livelong Day* (Ithaca, 1987), pp. 161–78.

sincere union representatives . . . had a hard time filing individual grievances." It is important to recognize that under these circumstances women may have chosen not to protest because to do so appeared futile. Mildred Jeffrey, noting the hostility of men and the general public toward women workers, claims that this too had its negative impact on women. "It was attitude setting," she notes; "it was the environment—it created a lot of pressures on women not to pursue their grievances." The treatment accorded those who did protest probably further discouraged women from seeking postwar employment in auto plants. Recalling the situation that existed at the Ford River Rouge plant during reconversion, Jeffrey remarks: "It was just so hard for women, although we had women who got their heads bloodied, figuratively speaking. . . . They had a hell of a time! It was really, really rough getting equal rights!" Says Jeffrey: "You had to be a very sturdy woman then to hang on."[37]

The ambiguous character of the relationship between the attitudes and behavior of female auto workers suggests the contingencies involved in working women's collective action in the immediate postwar period. In contrast to the experience of women in other industries and unions, the UAW's antidiscrimination policies and its commitment to the principle of seniority provided women auto workers with at least a legitimate platform for contesting the loss of their jobs during reconversion. But the initiative for challenging the violation of their rights as union members lay with the women themselves. The prospects for mobilizing a campaign both within the union and against management were as a result most favorable in those auto plants and UAW locals where there were contracts with single seniority lists; where there were women such as Pat McLean, Della Rymer, and Grace Blackett, who had acquired organizational and leadership skills during the war; and where there were women's committees such as the one in Local 400 which had been established before the war's end and could serve as bases for protest activities. These resources enabled women in some auto plants to overcome the forces that inhibited or precluded female protest elsewhere. Such strengths, however, were vulnerable to the rapid reduction of the female labor force and the consequent loss of women leaders as a

37. Interview with Ray Berndt, May 3, 1963, pp. 20–21, UAW Oral History Project; minutes of the IEB meeting, November 7–12, 1945, p. 38, Addes Collection, Box 25, Folder 6; interview with Jeffrey, pp. 70, 52, Twentieth Century Trade Union Woman Oral History Project.

result of layoffs during reconversion. Grace Blackett, for example, whom Jeffrey calls a "fireball" and an "agitator," was laid off from the staff of UAW Region 4 in August 1945 and soon after from her job at the Ford Willow Run plant. "We tried to have demonstrations of women," Jeffrey remembers. "That was kind of depressing because here we had worked so hard trying to develop leadership, but when it came to this period, it wasn't there. There weren't enough women."[38]

The absence of a feminist movement outside the plants also reinforced the political weakness of those who sought to secure for women postwar employment in basic industries. The women's movement that emerged in the unions during World War II was a vital and important force for change in the status of working women, but reconversion undermined its strength. By challenging the ideology of woman's proper place, other women's organizations might have given the protest of female defense workers additional and much-needed legitimacy. But race and class differences weakened gender solidarity among activist women in the 1940s, precluding a unified collective effort among feminists to secure wartime gains for women in the labor market.[39]

In light of the obstacles to both individual and collective action as well as the strength of opposition to the continued presence of women in the plants, it is perhaps surprising that any protest occurred. Yet too close attention to the relationship between the attitudes and behavior of women themselves may obscure the larger context. On the one hand, the manner in which many women were ousted from their jobs seriously threatened their chances of reclaiming or retaining their positions in the postwar period. On the other hand, without a transformation in the sexual division of labor in the

38. Interview with Jeffrey, p. 52, Twentieth Century Trade Union Woman Oral History Project; Gabin interview with Jeffrey, August 1, 1983. With the exception of the UE, most unions apparently did not witness overt or organized protest by women against the loss of their wartime jobs. See Milkman, *Gender at Work*, pp. 107–9, 117–18, 144–47; Amy Kesselman, "Hidden Resistance: Women Shipyard Workers after World War II," in Christine Bose, Roslyn Feldberg, and Natalie Sokoloff, eds., *Hidden Aspects of Women's Work* (New York, 1987), pp. 283–98. For the labor movement's disinterest in gender equality and wartime women workers during reconversion, see Anderson, *Wartime Women*, pp. 154–82; Philip Foner, *Women and the American Labor Movement from World War I to the Present* (New York, 1980), pp. 384–93; Frank, Ziebarth, and Field, *The Life and Times of Rosie the Riveter*, pp. 34–38; Susan Hartmann, *The Home Front and Beyond* (Boston, 1982), pp. 64–69.

39. On the women's movement in the 1940s, see Susan Hartmann, "Women's Organizations during World War II: The Interaction of Class, Race and Feminism," in Mary Kelley, ed., *Woman's Being, Woman's Place* (Boston, 1979), pp. 313–28.

auto industry, the vast majority of the women who worked in the plants after 1941 had little hope of remaining there after the war. Some progress had been made late in the war in more fully integrating women into the structure and organization of work in the auto industry, but it was simply too little, too late. Only a massive and sustained upheaval in the sexual division of labor could have ensured job opportunities for women. Some UAW men might have been willing to defend women's right to exercise seniority in transfers, layoffs, and recalls, but few were interested in undertaking the larger fight against employers determined to hire men. As a result, the action of union officials in behalf of women workers was often only a reluctant response to pressure rather than a voluntary expression of shared concern. "In retrospect, I think that I should have committed hari-kari when it came to the layoffs," Jeffrey observes. "I just think we should have been much more dramatic about it. I don't know anything except something like that that would have really commanded the union's attention." These barriers to postwar jobs indicate that the restoration of patterns of occupational segregation by sex in the years following World War II might better be read as evidence of the extent to which women were unable to make their own decisions regarding employment than as evidence of their preference for traditionally female occupations.[40]

The obstacles encountered by women seeking postwar employment in auto plants indicated the ambiguous legacy of the war years. As the proportion of women in the automotive labor force fell from a wartime high of 26 percent to 9 percent in 1947, a figure just two percentage points greater than that for the prewar period, the important role played by women in defense production for many faded into memory. Fifteen years after World War II, male UAW leaders reflected on what they clearly considered a unique if somewhat anomalous chapter in the union's history. Asked about the fate of the five thousand women who worked at Studebaker during the war, Ray Berndt thought that they simply—and contentedly—left the plant. "Most of them were wives of boys who had gone in the service and were trying to maintain the income of the family," he speculated. John McDaniel, a Local 190 officer who was more sensitive to the

40. Interview with Jeffrey, p. 70, Twentieth Century Trade Union Woman Oral History Project. For the recent debate over the extent to which women's choice of jobs explains patterns of occupational segregation by sex, see Ruth Milkman, "Women's History and the Sears Case," *Feminist Studies* 12 (Summer 1986): 375–400.

diverse character of the industry's female labor force and who tried to secure postwar jobs for women at Packard, recalled the dramatic and permanent drop in female employment. Referring to the seventeen thousand women who worked at Packard during the war, McDaniel averred that they all "went by the way," except for the original two hundred who had been employed there before the war. Norman Bully remembered that during the war "thousands and thousands" of women also worked at Buick in Flint, "but they have almost disappeared from the plant now." The only women working in the Nash-Kelvinator plant in Racine, Wisconsin, in 1963, according to Local 72 leader Jack Beni, were those "left from the wartime—war babies as we call them." The reassertion of women's marginal place in the auto industry after 1945 made those who had worked in defense jobs during World War II resemble relics from the past, odd and rather quaint anachronisms.[41]

Despite the restoration of prewar patterns of occupational segregation by sex, UAW women had a certain degree of success during reconversion. Women leaders gained from the reconversion experience a clearer understanding of the arbitrary and discriminatory character of the sexual division of labor. Lillian Hatcher, assistant director of the UAW Women's Bureau since October 1944, remembers, "We began to look a little differently at the whole question of equal job rights for women . . . when the . . . layoffs and recalls came and there were all sorts of innuendos about not calling back women because allegedly there weren't any jobs open that they could perform." According to Hatcher, women leaders realized that "to say that she wanted to be classified forever as a female worker was hurting the working woman . . . because there were many jobs that were tagged male occupations that women could perform as well as any other person." In this respect UAW women reflected shifting union perspectives on gender equality. As a result of the war and reconversion, some union women began to advocate equal rather than differential treatment as the appropriate strategy for obtaining gender equality in the workplace. Not all female union leaders rejected the longer-standing emphasis on gender differences. But the

41. Interview with Berndt, p. 21, UAW Oral History Project; interview with McDaniel, p. 12, ibid.; interview with Norman Bully, October 12, 1961, p. 20, ibid.; interview with Beni, March 4, 1963, p. 11, ibid. Berndt apparently forgot that women in Studebaker Local 5 protested the loss of wartime jobs to men and pressed for elimination of separate seniority lists for women and men. John Bodnar, "Power and Memory in Oral History: Workers and Managers at Studebaker," *Journal of American History* 75 (March 1989): 1211–12.

UE's campaign for comparable worth, waitress unionists' efforts to secure equal pay, and UAW women's criticism of sex-differentiated job classifications and seniority lists indicate the significance of the trend. The approach to the problem of gender inequality newly adopted by these women demonstrates that leaders of middle-class women's organizations were not the only advocates of equal treatment in the decades before the resurgence of feminism in the late 1960s. World War II influenced the history of the feminist movement in ways that most scholars have overlooked.[42]

The campaign against sexual discrimination in layoffs and recalls also consolidated the informal and loosely organized network of local women activists which had developed during the war. Mildred Jeffrey claims that the mobilization of the women's network was one of the most important accomplishments of the Women's Bureau, both because it increased the visibility of women in the UAW and because it provided a resource for collective action after reconversion. The resolution drafted by the Council of Women Delegates and adopted by the delegates to the 1946 convention was another achievement for union women, as it established an agenda for action by the UAW in the postwar years. Framed in the language of industrial unionism, this feminist perspective on the position of women in the auto industry received the endorsement of the UAW leadership. In June 1946 the IEB granted the Women's Bureau, which had been in limbo since the dissolution of the War Policy Division, permanent status by incorporating it into the newly established Fair Practices and Anti-Discrimination Department. William Oliver, co-director of the department, explained that although the unit was concerned principally with the employment problems of black workers, it would give "special emphasis . . . [to] women's problems in the automobile industry since [women are] unquestionably the largest single minority group within the jurisdiction of the UAW-CIO."[43]

42. Interview with Lillian Hatcher, p. 83, Twentieth Century Trade Union Woman Oral History Project; transcript, Official Report of Proceedings, Conference of Women Representatives of Labor Unions, RG 86/NA, Box 899, Conference Folder; Alice Kessler-Harris, "The Debate over Equality for Women in the Work Place: Recognizing Differences," in Laurie Larwood, Ann Stromberg, and Barbara Gutek, eds., *Women and Work: An Annual Review*, vol. 1 (Beverly Hills, Calif., 1985), pp. 141–61; Milkman, *Gender at Work*, pp. 77–83, 147–51; Dorothy Sue Cobble, " 'Practical Women': Waitress Unionists and the Controversies over Gender Roles in the Food Service Industry, 1900–1980," *Labor History* 29 (Winter 1988): 5–31.

43. Gabin interview with Jeffrey, August 1, 1983; Second Quarterly Report of the Fair Practices and Anti-Discrimination Department, 1946, UAW Fair Practices and Anti-Discrimination Department–Women's Bureau Collection, Box 2, Folder 17, ALUA.

The action by the IEB indicated the extent to which the war and reconversion had altered both gender relations and the role and status of women within the UAW. Before 1942 women were a marginal presence not only in the plants but in the union as well. By according women the status of a minority group, the UAW acknowledged the existence of discrimination based on sex in the auto industry and provided women with a legitimate platform for extending their gains. The introduction of a critique of the sexual division of labor, the consolidation of the women's network, the codification of antidiscrimination policies, and the institutionalization of an advocate of women's rights offset the losses sustained by women during the reconversion period.

CHAPTER FOUR

Postwar Problems and Prospects, 1948–1962

Caroline Davis, director of the UAW Women's Bureau, alerted the delegates at the 1955 UAW convention to a new employment crisis for women in auto plants. "Mass layoffs of women," she declared, "have become increasingly prevalent." She urged the union to seek the elimination of separate seniority lists in order to protect the jobs of female members. Anticipating that male workers would resist giving women access to men's jobs, Davis warned that gender conflict would weaken the union. "Experience has proven," she cautioned, "that when jobs are scarce management invents varied and devious methods to create confusion and disunity among our members." "Resorting to outworn prejudices against women," Davis continued, "employers seek to divide us and . . . divert our attention from the real issue at hand—that of providing for full employment."[1]

Caroline Davis's impassioned speech reflected her great concern for the future of women in the auto industry. Following World War II, women's advocates in the UAW tried to salvage what reconversion nearly wrecked. Seeking to consolidate wartime gains, they engaged

---

1. Women's Bureau Report, *President's Report to the Fifteenth Constitutional Convention, UAW-CIO, March 27, 1955* (hereafter cited as *President's Report to the 1955 Convention*), pp. 94D–95D. When Mildred Jeffrey resigned from the Women's Bureau in the fall of 1947, Walter Reuther appointed Davis as director of the unit. Davis, an auto worker herself and president of Local 764 from 1944 until her ascension to the international staff, was director of the bureau until her retirement in the early 1970s.

in female institution building while formulating a penetrating critique of the sexual division of labor in the auto industry and devising an agenda for union action against gender inequality. The events of the 1950s, however, undermined optimism about the prospects for improving the status of women in auto plants. The combination of intraindustry trends, such as automation, decentralization, and corporate mergers, and a series of economic recessions exacerbated the persistent problem of irregular employment for auto workers. Both men and women suffered in these years, but women were made especially vulnerable in times of layoffs and job dislocations by the still widespread existence of sex-based seniority lists and job classifications. Restricted to an already small number of jobs, women would find themselves on the street while men with less seniority remained on or even were newly hired for jobs that women were capable of performing. It seemed to some that women had become, in the words of one observer, the "shock absorbers" for the problem of layoffs in the auto industry.[2]

The varied responses of auto unionists to the impact of industrial change on women indicate both the problems of and the prospects for gender advocacy in postwar America. The analysis of women's status in the auto industry made by Davis and other leaders was astute. In a period generally regarded as the nadir of modern American feminism, a group of women in the UAW advocated sex-blind treatment as a means of achieving gender equality in the workplace. Their success in legitimizing union concern about sexual discrimination ensured not only that a debate over woman's place would occur in the 1950s but that it would be grounded in terms of feminism as well as unionism. Thus the events of the 1950s were a measure of how far the union had come since the late 1930s and early 1940s, when women's concerns about job security merited little attention. The circumstances and consequences of these postwar conflicts, however, also revealed how far the UAW had to go.

In a report to the International Executive Board (IEB) of the UAW in December 1946, the Women's Bureau assessed the progress made by the union toward the elimination of sexual discrimination in the auto

2. Robert A. Zaban, "Internal Union Frictions Created by a Job Security Issue: A Case Study of a UAW Internal Dispute Involving Seniority Division by Sex," master's thesis, Purdue University, 1964, p. 106.

industry. The presence of 63,900 women in the plants, the greater extent of equal wage rates, and the preservation of the bureau itself offered "proof of a job well done." The report noted, however, that there were "many problems to be licked." Citing the persistence in some contracts of dual seniority lists and sex-differentiated wage scales, the absence of provisions for maternity leaves, and the limited availability of upgrading and promotional opportunities for women, the bureau chided the "laxness" of union officials in eliminating discrimination from collective-bargaining agreements and in enforcing contract clauses that protected women's right to fair and equal treatment. The Women's Bureau stated the problem more forcefully in an April 1947 report on the status of women foundry workers in the auto industry. "No one but a blind fool would believe that in the UAW-CIO prejudice against women working, against equal pay, against women holding the same or comparable jobs as men, against women's participation on an equal basis with men in the local union has been eliminated." Emphasizing the importance of educating male unionists "as to the rights of women to work and hold a job," the report observed that the bureau *alone cannot solve all of these problems*. It will take the united support and mobilization of all forces within our union to change the one factor which is most difficult— the question of *changing human nature*."[3]

The Women's Bureau was not sanguine about the prospects for a thoroughgoing postwar challenge to sexual discrimination by union men. The unit itself had been in limbo for almost a year, after its sponsor, the War Policy Division, was disbanded in August 1945. The twelve months following V-J Day were tumultuous for the UAW, as it responded to the confusion of reconversion, negotiated with employers, and conducted a nationally important 113-day strike against General Motors. The marginality of the Women's Bureau and its mission was evident in the silence of the UAW and GM on the issue of gender equality during the strike. The issue gained some prominence at the local level during negotiations over the equal-pay principle and the determination of rates for male and female job classifica-

---

3. Fair Practices Department Report, December 10, 1946, pp. 17–19, UAW Fair Practices Department–Women's Bureau Collection, Box 2, Folder 17, Walter P. Reuther Library, Archives of Labor and Urban Affairs, Wayne State University, Detroit, Michigan (hereafter cited as ALUA); Conditions Affecting the Equal Status of Women Foundry Workers, n.d. [April 1947], pp. 3, 15, Walter P. Reuther Collection, Box 89, Folder 12, ALUA.

tions. The UAW's public relations campaign, however, ignored this issue and that of women's place in the postwar labor force, emphasizing instead women's participation on picket lines and in strike kitchens.[4]

Like the GM strike, internal divisions consumed a great deal of auto unionists' energies in the mid-1940s. Factionalism was endemic to the UAW, but the end of the war renewed and intensified a struggle over the union's direction and who would lead it. Riding the crest of the wartime and postwar strike wave, Walter Reuther wrested the presidency of the UAW from R. J. Thomas at the March 1946 convention. During the next twenty months, Reuther battled with Thomas, now first vice-president, and George Addes, who continued as secretary-treasurer, for control of the union. Communism was a central issue in the struggle, Reuther attacking the alliance of the Thomas-Addes leadership with the Communist faction, whose loyalty to the union, he claimed, was suspect. Effectively deploying political as well as ideological weapons, Reuther secured control at the November 1947 convention. Women participated on both sides of the battle for power in the UAW. But it is striking that both the left-wing Addes-Thomas coalition and Reuther's anti-communist, right-to-center alliance rarely tried to use gender-specific issues to gain political capital. Appeals occasionally were made to women in locals where they were numerous enough to attract special attention, one side or the other claiming to be the more militant advocate of the interests of female workers in higher wages and better working conditions. It is significant, however, that these appeals did not challenge occupational segregation by sex. Neither side advanced the idea of sex-blind treatment or called for the abolition of sex-based wage rates, job classifications, and seniority lists. Indifference to gender inequality was the special province of neither the right nor the left.[5]

4. For local action on equal pay during the GM strike, see minutes of Meetings on Local Demands, March 24, 1946, UAW Local 602 Collection, Box 6, Folder 20, ALUA; E. S. Patterson to Senator Pritchard, May 6, 1946, ibid., Folder 23; minutes of meeting, May 24, 1946, ibid., Folder 28; Patterson to Pritchard, June 20, 1946, ibid., Folder 23; minutes of meeting, June 27, 1946, ibid., Folder 29; Neal Edwards to George Coburn, September 21, 1945, Neal Edwards Collection, Box 1, Folder 1, ALUA; Delco Remy Division Local 662 Agreement, June 5, 1946, ibid., Box 3, Agreements-Seniority Folder; and Local 662 strike leaflet, October 8, 1945, Cecil Roeder Collection, Box 2, Local 662 Strike Folder, ALUA. On the strike generally, see Barton Bernstein, "Walter Reuther and the General Motors Strike of 1945–46," *Michigan History* 49 (1965): 260–77.

5. On UAW factionalism, see Martin Halpern, *UAW Politics in the Cold War Era* (Albany, N.Y., 1988); Bert Cochran, *Labor and Communism* (Princeton, N.J., 1977). For

Aware of the disinterest of the union's male majority, the Women's Bureau decided that the initiative for preserving and extending wartime gains lay with women themselves. Because the bureau lacked the power to implement or enforce the UAW's official antidiscriminatory policies, the elimination of the disparity between policy and practice was to a great extent contingent on women's own efforts at the local level. The bureau also recognized that unless the female membership evinced interest in obtaining equal rights and opportunities, the international leadership would have little reason to insist on adherence to official policies. "The best we could do," explains Mildred Jeffrey about this period, "was to work with the women, to try and get them activized and militant, very demanding in their own local unions, and as they did that to be supportive of them."[6] Hoping to sustain the momentum of the wartime movement for equal rights among women in the UAW, the Women's Bureau devoted its energy and resources in the late 1940s to increasing women's participation in the local unions and encouraging women to act individually and collectively in defense of their interests as workers and union members.

As it confronted the task of mobilizing a rank-and-file women's movement, the bureau was encouraged by the efforts of activists in several UAW locals to sustain gender-conscious protest in the aftermath of reconversion. The Local 154 Women's Committee, for example, mounted a successful campaign in 1947 to include an equal-pay-for-equal-work clause in the local's contract with the Hudson Motor Car Company. Enforcing an arbitrary sexual division of labor, Hudson was paying women in jobs classified as "female" 90 cents an hour but paying men in comparable operations classified as "male" an hourly rate of $1.20. Women employed in "men's" jobs were the victims of more blatant discrimination: they received $1.11 an hour, while their male counterparts received $1.60. To demonstrate support for the principle of equal pay, the Women's Committee held meetings that were attended by hundreds of female employees. The all-male bargaining committee bowed to pressure and included an equal-pay clause in its list of demands. Although jobs remained

an example of a local engaged in gender-specific politics during the factional fight of the mid-forties, see the material in UAW Local 45 Collection, Box 6, Folder 21, ALUA.

6. Interview with Mildred Jeffrey, p. 63, The Twentieth Century Trade Union Woman: Vehicle for Social Change Oral History Project, Institute of Labor and Industrial Relations, University of Michigan, Ann Arbor.

separately classified as "male" and "female," the new agreement equalized wage rates for work performed by both sexes.[7]

The action taken by the Local 653 Women's Committee in the winter of 1946–1947 to protest the arbitrary dismissal of 150 female employees at the Pontiac Motor Division of General Motors also demonstrated the vitality of feminist principles in the immediate postwar period. The scarcity of male labor in the summer of 1946 forced the company to hire women. Regarding this as a temporary expedient, management fired all the women on the ground of inefficiency in December, just a few weeks before their probationary period was to expire. Although the women technically were ineligible for union protection, the local—at the urging of Della Rymer, a member of the local executive board, chair of the Women's Committee, and veteran of the reconversion struggles—filed a grievance on their behalf. When plant management rejected the complaint, the Women's Committee marshaled support for the discharged women, holding public meetings at the Pontiac YWCA, issuing press releases condemning management's action, and seeking the support of community women's organizations and the Pontiac city council. The UAW's General Motors Department and Region 1B office submitted an appeal to Ralph Seward, the union-management umpire. Noting that the mass dismissal had not been occasioned by a reduction in force or "any individual misconduct or inefficiency on [the women's] part," Seward asserted that the action stemmed solely from the renewed availability of a male labor supply. Seward informed GM that "an employee's sex alone does not constitute good cause for discharge" and ordered the women reinstated. The UAW's Fair Practices Department hailed Seward's decision as "the first real victory toward elimination of discrimination against women in industry."[8]

7. The Local 154 Women's Committee also wanted a single seniority list and elimination of sex-based job classifications. The local bargaining committee, however, was not supportive of these demands. The supplemental agreement that was drawn up in February 1948 did provide that, in the event of a plantwide layoff, male and female occupational groups would be considered interchangeable. Local 154 Proposed Contract, December 29, 1944, Proposed Agreement between Local 154 and Hudson Motor Car Company, n.d. [July 1947], and Local 154 Supplemental Agreement, February 13, 1948, Emil Mazey Collection, Box 37, Folder 3, ALUA; "Dorothy Scott of Hudson," *Ammunition* 5 (September 1947): 9–11.

8. *Detroit News*, February 12, 1947, clipping in UAW Research Department Collection, Box 32, Folder 19, ALUA; Fourth Quarterly Report of the Fair Practices Department, June 9, 1947, pp. 10–11, Fair Practices Department–Women's Bureau Collection, Box 2, Folder 18; *Fair Practices Fact Sheet* 1 (March 1947): 4, and 1 (May 1947): 1; "What Happens When 150 Women Are Fired," *Ammunition* 5 (May 1947): 1–4; Umpire Decision E-81, March 19, 1947, *GM Umpire Decisions* (Detroit, n.d.).

The Women's Bureau embarked on a program designed to inspire women in the local unions to imitate the efforts of women in Locals 154 and 653. Regional women's conferences, attended by groups of 50 to 140 women, were a central feature of this program. As an educational device, they alerted women to the character and consequences of sexual discrimination and acquainted them with international policies protecting their right to fair and equal treatment. The conferences also offered guidance in filing grievances and appeals, organizing local women's committees, and seeking election to local office. In addition, the conferences served as a forum where women could meet, express concerns, and exchange information. Providing a uniquely supportive environment, they engendered a sense of purpose and solidarity among women in the UAW.[9]

To reach women who did not attend the regional conferences, the Women's Bureau featured articles about women activists in such UAW publications as *Ammunition* and *Fair Practices Fact Sheet*. The women selected for recognition were all active in their local unions, both as elected officers and as volunteers on special-interest committees; many were also committed to challenging sexually discriminatory employment practices. Betty Jaskierny, for example, merited attention not only because she was the first woman elected to a top office in Local 490 but also because she was the first officer to demand the upgrading of female employees. An article in *Ammunition* similarly praised Dorothy Scott for her role, as fourth vice-president of Local 154, in seeking to win equal pay for women employed at the Hudson plant. By her own account, Dorothy Haener first was inspired to become involved in the union during reconversion, when Kaiser-Frazer refused to recall wartime women workers in line with seniority.[10]

Intended to inspire self-confidence as well as admiration, the stories about women activists emphasized not just their exceptional achievements but the traits they shared with all women. The article

9. The first regional women's conference was held in Region 2B (Toledo) in December 1945. By 1950 the Women's Bureau was conducting women's conferences in all regions of the UAW; in many regions, conferences were convened on an annual basis. Information about the conferences was found in Fair Practices Department–Women's Bureau Collection, Box 5, Folder 3; Fair Practices Department Reports to the IEB; Women's Bureau Reports to the UAW conventions; and issues of the *Fair Practices Fact Sheet*.

10. *Fair Practices Fact Sheet* 2 (January–February 1948): 2; "Dorothy Scott of Hudson," *Ammunition* 5 (September 1947): 9–11; "How Dorothy Haener Got on the Fair Practices Committee," *Ammunition* 6 (November 1948): 29–31.

about Scott, for example, sympathetically described the leader's shy-
ness and reluctance to speak at the Local 154 general assemblies.
"Part of my work with the women of the local," Scott explained, "is a
struggle with myself." Articles about married women always men-
tioned how many children they had and lauded their willingness to
combine domestic responsiblities with union activities. Camille Gordon, recording secretary and member of the bargaining committee of
Local 837, kept house for her husband and five children and also was
active in her church and PTA. Gordon's activism, the *Fair Practices
Fact Sheet* remarked, "is striking evidence that one can combine moth-
erhood and trade unionism." As the article about Gordon suggests,
another purpose of the biographical features was to counter the
notion that employment and participation in union affairs were unfeminine pursuits. Stella Ulrich, for example, worked "to provide a
fuller life for her children" and was "one of the thousands of women
in the auto industry who have successfully combined their activities
as mother and trade unionist."[11]

The efforts of the Women's Bureau to promote and cultivate activism among women auto unionists bore results. With the bureau's
encouragement, ten female delegates to the 1947 UAW convention
drafted a resolution reaffirming the union's commitment "to further
women's struggle for equal opportunities in the auto industry" and
mandating the convocation of annual women's conferences in all
regions. Since the resolution did not make it to the convention floor
for debate and ratification, it was referred to the IEB for approval.
Despite the support of Emil Mazey, the UAW secretary-treasurer, the
resolution was strongly opposed by several regional directors, who,
with the top four officers of the union, made up the IEB. Speaking for
the opposition, Richard Reisinger initially argued against the resolution in the interest of economy. In subsequent statements, however,
the director of Region 2 (Cleveland) revealed that his opposition
reflected an insensitivity to the extent of sexual inequality in the
plants. "Now there are problems, I assume, in some regions," Reisinger remarked, "and some where there aren't." Objecting to the
calling of women's conferences "where they may not be necessary,"
Reisinger added derisively that the resolution would benefit "every
little minority group that wants to have a conference." The resolution

11. "Dorothy Scott of Hudson," p. 11; *Fair Practices Fact Sheet* 3 (March–April 1949):
2, and 3 (May–June 1949): 4.

was rejected by the IEB because it lacked the unanimous support of the board members.[12]

Offended and dismayed by the board's action, women in several Detroit-area locals organized a regional women's committee to dramatize the issue of women's rights within the UAW. The formal announcement of their organization was, despite their anger, conciliatory in tone. Established "for the purpose of giving to the women workers . . . a medium through which they may discuss their mutual problems," the Region 1–1A Women's Committee, the group stated, would seek to resolve those problems "in a manner amicable to the best interests of the trade labor movement." In contrast to Reisinger, the directors of Regions 1 and 1A offered the women support and cooperation. "We want this committee to have full freedom to plan its own program," asserted Norman Matthews, co-director of Region 1. "We want this committee to bring in ideas and suggestions to improve working conditions and the status of women generally both in the union and in the plant."[13]

In June 1948 the sixteen members of the Region 1–1A Women's Committee submitted a proposal to the IEB for the establishment of similar committees in all the regions. Anticipating an unsympathetic response, the committee linked the particular problems then being experienced by women auto workers to the general concerns historically shared by all American women. In view of "the progress and achievements women have made since the first Women's Rights Convention in Seneca Falls, New York, in 1848 and acknowledging their present role as citizens, trade unionists, workers and homemakers," the proposal stated, it was incumbent upon the IEB to "recognize the complexities of women workers' responsibilities." The regional women's committees were to serve several purposes. They would enable women leaders to discuss problems and recommend policy to the regional directors, stimulate the participation of rank-and-file women in union activities and political action, channel information on women's problems from the Women's Bureau to the

12. *Fair Practices Fact Sheet* 2 (January–February 1948): 8; minutes of the March 1–5, 1948, meeting of the IEB, pp. 796–99, UAW IEB Collection (processed), Box 10, March 1948 Folder, ALUA. The ten women were Scott, Jaskierny, Rymer, Caroline Davis, Nettie Nielson of Local 247, Mildred Szur of Local 174, Evelyn Siterlet of Local 684, Eloyse Rivers of Local 365, Helen Moore of Local 602, and Zita Bowers of Local 195.

13. Second Quarterly Report of the Fair Practices Department, June 7, 1948, p. 10, Fair Practices Department–Women's Bureau Collection, Box 2, Folder 19; *Fair Practices Fact Sheet* 2 (March–April 1948): 6.

regional offices, and "give increased recognition of the women's contribution to the Union." The IEB not only approved the proposal but subsequently sanctioned the establishment of a National Advisory Council to the Women's Bureau. Composed of representatives of the regional women's committees, the council met annually to hear reports of regional problems and activities, discuss mutual concerns, and evaluate union policy and practice.[14]

The formation of regional women's committees and the establishment of the National Advisory Council increased the visibility of women within the UAW and institutionalized a communication and support network for female unionists. The group of women who had campaigned for changes in UAW policy during the war and had spearheaded the movement protesting discriminatory layoffs and recalls after the war did not emerge intact after reconversion. Grace Blackett and Trilby Riopelle, for example, did not return to the plants after they were laid off, in 1945 and 1946 respectively; Blackett left the Detroit area, and Riopelle simply disappeared from union records. Irene Young, one of the most important proponents of women's rights in the prewar and early war years, worked at the Ford River Rouge plant during the war but left the labor force in 1945. Other women, such as Patricia McLean of Local 400, found jobs in other auto factories after reconversion and needed time to orient themselves to new work environments and local union politics. The membership lists of the regional women's committees and the National Advisory Council nevertheless indicate continuity between wartime and postwar female activism in the UAW. Such women as Emma Murphy, Della Rymer, Gwendolyn Thompson, Gertrude Kelly, and Jennie Taylor survived the ravages of reconversion and made valuable contributions to the Women's Bureau as it sought to promote and cultivate collective action among women in the late 1940s.

The network of activists that acquired formal institutional status within the UAW in the period 1947 to 1950 also included women who had not participated in the wartime campaigns. Dorothy Scott, for example, attended the first national UAW women's conference, sponsored by the Women's Bureau in December 1944, as a Local 154 delegate but did not become actively involved in her local women's committee until 1947. Dorothy Haener attributed her interest in

14. Women's Committee Proposal, n.d., Fair Practices Department–Women's Bureau Collection, Box 5, Folder 8.

women's rights to actions taken by Kaiser-Frazer and Local 142 during reconversion. Kaiser-Frazer, which bought the Willow Run, Michigan, bomber plant from the Ford Motor Company in 1945, refused to honor an agreement with Local 50 giving hiring preference to bomber-plant workers. Women's rehire rights were most conspicuously violated. Women had worked at the Ford plant as drill-press operators, inspectors, and tool-crib attendants, but Kaiser-Frazer wanted women for "female" jobs only. Ignoring women's seniority rights, the company hired men with no history of employment with either Ford or Kaiser-Frazer for jobs women were eminently capable of performing; it restricted women to sewing machine operations and small parts assembly. Haener had worked at the bomber plant and had been minimally active in Local 50 during the war. Hired as a clerk by Kaiser-Frazer in 1946, she spearheaded an organizational drive among the clerks and engineers. After the group joined Local 142, Haener won election to the local's bargaining committee and, over the objections of men who had supported her campaign, demanded that Kaiser-Frazer recall former Ford female employees to "male" jobs. "The men were very angry at me," Haener recalls. "It was a terribly awakening experience for me. I really believed all this stuff we preached and believed that everybody was going to do it." The unwillingness of male unionists to defend the interests of women workers dismayed Haener but also inspired her to greater activity.[15]

The status of the international's antidiscriminatory policies was enhanced not only by the reinvigoration and expansion of the female leadership network but by the evidence of rank-and-file interest in

15. "Dorothy Scott of Hudson"; "How Dorothy Haener Got on the Fair Practices Committee"; *Fair Practices Fact Sheet* 3 (September–October 1949): 2; interview with Dorothy Haener, pp. 29–34, 37–38, 46, Twentieth Century Trade Union Woman Oral History Project. Of the eleven members of the first Region 1–1A Women's Committee, seven had participated in the wartime campaigns: Nora Shonk, Anna Pastuszka, Gertrude Kelly, Gwendolyn Thompson, Agnes Loveland, Betty Jaskierny, and Emma Murphy. The four women who were new to the Detroit-area network were Lucille Campbell, Dorothy Haener, Stella Deakins, and Evelyn Siterlet. Of the thirteen members of the first National Advisory Council to the Women's Bureau, seven had started their activity during the war: Jaskierny, Loveland, Pastuszka, Della Rymer, Loretta Schillinger, Shonk, and Grace Sturk. Six of the women became active participants after the war: Zita Bowers, Bessie Burge, Grace Davis, Evelyn Nelson, Henrietta Vos, and Martha Willoughby. Biographical data have been culled from a variety of sources, including attendance lists of women's conferences, UAW convention delegate rosters, reports of meetings, articles in UAW publications, local union records, and oral histories.

challenging gender inequality. The Women's Bureau received an increasing number of unsolicited complaints by women workers of
discriminatory employment practices. Several local unions also requested the bureau's assistance during contract negotiations in eliminating sexual discrimination. Having increased the visibility of
women and issues of concern to them, the Women's Bureau peti-
tioned Walter Reuther to strengthen efforts to put policy into practice
and abolish sexual discrimination in auto plants under contract with
the UAW. Encouraged by Reuther's offer of support and cooperation,
the bureau inaugurated a campaign to extend equal rights and opportunity to women in the auto industry. Reflecting on the history of
women in the UAW, Lillian Hatcher, assistant director of the bureau
in these years, recalls that the early 1950s "is when we were really
down to [the] serious business of eliminating discrimination as it
might have been directed in contracts."[16]

The bureau soon found itself engaged in a defensive battle to save
women's jobs rather than the offensive attack on sexually discriminatory practices that it had anticipated. The seasonal and cyclical character of automobile production had always made periodic fluctua-
tions in employment inevitable. But beginning in the mid-1950s, a
series of economic recessions, combined with company mergers,
increased automation, and the decentralization programs introduced
by the Big Three auto producers, exacerbated the situation. Rising
from 677,100 workers in 1950 to a postwar high of 739,400 in 1953, the
last year of the Korean conflict, employment in the industry fell to
601,500 in the 1954 recession year. Employment recovered to 718,300
in 1955, only to begin a three-year decline, reaching a decade low of
452,500 in 1958, another recession year. After a two-year rise, there
was another drop, to 479,100 in 1961, after which employment in the
auto industry finally stabilized and steadily increased. It is not surprising that the problem of unemployment was a principal concern of
all auto workers and the UAW in this period. Overall figures also
indicate that neither sex suffered disproportionately the effects of
unstable employment. Women's share of the labor force in the auto
industry was a remarkably consistent 12 percent, with the exception

16. Lillian Hatcher to William Oliver and Caroline Davis, April 28, 1949, Fair Practices Department–Women's Bureau Collection, Box 5, Folder 8; Oliver to Walter Reuther, May 26, 1949, ibid., Box 6, Folder 8; Hatcher interview, p. 32, Twentieth Century
Trade Union Woman Oral History Project. Information regarding complaints and
requests received by the Women's Bureau in the late 1940s is found in the Fair Practices
Department reports to the IEB and the bureau's reports to the UAW convention.

of 1952 and 1953, when the greater demand for defense production slightly increased the proportion to 15 percent.[17]

Despite the evidence that unemployment did not discriminate on the basis of sex, there was growing concern that women were bearing the brunt of labor-force reductions. The Women's Bureau received reports that auto manufacturers refused to hire women, claiming that "female" jobs were already filled. Recalling the great demand for women workers during World War II, even the *Detroit Free Press* remarked in 1953, "Rosie feels something like Typhoid Mary when she applies for a factory job." Additional evidence of the disinterest of employers in hiring women was the common complaint that women over the age of thirty-five now were finding it difficult to secure jobs in auto plants. There also were charges that married women either were being denied employment or, if they held auto jobs, were being laid off without regard to seniority.[18]

Employers also were criticized for using protective labor laws to reduce the number of women on payrolls and as a smokescreen for discrimination. The president of Local 1055 told the 1955 convention that the number of women in his plant "grew less every day" because the company combined lighter jobs held by women with heavier jobs held by men and then denied women access to the new jobs, claiming that state laws forbade their employment on such work. With "all the women squeezed out into the street," the local president "won the battle" when, at his insistence, a representative from the Connecticut Department of Labor inspected the jobs and declared them suitable for women. Women employed as punch-press operators in the power-brake division of Midland Steel met with a less happy fate. Automation had progressively reduced the number of jobs available to women; in the mid-fifties the company transferred the entire operation to its new plant in Owosso, Michigan. Already having had "a problem finding jobs which the women are capable of performing," Local 410 negotiated an agreement with the company whereby the "displaced" women would quit, surrender their seniority rights, and receive severance pay. Anxious to retain their employment, two women requested transfers to crane operation, a male-classified job

17. U.S. Bureau of Labor Statistics (BLS), *Employment and Earnings, United States, 1909–75*, Bulletin No. 1312–10 (Washington, D.C., 1976), pp. 302–3.

18. *Detroit Free Press*, August 30, 1953; *Proceedings of the Fourteenth Constitutional Convention of the UAW-CIO, March 22–27, 1953* (hereafter cited as *1953 Convention Proceedings*), pp. 62–64; *Proceedings of the Fifteenth Constitutional Convention of the UAW-CIO, March 27–April 1, 1955* (hereafter cited as *1955 Convention Proceedings*), p. 53; *President's Report to the 1955 Convention*, p. 93D.

but one that women had ably performed during the Korean War. Management representative John Perry affirmed the company's willingness "to promote and upgrade employees to jobs where possible and where they possess the required ability" but reported that "restrictions that govern female employees" prevented Midland Steel from employing women as crane operators. Unable to specify what those "restrictions" were, Perry claimed that it was "not advisable for women to operate cranes because of the climbing, jarring, and shaking involved in this work." He contended that Midland had hired women as crane operators during the war "only because no men were available for employment at that time." "We were not satisfied with their work then or now," Perry lamely protested, "but it was one of those conditions we had to live with."[19]

On the basis of such evidence, some concluded that efforts were under way purposefully to exclude women from auto plants. Caroline Davis, for example, decried "the growing propaganda aimed at discrediting women workers" and urged auto unionists not to make women the scapegoats for unemployment.[20] The practices deplored by Davis and others, however, were neither unprecedented nor especially unusual. They simply confirmed the extent of occupational segregation by sex in the auto industry. Separate seniority lists and sex-based job classifications had always disadvantaged the women competing for jobs in auto plants. To a certain extent, what was new in the 1950s was the more widespread perception of gender hierarchy as unfair and discriminatory. Having only recently acquired a critical perspective on the dynamics of sexual inequality in the labor market, sympathetic observers in the postwar era incorrectly attributed the consequences of long-standing patterns of occupational segregation to an innovative attempt to deprive women of employment.

Although there was no conspiracy to eliminate female auto workers, the still widespread existence of sex-based seniority lists and job classifications could make women especially vulnerable in times of layoffs and job dislocations. Where the sexual division of labor was not explicitly codified in the organization of work, de facto segregation in the form of departmental or noninterchangeable occupational

19. *1955 Convention Proceedings*, p. 53; Zigmunt Mizejeski to Emil Mazey, May 3, 1956, and Grievance #1741, May 9, 1955, UAW Local 410 Collection, Box 17, Kay Darvin et al. Folder, ALUA.
20. *President's Report to the 1955 Convention*, p. 95D.

group seniority accomplished the same results. Restricted to an already small number of jobs, women might find themselves unemployed while men with less seniority held jobs that the displaced women were capable of performing. As this scenario was played out in many plants during the 1950s and early 1960s, activists in the Women's Bureau and the National Advisory Council reasserted their preference for sex-blind treatment as a strategy for obtaining equality in the workplace. The plight of women auto workers, they contended, would best be remedied by equal treatment in employment.

Although women's rights advocates emphasized collective bargaining as the principal means of obtaining equality, the obstacles to female employment heightened their interest in government action. Discrimination at the hiring gate, for example, was a particular concern. Although employers varied in their response to negotiations over contractual rules regulating the treatment of employees, as a group they refused to concede their prerogative in hiring, asserting that the union's relationship was with job holders not job seekers. Turning to the government for assistance in combating this form of employment discrimination, the UAW participated in the unsuccessful campaign at the end of World War II to give permanent status to the president's Fair Employment Practices Committee, which had monitored the hiring of blacks by companies with federal defense contracts. When United States involvement in the Korean War revived demands by civil rights advocates for a federal fair-employment-practices policy, Harry Truman created the Committee on Government Contract Compliance in December 1951. Women auto unionists, with the support of the union leadership, sought to have sex included in the compliance code's Section 18, which required government contractors not to discriminate against job applicants or employees on the basis of race, creed, color, or national origin. But despite evidence that government contractors were refusing to hire women for defense jobs, the effort to include sex in the new compliance code could not overcome employer opposition and disinterest on the part of Labor Department officials. Women's rights advocates in the UAW again tried to no avail in 1961, when they urged that sex be included in President Kennedy's Executive Order 10925, which prohibited discrimination in hiring by employers with government contracts "as the most expeditious method of removing the scourge of discrimination" from women workers.[21]

21. Administrative Letter 4 (November 24, 1952), *UAW Administrative Letters*, vol. 1–

To secure sex-blind treatment for women in the labor market by political means, auto unionists also began to question the benefits of state laws designed to protect the health and safety of women workers. They first asserted the disadvantages of these laws after World War II, when states reimposed restrictions on the employment of women which had been suspended for the duration of the war. Citing protective laws, employers dismissed wartime female employees and replaced them with men with less seniority. After reconversion, protective legislation denied women hiring and promotional opportunities. According to Lillian Hatcher, women union leaders realized as early as the late forties that protective laws "negated opportunity for women to move up into better paying jobs and to receive equal pay for equal work." Caroline Davis voiced frustration with the legal obstacles to gender equality in her report to the 1957 UAW convention. Hailing the elimination of sexually discriminatory features from many collective-bargaining agreements, Davis cited state laws as undermining the UAW's efforts. A law limiting the number of hours women could be employed or the number of pounds women could lift might appear "liberal toward working women," she explained, but "is in reality often used by unscrupulous employers to discriminate against women." Such laws, Davis maintained, "are being used effectively when employers are seeking ways to prevent women from being upgraded, hired or retained on their jobs."[22]

The position taken by women's rights advocates in the UAW on federal fair-employment-practices policy and protective legislation for women workers branded them as mavericks in the postwar period. UAW women were not naive. They recognized that employers discriminated on the basis of race in hiring women for female jobs in the auto industry. But black women, they argued, suffered double

---

10A (Detroit, n.d.), pp. 291–92; Women's Bureau Report, *President's Report to the Fourteenth Constitutional Convention, UAW-CIO, March 22–27, 1953* (hereafter cited as *President's Report to the 1953 Convention*), pp. 204–5; *President's Report to the 1955 Convention*, p. 93D; Summary of Actions Taken by the Women's Advisory Committee on Defense Manpower, n.d. [1953], Papers of the U.S. Women's Bureau, Record Group 86, National Archives, Washington, D.C. (hereafter cited as RG 86/NA), Box 965, Equal Pay Folder; U.S. President's Commission on the Status of Women, *Report of the Committee on Private Employment* (Washington, D.C., 1964), p. 18.

22. Hatcher interview, p. 52, Twentieth Century Trade Union Woman Oral History Project; Women's Bureau Report, *President's Report to the Sixteenth Constitutional Convention, UAW, April 7–12, 1957,* (hereafter cited as *President's Report to the 1957 Convention*), p. 181D.

jeopardy on account of their race and gender; unless employers were compelled to increase job opportunities for women in basic industries, neither racial nor gender segregation would be eliminated. As a public statement of concern for the double burden borne by black women, the Women's Bureau always had at least one black woman on its three-to-four-person staff. Black women themselves, recognizing the obstacles to their employment in the auto industry, continued to play a prominent role in the UAW network of women's rights advocates and to demand gender equality at the local level. But the persistent attempts by UAW women to have sex included in government contract compliance policy caused conflict with civil rights activists outside the union. In 1945 Mildred Jeffrey reported to Frieda Miller, director of the United States Women's Bureau, that the inclusion of sex as a category "has been battled back and forth in Michigan for the past two years. Our ardent feminists have insisted that sex be included; however, everyone capitulated when it was emphasized that inclusion of sex would make the passage of FEPC legislation more difficult." When civil rights supporters campaigned for fair-employment-practices committees at the state level during the 1950s, women in the UAW now pressed for the inclusion of sex in antidiscrimination guidelines. But fearing that this would either jeopardize passage of legislation or distract attention from racial discrimination, Will Maslow, director of the American Jewish Congress's Commission on Law and Social Action, warned the secretary of the Michigan Coordinating Council for the FEPC to "resist any efforts [by women auto unionists] to include sex as a prohibiting ground" in a Michigan legislative initiative. UAW women again raised hackles when President Kennedy's Commission on the Status of Women refused to comment on the absence of sex as a category in Executive Order 10925 because, commission members believed, the elimination of racial discrimination should receive priority. Caroline Davis, a member of the commission's Committee on Government Contracts, was so angered by the failure of the committee to recognize or acknowledge the problem of sexual discrimination in the labor market that she filed a minority report strongly condemning the omission of gender in the order.[23]

23. Jeffrey to Miller, November 4, 1946, RG 86/NA, Box 867, Autoworkers Folder; Maslow to Marvin Meltzer, February 8, 1955, Jewish Labor Committee Collection, Box 8, Folder 13, ALUA; transcript of proceedings, Committee on Government Contracts meeting, April 4, 1962, Papers of the President's Commission on the Status of Women, Committee on Private Employment Files, Department of Labor Library, Washington, D.C.; Committee on Government Contracts Document No. 30, February 6, 1963, ibid.;

The labor movement's support for protective labor legislation similarly placed auto unionists in an awkward position. UAW women were among those attending the National Manpower Council meetings in the mid-fifties who contended that "the existence of differential legislation provides employers with a justification for hiring men for work which women have in fact done or could undertake" and recommended review of "the consequences and adequacy of existing Federal and state laws which have a direct bearing on the employment of women." But conflict over the Equal Rights Amendment (ERA) had long polarized the women's movement, and organized labor steadfastly refused in the 1950s to consider that protective laws might discriminate against women. Nor could UAW women seek more likely allies in feminist organizations. ERA supporters in the 1950s had a class-bound perspective and, according to Leila Rupp and Verta Taylor, regarded all organized labor "as an enemy whose opposition [to ERA] had to be neutralized." The UAW Women's Bureau, therefore, had to tolerate the inconsistency of simultaneously denouncing the ERA as "a pernicious and anti-social piece of legislation which will perpetuate exploitation and discrimination" while seeking at least to debate the issue of protective legislation within and without the union.[24]

Opposition outside the UAW to the idea of gender equality and the unsuccessful search by auto union feminists for allies meant that the real test of the Women's Bureau agenda in the 1950s was the response of the union's membership and leadership. In certain respects the

U.S. President's Commission on the Status of Women, *Report of the Committee on Private Employment*, pp. 8, 15–18; Cynthia Harrison, *On Account of Sex* (Berkeley, Calif., 1988), pp. 146–51. For material on discrimination against black women at the hiring gate, see *Pittsburgh Courier*, November 15, 1952, clipping in Reuther Collection, Box 90, Folder 9; meeting on Discrimination in Employment, November 19, 1952, ibid.; William Oliver to Walter Reuther, November 19, 1952, ibid.

24. National Manpower Council, *Womanpower* (New York, 1957), pp. 6, 336; Harrison, *On Account of Sex*, pp. 37–38; Leila Rupp and Verta Taylor, *Survival in the Doldrums* (New York, 1987), pp. 144–53; UAW brief in regard to the ERA, n.d. [1945–1946], p. 12, UAW Research Department Collection, Box 11, Folder 14. The paucity of research on women and unions in the post–World War II period makes it difficult to generalize much beyond the UAW about other unions' attitudes toward laws concerning female labor. Ruth Milkman and Bruce Fehn indicate that the United Electrical Workers, the International Union of Electrical Workers, and the United Packinghouse Workers were beginning to endorse equal treatment for women and men in the workplace in the postwar years. Additional evidence from the early to middle 1960s confirms this view. Ruth Milkman, *Gender at Work* (Urbana, 1987), pp. 144–52; Bruce Fehn, "Women of the United Packinghouse Workers of America, 1946–1956," unpublished paper in author's possession.

international leadership was supportive of the efforts of the Women's Bureau and the National Advisory Council. President Reuther's public statements on international policy were strongly worded and often eloquent on the subject of women's right to fair and equal treatment. "We in the UAW-CIO believe that unless everyone is given an opportunity to find employment without regard to race, creed, color, or sex," Reuther stated in 1952, "we cannot really claim that we are free in America. We believe that unless everyone enjoys freedom to work and earn a living, no one's freedom will be secure."[25] To demonstrate its support for the goal of eliminating sexual discrimination, the IEB granted the Women's Bureau independent departmental status in 1955 and augmented the size of its staff. The IEB also advanced some of the bureau's collective-bargaining objectives. To cite a notable example of this type of effort, the UAW made a single seniority list a central demand in its negotiations with General Motors in 1955.

The IEB's renunciation of discrimination against married women expressed a measure of shared intent and purpose with female activists in the postwar period. The scarcity of jobs during the Great Depression had made the position of married women in the plants especially tenuous, and discriminatory practices had been written into many early collective-bargaining agreements. The demand for labor during World War II eased restrictions on the employment of married women, and the entrance of large numbers of married women into the work force began, in turn, to undermine the ideology of the family wage. Demobilization, however, revived hostility toward the presence of married women in some auto plants. The threat of unemployment in the 1950s similarly spurred on opposition to the presence of married women in the plants. Such attitudes inspired a number of employers and local unions to enter into verbal and written agreements after World War II which reinstated discriminatory practices. Some contracts forbade the hiring of married women and required single female employees who married to resign. Other agreements stipulated that in the event of job cutbacks, married women workers were to be laid off first regardless of their seniority. For their part, international union leaders had adopted an ambivalent policy in the 1930s, deferring to local autonomy and the

25. Administrative Letter 4 (November 24, 1952), *UAW Administrative Letters*, pp. 291–92.

power of the family-wage ideology rather than taking a principled stand on the issue. But after World War II the top leadership of the union made discrimination against married women a violation of the UAW's fair-practices policy and condemned attempts to make married women the scapegoat for the problem of unemployment in the industry. Abandoning the earlier concessions to local autonomy, the IEB now directed local unions to comply with international policy and abolish practices that discriminated against married women.

The international union made Racine, Wisconsin, a test case for its postwar challenge to local union discrimination against married women. The six UAW locals in Racine were conspicuous for their collective opposition to the employment of married women. Several local agreements simply forbade the hiring of married women and provided for the discharge of single women who married. Other contracts provided that if a married woman could show cause for employment—for example, if her husband was incapacitated or in the service—she might be allowed to work, but only under certain onerous constraints. The contract between Local 72 and the Nash-Kelvinator Company allowed married women thus hired to accumulate seniority only in the department in which they worked rather than in accordance with the contract's provision for plantwide seniority. They were, moreover, the first to be laid off regardless of any seniority they might have accumulated. Local 391 had a particularly insulting way of ensuring a married woman's gratitude: she had to pay the local $1 per week for permission to work. Exercising its prerogative, the international disapproved the 1946 contracts of Locals 225 and 391 and the 1948 contract of Local 642 and instructed the locals to eliminate the objectionable clauses. When Local 642 refused to comply and proceeded to operate under a contract lacking the signature of the international, the IEB redoubled its effort in Racine. The Women's Bureau conducted an educational campaign in the various locals, and Walter Reuther personally pressured the regional director to reverse his lenient policy toward the Racine locals. In 1949 the IEB announced that all the UAW locals in Racine had abolished the offensive contract provisions.[26]

26. William Oliver to Davis and Hatcher, April 12, 1949, Fair Practices Department–Women's Bureau Collection, Box 5, Folder 8; Fair Practices Department Report, July–December 1949, p. 6, ibid., Box 2, Folder 20; Oliver to Mazey, Pat Greathouse, Walter Reuther, and Jack Conway, May 2, 1949, Reuther Collection, Box 90, Folder 7; Davis to Reuther, May 16, 1949, ibid.

In the 1950s the IEB continued exerting pressure on local unions that did not conform to international policy regarding married women. When moral suasion failed to produce the desired results, the IEB intervened in behalf of married women whose job rights were violated. In its review of an appeal case involving the discharge of four married women from the Nash-Kelvinator plant in Grand Rapids, Michigan, for example, the IEB noted with annoyance that the local union officers "seem to have their own definition of the word 'discrimination.' One of the local union witnesses went so far as to state that the International Union might continue to follow its policy with no complaint from Local 206 so long as the Local Union was permitted to follow its policy." Reminding the local officers that the IEB had taken "drastic action" and revoked the charter of Local 1014 in Dallas, Texas, for colluding with Braniff Aircraft to discriminate against blacks, the IEB directed Local 206 to negotiate the reinstatement of the four women with compensation for time lost and to "cease and desist from this practice in the future."[27]

Layoffs of thousands of auto workers in the recession of 1954 prompted renewed demands for the discharge of married women workers regardless of their seniority. Emil Mazey told fellow IEB members, "I firmly believe that a married woman is an economic citizen in her own right and that the policy of our Union is correct." Urging the board "to see that our staff is straightened out on this policy," Mazey asked Reuther to issue a statement to the membership defending the right of married women to work and to receive protection under union contracts. In June 1954 Reuther released the first UAW presidential statement addressed specifically to the issue of married women's rights in the UAW. Admitting that employment continued to be "the Union's gravest problem," Reuther nevertheless warned that "destruction of our hard-won seniority system could be the result of adoption of proposals based on alleged need of workers." Reuther asserted that there was "no good reason for us to wander off on a by-path seeking to find ways to share scarcity—how to divide up what's left over after an economic cyclone hits us. We must not let fear and economic insecurity blind us to the damaging consequences of evading our responsibilities in carrying out the

27. Appeal Hearing Report, May 20, 1952, Mazey Collection, Box 40, Folder 9. Two other important IEB decisions regarding discrimination against married women involved Locals 85 and 1020. See Appeal Hearing Report, April 28, 1954, Mazey Collection, Box 32, Folder 9; Appeal Hearing Report, April 29, 1954, ibid., Box 35, Folder 9.

policies and contract provisions of equal seniority protection for all our members."[28]

The combined efforts of the Women's Bureau and the IEB contributed to the decline of contractual discrimination against married women in the auto industry. Because much of the discrimination was codified in verbal agreements, it is impossible to know the extent to which discriminatory practices actually persisted. For example, an appeal filed in 1953 by two women who had been discharged by the Walker Manufacturing Company in Racine after they had married revealed that Local 85, having eliminated the contract clause forbidding the employment of married women, had entered into a verbal agreement with management in 1947 to perpetuate the policy. Each economic downturn and rise in unemployment revived calls for the dismissal of married women workers. As late as 1961 international representatives who visited General Motors local unions to sound out the rank and file on issues for the UAW's upcoming contract talks with the corporation remarked on the persistent hostility toward married women's presence in plants afflicted with extensive layoffs. The increase in the relative number of married women employed in auto plants between 1940 and 1960, however, does offer evidence of a substantial decrease in the extent of discrimination. Between 1940 and 1950 the proportion of married women in the female automotive labor force rose from 51 percent to 61.5 percent. In 1960, 68 percent of all women auto workers were married.[29]

Although the IEB promoted the principle of gender equality after World War II, it was inconsistent in practice. One measure of the

28. Minutes of the May 3–7, 1954, meeting of the IEB, pp. 103–4, IEB Collection (processed), Box 6, May 1954 Folder, ALUA; Administrative Letter 6 (June 16, 1954), *UAW Administrative Letters*, pp. 419–21.

29. Appeal Hearing Report, April 28, 1954, Mazey Collection, Box 32, Folder 9; notes on 1961 GM Negotiations and Local Union Demands, Leonard Woodcock Collection, Box 47, Folders 12–13, ALUA; U.S. Bureau of the Census, *United States Census of Population, 1940*, vol. 3, Pt. 1 (Washington, D.C., 1956), pp. 96, 98; U.S. Bureau of the Census, *United States Census of Population, 1960*, vol. 2, pt. 7, chap. A (Washington, D.C., 1963), p. 180. The percentages of married women in the automotive labor force are based on figures for "married women, husband present." In contrast, the proportion of "married women, husband present" in the female labor force nationally was 13.8 percent in 1940, 21.6 percent in 1950, and 30.6 percent in 1960. The discrepancy between the percentage of married women in the auto industry and the percentage in the female labor-force in general can best be explained if it is noted that female auto workers were working-class women. The extent of labor force participation among middle-class married women historically has been less than that among working-class married women.

board's commitment to extending equal rights and opportunities to women was the refusal of most of its members to offer women international staff positions. The few women who did obtain positions on the staff, moreover, experienced the effects of male prejudice. Dorothy Haener, an international representative from 1952 until her retirement in 1982, remembers how "depressing" it had been to learn that the staff at Solidarity House, the UAW's headquarters in Detroit, was just as "bitterly opposed to the concept of women moving upward or having a job" as the men in the rank and file. Excluded from direct participation in contract negotiations, female staff members were themselves unable to press the job status of women auto workers at the bargaining table. "I learned about sex discrimination at Solidarity House," says Florence Peterson, one of the mere handful of female international representatives. "Any woman who has worked for the union has to fight to avoid being tied to the desk because, at least in those years, that was the appropriate place [for women]."[30]

The attitude of many of the UAW's powerful regional directors toward the goals and purposes of the Women's Bureau also ranged from disinterest to disapprobation. Raymond Berndt, the director of Region 3, indicated his understanding of the role of women in the UAW in his opening remarks to a regional women's conference in April 1949. "Since our Union has over a million members we are 'Big Business,'" Berndt observed. Informing the women that it was their responsibility to clean up local union halls, Berndt explained, "Our offices and halls should be dressed up to the point where we are in a position to invite all civic leaders into our offices and halls for discussion." Other regional directors were hostile rather than condescending toward women, approving contracts that contained sexually discriminatory clauses and obstructing appeal procedures. Regional director Charles Ballard, for example, signed a 1950 agreement between the Newport Steel Corporation and Local 750 which provided for separate male and female job classifications. When several women protested a supplemental agreement that further reclassified as male jobs those that previously were allotted to women, Ballard disapproved of their action. Florence Butcher was unable to meet with Ballard to discuss the grievance and appeal procedures, as

30. Haener interview, p. 34; Peterson interview, p. 37, Twentieth Century Trade Union Woman Oral History Project.

Caroline Davis had directed her to do. Davis herself encountered difficulty in dealing with Ballard. In a letter to Emil Mazey, Davis stated that she had been "unable to impress [Ballard] sufficiently" with the seriousness of the women's charges and could not get him to arrange a date for a meeting between the local union and the Women's Bureau to investigate the problem.[31]

The antagonistic relationship between the Women's Bureau and several regional directors reflected the undercurrent of tension regarding gender relations within the UAW in the postwar period. To a certain extent, the criticism made by regional directors of the bureau's activities stemmed from an ongoing struggle within the union over spheres of authority rather than from a limited commitment to gender equality. Concerned to preserve their autonomy from international headquarters in Detroit, regional directors tended to regard the Women's Bureau staff, which was appointed by Walter Reuther, with suspicion. Regional directors thus protested as a matter of principle when the bureau bypassed the chain of command and dealt directly with a local union. Mildred Jeffrey recalls that Richard Gosser, director of Region 2B, often complained to Reuther that "Millie had jumped over the fence." The defense of prerogatives by regional directors, however, also concealed an aversion to conflict and controversy and a fear of exposure. Caroline Davis urged the members of the National Advisory Council to "be diplomatic" when bringing problems to the attention of the regional directors. "It is going to be [a] tough job," she warned. "Contact your regional directors and they will try to brush you off." Not at all sanguine about the motives of the regional directors, Dorothy Haener claims, "There was really a reluctance . . . on the part of the regions always, to have us come in and get involved in what they called 'the women's problem' because they really felt that we tended to incite people."[32]

Because the Women's Bureau was deprived of enforcement power, it depended on the leaders of the IEB to implement the union's antidiscriminatory guidelines. The failure of these men to promote women's right to fair and equal treatment, therefore, limited the

31. Report of Women's Conference, April 24, 1949, p. 2, Fair Practices Department–Women's Bureau Collection, Box 5, Folder 3; Davis to Butcher, September 6, 1951, and Davis to Mazey, October 29, 1951, Mazey Collection, Box 31, Folder 8.

32. Jeffrey interview, p. 63, Twentieth Century Trade Union Woman Oral History Project; minutes of the July 13, 1950, National Advisory Committee meeting, p. 6, Fair Practices Department–Women's Bureau Collection, Box 4, Folder 16; Haener interview, p. 64.

bureau's effectiveness after World War II. The Fair Practices Department urged the IEB to "recognize the difficulties incumbent upon this department when, on one hand clearly defined policies are to be observed as they appear in the constitution and official records of the Union; and on the other hand observances of these policies are ignored and even flaunted." The department reminded the IEB of the fundamental principle of the UAW-CIO: "It behooves the International Executive Board to give serious consideration to this aspect of our internal discipline in order that democracy and fair play will be something more than window dressing." The Women's Bureau "wanted to be effective," Florence Peterson, an international representative, asserted, "but the cards were stacked against it." Endowed with only "the power of moral persuasion," the department itself could do little to eliminate discrimination at the local level. "If I had been Caroline Davis," Peterson remarked bitterly, "I think I would have wanted to go out and shoot myself."[33]

The IEB's handling of the issue of equal pay also indicates the limits of its commitment to gender equality. The UAW did make some important advances with regard to equal pay in the postwar period. Its most notable efforts involved General Motors, the largest single employer of women in the automobile industry and the only one of the Big Three auto producers to continue to resist the principle of equal pay for equal work. Having been required by the National War Labor Board to establish equal rates for "comparable quantity and quality of work on comparable operations," the company sought to eliminate this clause from its contract with the UAW in 1946. Although the UAW was successful in reinstating the clause in the new contract, its ambiguous wording, together with the provision for sex-based occupational and wage classifications, enabled GM to continue paying its female employees wages consistently lower than those of men. Women working at the Delco-Remy plant in Anderson, Indiana, and the Delco Radio plant in Kokomo, Indiana, thus received 16 cents less per hour than men in the same job categories. After the historic five-year UAW-GM agreement was signed in 1950, local leaders in six GM plants made equal pay for women a principal goal of negotiations for the 1955 contract; and with the assistance of the Women's Bureau they launched a campaign to mobilize membership

33. Fourth Quarterly Report of the Fair Practices Department, 1947, pp. 1–2, Fair Practices Department–Women's Bureau Collection, Box 2, Folder 18; Peterson interview, p. 46.

support for the demand. The six locals won a partial victory in the 1955 contract, which narrowed by one-half differentials ranging from 10 to 26 cents an hour.[34]

Despite the importance of these and similar efforts, wage-rate discrimination persisted in the postwar years. A comparison of the wages paid women and men performing the same jobs in automotive-parts plants in 1940 and 1963 indicates that sex differentials were reduced but not erased in this period. Women employed as Class C inspectors made the most dramatic gain, their proportion of the rate paid similarly employed men increasing from 71 percent to 87 percent. Female Class C small-parts assemblers and Class C drill-press operators earned 76 percent and 73 percent, respectively, of the hourly rates paid men in those jobs in 1940, but 80 percent and 82 percent of the rates paid male small-parts assemblers and drill-press operators in 1963. The gap between men's and women's rates for light and medium punch-press operation, however, actually increased by two percentage points between 1940 and 1963. As the example of GM suggests, management resistance accounts in large part for the persistence of wage inequality after World War II. The UAW's limited commitment to gender equity, however, also minimized the prospects for a thoroughgoing challenge to unequal pay for equal work. To its credit, the UAW officially forbade the inclusion in contracts of the most blatant forms of discrimination, such as unequal hiring rates and dual wage scales without reference to job assignment. But the widespread use of separate "male" and "female" job classifications, which enabled employers to pay women less than men for equal and comparable work, did not receive the UAW's censure.[35]

The experience of women employed at the Auto-Lite Corporation plant in Vincennes, Indiana, demonstrated the ways in which male

34. Howell John Harris, *The Right to Manage* (Madison, Wis., 1982), pp. 141–42; Provisions Reinstated in New Contract, n.d. [March 1946], George Addes Collection, Box X, Folder 3, ALUA; Drennon to Frieda Miller, November 16, 1953, RG 86/NA, Box 965, Equal Pay 1952–1953 Folder; *1955 Convention Proceedings*, p. 54; *Kokomo Tribune*, January 28, 1955, clipping in Bruce Kingery Collection, Scrapbook, ALUA; Women's Bureau Report, *President's Report to the 1957 Convention*, p. 172D; U.S. Bureau of Labor Statistics (BLS), *Wage Chronology: General Motors Corporation, 1939–63*, Report No. 185 (Washington, D.C., 1964), p. 8.

35. Harold Hosea and George Votara, *Wage Structure of the Motor-Vehicle Industry*, BLS Bulletin No. 706 (Washington, D.C., 1942), pp. 38–39; U.S. Bureau of Labor Statistics (BLS), *Motor Vehicle Parts Industry Wage Survey, April 1963*, Bulletin No. 1393 (Washington, D.C., 1964), pp. 23–24.

unionists at the international as well as the local level undermined the effort to achieve wage parity for female auto workers after World War II. Because Local 675's agreement with Auto-Lite provided for separate "male" and "female" job classifications and sex-differentiated wage scales, the day and evening shifts of the punch press operation were classified as "female" and assigned the rate of $1.05 per hour whereas the graveyard shift of the same operation was classified as "male" and accorded the rate of $1.25 per hour. In July 1951 an international representative informed the local that its agreement did not comply with either the UAW's equal-pay policy or the national contract with the Electric Auto-Lite Corporation, which stipulated that women employed in jobs "normally performed by men" were to receive equal pay. The predominantly male local leadership and membership ignored the representative's appeal. Eight women punch-press operators, however, "having been sold the idea of equal pay for equal work," filed a grievance demanding that they receive the $1.25 hourly rate paid to male punch-press operators.[36]

The company cited the local agreement's provision for separate wage scales and rejected the women's complaint. Asserting that it was acting in the interest of consistency and contractual conformity, the company offered to pay male rates on the punch-press job only if the local union agreed to put men on all the shifts. If the local union refused to do so, the job was to remain in the "female" classification and receive the lower rate. The company preferred to pay higher wages for the one job rather than concede the point and risk having later to pay higher wages to female employees in other jobs. The local, for its part, not only saw an opportunity to provide more work for men but also feared that advocating women's right to equal pay in the one instance would set a precedent for women to be hired for other "male" jobs. Instead of defending the female members, the local membership accepted the company's proposal, whereupon women on the two shifts were laid off.

Requesting assistance from the Women's Bureau, the laid-off women protested the local's action. "We have been holding our present jobs since the factory started, paying dues as required for the protection of our jobs," they complained. "We feel this is a discrimi-

36. Agreement, Auto-Lite Battery Corporation and UAW-CIO Local 675, March 7, 1951, Mazey Collection, Box 39, Folder 1; National Agreement, Electric Auto-Lite Company and UAW-CIO, 1951, ibid.; Fair Practices Appeal, February 12, 1951, ibid.; Women's Bureau Appeal Hearing Report, October 15, 1951, ibid.

nation against the women." The Women's Bureau stated in its report on the matter that in light of both the national agreement and the international's "firm equal pay policy," Local 675 "should have had the grievance processed to a successful conclusion and with the local membership support." Local 675, however, refused to follow the bureau's recommendation to negotiate with the company for the reinstatement of the women to the day and evening shifts with pay equal to that of men on the night shift. "We have been treated wrong by our local," the women told Caroline Davis in November 1951. In desperation, however, they stated that they would accept the lower rate of pay if they could get their jobs back.[37]

Lacking the power to enforce its rulings, the Women's Bureau referred the women's case to the IEB for adjudication. The IEB Appeals Committee found that the women had lost their jobs "solely because of the fact that they made a demand for equal pay for equal work in accordance with the well-established policy of the Union," and it ruled that they be reinstated in their former jobs with the higher male rate of pay. The committee, however, also recommended that the punch-press operation remain classified as a "male" job and that "future additions or replacements shall be made on the basis of a classified male job." Presenting the committee's report to the IEB, Leonard Woodcock explained, "That's necessary because in the Auto-Lite master agreement you have male jobs and all jobs are classified as one or the other." No member of the IEB questioned the relevance of separate classifications for the same job or seemed concerned that the practice discriminated against women by denying them both equal pay and equal access to employment. Concerned only to preserve the highest rate possible, the IEB took the path of least resistance, rendering its decision a pyrrhic victory for women auto workers.[38]

The failure of the IEB to take advantage of opportunities to make a thoroughgoing challenge to the sexual division of labor was also evident in its action on an appeal filed by nineteen women from Local 750. The September 1950 agreement between the Universal Cooler Division of the Newport Steel Corporation and Local 750 in Marion,

37. William Groeber to William McMahon, August 10, 1951, ibid.; Fair Practices Appeal, September 12, 1951, ibid.; Women's Bureau Appeal Hearing Report, October 15, 1951, ibid.; Dorothy Williams to Davis, November 1, 1951, ibid.

38. IEB Appeal Committee Report, September 9, 1952, ibid.; minutes of the September 15–18, 1952, meeting of the IEB, pp. 326–27, IEB Collection (processed), Box 6, September 1952 Folder.

Ohio, provided for plantwide seniority irrespective of sex but also provided that jobs would be designated as either male or female. When the Tecumseh Products Company bought Newport Steel five months later, the new president of the company, which remained under contract with the UAW, made it clear to the local union that he did not approve of women working, stating that he thought women "should be home in the kitchen." He told the local that he wanted to eliminate the female employees, a proposal with which the male leadership agreed. A supplemental agreement was therefore drawn up; it arbitrarily, and without reference to job content, revised the classification of some female jobs to male and granted corresponding rate increases. The remaining female-classified jobs were "to constitute the job classifications to which all female employees shall be limited." The women working on the jobs newly classified as male were laid off.[39]

The women promptly filed grievances to protest what had occurred. Rachel Shaffstall, a woman working on one of the few remaining female-classified jobs, demanded a rate of pay equivalent to that paid men on the same but male-classified jobs. Betty Delaney asserted that the installation of a conveyor belt actually made one of the reclassified soldering jobs less burdensome than when it had been designated a female position. Citing the contract's provision for plantwide seniority, Glenna Clements charged that she had been laid off out of line with her seniority and requested reinstatement with back pay. The company and the local rejected the grievances and superciliously advised all the women to "thoroughly acquaint yourselves with the contract and the supplement in regards to female classifications." Evading the women's complaints of violation of the contract, the grievance committee claimed, "Past practice and precedent have always dealt with female classifications independently of male classifications."[40]

The women sought the assistance of the Women's Bureau. When

39. Agreement between Universal Cooler Division–Newport Steel Corporation and Local 750, September 20, 1952, Mazey Collection, Box 39, Folder 6; Supplemental Agreement between Universal Cooler Division–Tecumseh Products Company and Local 750, January 19, 1951, ibid., Box 31, Folder 8; Schedule A of New Hourly Rates, March 26, 1951, ibid., Box 39, Folder 6; Florence Butcher to Caroline Davis, August 28, 1951, ibid., Box 31, Folder 8.

40. Shaffstall grievance, June 11, 1951, Mazey Collection, Box 39, Folder 6; Clements grievance, July 17, 1951, ibid.; Eva Bindle grievance, September 24, 1951, ibid.; Carrie Parker grievance, September 24, 1951, ibid.; Delaney grievance, n.d., ibid.; Grievance Committee to Bindle et al., October 30, 1951, ibid.

Caroline Davis conducted an investigation in Marion in March 1952, the local president, who admitted that 60 percent of all jobs in the plant could be performed by women, blamed management for refusing to employ women. In her report to the IEB, Davis dismissed the local president's charge, noting that male workers had submitted a petition in 1946 demanding the elimination of female employees. The male union members, who outnumbered the women seven to one, also voted down a motion at a December 1951 meeting to classify all jobs that women were able to perform according to state law as either male or female so that women could continue working in line with seniority. "There seems to be little doubt," Davis concluded, "that the policy of both Newport Steel and Tecumseh had been directed toward the elimination of female employees [and] that the male employees . . . are in accord with this policy."[41]

The IEB Appeals Committee directed Local 750 to seek the reinstatement of nineteen women. "There is little question," the committee stated, that the women "were dealt a serious injustice since their inability to return to work is brought about not by a lack of seniority but by the manipulation of jobs which deprived them of employment." The committee, however, did not order the local to seek the elimination of sex-based job classifications from its contract with Tecumseh. Just as in the decision in the Local 675 case, the IEB sought only to remedy the one instance of discrimination rather than take advantage of an opportunity to implement international policy and dictate a restructuring of the organization of work in the factory in accord with that policy.[42]

The IEB's action in the Local 675 and 750 cases illustrates the way in which the IEB contributed to the persistence of gender inequality in the auto industry after World War II. Arbitrarily defining women's place in the plants, sex-based occupational classifications were discriminatory not only because they denied women equal pay for equal work but because they limited women's job prospects, prevented women from exercising seniority rights in layoffs and recalls, and excluded women from training and promotional opportunities. Activists in the Women's Bureau and the National Advisory Council were fully aware of the threat that sex-based job classifications posed to the goal of achieving gender equality in the industry. They repeat-

41. Women's Bureau Folder, n.d. [October 1952?], ibid., Box 31, Folder 8; minutes of Local 750 Membership Meeting, December 1951, ibid., Box 39, Folder 6.
42. IEB Appeal Hearing Report, February 12, 1953, ibid., Box 39, Folder 6.

edly emphasized that unless the UAW pressed employers to determine wage rates on the basis of job content rather than on the sex of the operator, its equal-pay policy was meaningless. Alert to the way in which the labeling of jobs as male or female endowed the sexual division of labor with an aura of legitimacy, they also demanded the elimination from contracts of occupational classifications based on sex. UAW leaders may have committed themselves verbally to extirpating the sources of women's separate and unequal status in the auto industry, but in practice they confirmed the codification of that status in contracts.

In assessing the IEB's efforts in behalf of women auto workers, it is necessary to acknowledge the constraints placed on the union by auto management in this period. To a certain extent, many demands were casualties on "the industrial battleground" of labor-management relations after World War II. The UAW accomplished a great deal for its members in the postwar era, but it lost a measure of control over shop-floor issues while securing higher wage and benefit packages. The UAW won cost-of-living increases, the annual wage-improvement factor, pension plans, and supplemental unemployment benefits at the bargaining table in exchange for agreeing not to contest management's prerogative to determine the structure and organization of work in auto plants. According to labor historian David Brody, "When it took up the problem of unstable employment in the auto industry, the UAW had two choices: either to deal with the causes, or to protect its members from the consequences. By choosing the latter, the UAW actually conceded away its interest in the former." The elimination of job classifications and seniority rosters based on sex, practices that made women especially vulnerable in layoffs, was an explicit challenge to managerial prerogatives, a challenge that the UAW was incapable of, if not uninterested in, making in the postwar period.[43]

But quite apart from the intents and purposes of auto management, the IEB's disinterest in fully implementing official UAW policy sent a signal to local leaders and the rank and file. The response of the IEB to locals that engaged in discrimination against married women

---

43. David Brody, *Workers in Industrial America* (New York, 1980), p. 194. For discussions of collective bargaining in the auto industry after World War II, see also Harris, *The Right to Manage*; Steve Jeffreys, *Management and Managed* (Cambridge, England, 1986); Robert M. Macdonald, *Collective Bargaining in the Automobile Industry* (New Haven, 1963); Sumner Slichter et al., *The Impact of Collective Bargaining on Management* (Washington, D.C., 1961).

clearly contrasted with its unwillingness to do much more than admonish local unions that colluded with employers in denying women equal pay and job opportunities. To a certain extent, the greater presence of married women in the labor force after World War II made it easy, if not inevitable, for the international to change its policy regarding the employment of married women. Too, the pervasiveness of the sexual division of labor meant that a defense of the right of married women to work did not in and of itself threaten the principle of gender hierarchy or men's dominant position in the auto labor force. The president of the UAW indicated his own ambivalence about women's right to equal treatment by minimizing the significance of a section of a 1955 convention resolution on job security for female auto workers which instructed regional directors "to disapprove any contract that discriminates in any way against women workers." In response to a male delegate who wondered "if we still retain our autonomy if the resolution is accepted," Walter Reuther explained that the principle of gender equity might be sacrificed in "a practical collective bargaining decision." Although large numbers of women were adversely affected by job dislocation and unstable employment in the 1950s and early 1960s, the IEB's phlegmatic approach to the problem of occupational segregation by sex left local leaders and members to their own devices in dealing with female unemployment.[44]

The problem of unemployment for women auto workers was both bane and boon to UAW advocates of gender equality. On the one hand, it intensified the marginality and vulnerability of women in auto plants, evoking latent hostility toward the presence of married women in the plants and reinforcing conservative and prevailing notions about woman's proper place. "The sacrament of matrimony bears out the fact that the man has the responsibility of providing for his family," asserted one male delegate at the 1955 convention. "Let's not leave this convention with the understanding that a woman has the right to compete with a man for a job."[45] Male unionists also expressed their resistance to women's demands for equal-employment opportunities by negotiating contracts, supplemental agreements, and verbal agreements that codified the separate and unequal status of women in the auto industry. Whether they regarded women workers as competitors for jobs, threats to wage standards, or viola-

44. *1955 Convention Proceedings*, pp. 54–55.
45. Ibid., p. 61.

tors of social conventions, men contributed to the plight of women in auto plants in the postwar period.

At the local level, male unionists indicated their hostility to equal-employment opportunity for women in a variety of ways. Some men manipulated contractual provisions to deprive women of employment. An appeal case heard by the IEB in 1953 illustrates how vulnerable women were to this kind of harassment at the local level. To reduce the number of women working in his district, Johnnie Kallos, a chief shop steward, availed himself of a clause in Local 154's contract with Hudson Motors providing him and the general foreman with the power to determine which of the sex-based job classifications were interchangeable. Placing eight of twenty-two female employees on heavy operations, Kallos gave the women's former jobs to men with less seniority. Kallos added insult to injury by using verbal harassment and threats to coerce the women into quitting and to prevent them from protesting his action. Nina Maynard reported that after she told him she was pregnant, Kallos "had the gall to walk up and down the line with his stomach stuck out pretending he was me on the job." Kallos also told Mildred Westbrook that he wanted no women in the department and that it would be best for her to find employment elsewhere. Grace Curcuri, who had been laid off from one of the heavy jobs, testified that when she refused to date Kallos, he told her she would not be recalled to work as long as he was chief steward in the district. Kallos's flagrant abuse of power led to his censure by both Local 154 and the IEB. But other complaints received by the Women's Bureau and appeals heard by the IEB indicate that such behavior not only was not rare but was tolerated by local members and leaders.[46]

Men in other locals expressed their negative attitudes toward women more covertly than Kallos did. Women who protested that certain contractual provisions were discriminatory in effect if not in intent provoked the opposition of male unionists. When nearly all the women working at Midland Steel Products in Detroit were laid off, they asked Local 410 to seek an exception to the provision in the contract dictating that laid-off employees could exercise seniority only by "bumping" those workers with the least seniority in the plant. Since the workers with the lowest seniority were employed on

46. Maynard to Richard Gosser, September 16, 1952, Mazey Collection, Box 37, Folder 3; Westbrook to Dear Sirs, September 16, 1952, ibid.; Curcuri to To Whom It May Concern, September 16, 1952, ibid.

heavy operations, the women faced certain dismissal. They argued in defense of their petition that their layoff was the result not of any ordinary reduction in force but of the company's decision to transfer the operation on which they worked to another plant. Appealing to the local to defend them, the women also noted that men with less seniority were still employed in other departments on jobs that women were capable of performing. The local adamantly refused to acknowledge the women's complaint as legitimate. When the women hired a lawyer and threated to take legal action against both Midland Steel and Local 410, the men retaliated by charging them with conduct unbecoming to union members. Confronted with the prospect of suspension, the women withdrew their complaint.[47]

The unemployment crisis for women, however, also dramatized the issue of women's rights and was a means of gaining the attention of auto unionists. In contrast to women in the period of demobilization and reconversion after World War II, women employed in the plants in the 1950s could not be regarded as temporary interlopers with limited legitimate claims to auto jobs. Their status as workers and union members commanded attention in ways that the status of World War II defense workers never did. Signifying the shift in attitude about gender within the UAW, activists in several local unions pressed for modification or elimination of separate seniority lists, departmental or occupational group seniority agreements, and sex-based job classifications to afford women workers access to a greater number and variety of jobs. Thus, although the problem of unemployment to a certain extent exacerbated gender conflict and reinforced women's marginal position within the UAW, it also compelled some unionists to reconsider their assumptions about gender hierarchy and the place of women in auto plants.

Some local unions, for example, debated the problem of occupational segregation by sex even if they did not challenge the concept. The vast majority of the approximately nine hundred female production workers at the General Motors Fisher Body plant in Cleveland, Ohio, were employed as sewing-machine operators and bench assemblers in the trim department. Although restricted to that department, they and the relatively smaller number of men working there were numerous enough to warrant special attention from local union

47. Wendell Flynn to Zigmunt Mizejeski, April 13, 1955, UAW Local 410 Collection, Box 17, Kay Darvin et al. Folder.

officers. During local elections the various candidates vied with one another for the support of the women, who represented one-fifth of all workers in the plant. In certain respects, local leaders did well by their female constituents. Local 45 records reveal persistent discontent in the trim department over speedups, automation, and layoffs. Union officials were responsive to women's complaints, challenging management practices at every turn. But the tension among trim employees often found expression in conflict among women over scarce jobs; it did not find resolution in union attempts to expand the number of jobs available to women employed at Fisher Body. Despite continuous wrangling over layoffs and recalls, only occasionally did local leaders even consider the extent to which the practice of labeling all jobs as male or female benefited younger men with less seniority at the expense of older women with more seniority.[48]

In 1960 some women laid off from their jobs sought the opportunity to work on inspection in the trim department, a male-classified job. Several members of the local executive board supported the plan to give women access to the jobs. "If we believe in seniority equality," one man said, "they have the right." However, the local president, Charles Beckman, claimed that the precedent of "breaking down" the established noninterchangeable occupational groups that determined layoff and recall procedures throughout the plant was "too important" and would have to be handled "diplomatically," a veiled reference to the inevitably negative reaction of male union members. Beckman prevailed, and the local union did not challenge the division of labor. Eighteen months later one of the minority of local officers who had supported the women seeking the inspection jobs wondered "why we can't work out something that would allow the women to come into the press room and work on small presses rather than hiring new men from the street." But although the Local 45 executive board had declared its opposition to the scheduling of overtime for some plant workers while others remained laid off,

48. Charles Beckman to Caroline Davis, August 5, 1955, UAW Local 45 Collection, Box 5, Folder 8, ALUA; Election campaign flyers, n.d., ibid., Box 6, Folder 21; Bert Foster to Sisters in the Trim Shop, n.d. [1953], ibid., Box 7, Folder 6; minutes of Stewards' meetings, June 10, 1956, and September 8, 1957, ibid., Box 11, Folder 5; minutes of Executive Board meeting, June 27, 1954, ibid., Box 10, Folder 3; minutes of Executive Board meeting, February 24, 1957, ibid., Folder 5; minutes of Membership meeting, February 7, 1954, ibid., Folder 17; minutes of Membership meeting, March 27, 1960, ibid., Folder 21.

Beckman would not at the same time countenance the idea of placing laid-off women in "male" jobs.[49]

Other locals addressed the problem of occupational segregation more aggressively. In the winter of 1956 management at the Oldsmobile plant in Lansing, Michigan, began to transfer all the operations in the cut-and-sew department to other GM plants in Livonia and Grand Rapids, Michigan. Several hundred women, a good number of whom had worked in the plant since the early 1930s, were affected by this decision. An agreement between the company and Local 602 provided those laid off as a result of the action with the right either to transfer to the plants in Livonia and Grand Rapids or to displace employees with less seniority, regardless of sex, from jobs in the Lansing plant specifically labeled "male-female." Not surprisingly, few women accepted the offer to move east to Livonia or west to Grand Rapids, both cities more than an hour's drive from Lansing. Soon there were too many women demanding recall and too few jobs labeled "female" or "male-female." In the spring of 1957 the local shop committee asked plant management to increase the number of "male-female" operations, asserting, "We don't want any female out in the cold." There was resistance to the shop committee's request, both from men who would be displaced by the women and from plant management, which assigned laid-off women to very difficult jobs in the hope that they would disqualify themselves from reemployment. But by December 1960 a hundred women had been integrated elsewhere in the plant and seventy more were promised reemployment, a not inconsiderable achievement in light of the obstacles.[50]

There is even more compelling evidence of the extent to which women's concerns and the issue of sexual inequality were not wholly ignored at the local level in the 1950s. In contrast to the leaders of Local 602, other locals launched more radical attacks on the sexual division of labor. Automation and production slowdowns during the recessions of the 1950s led to many layoffs on "women's" jobs at Delco-Remy, a GM plant in Anderson, Indiana. Men's jobs, however,

49. Minutes of Executive Board meetings, June 26, 1960, June 25, 1961, November 26, 1961, and December 17, 1961, ibid., Box 10, Folder 7.
50. Minutes of meeting, January 12, 1956, Local 602 Collection, Box 25, Folder 31; Local agreement, January 27, 1956, ibid., Box 26, Folder 1; minutes of Shop Committee and Management meetings, May 27–28, 1957, ibid., Box 29, Folder 7; minutes of Special Executive Board meeting, October 6, 1959, ibid., Box 34, Folder 17; minutes of Executive Board meetings, December 10, 1959, and January 7, 1960, ibid.; minutes of Membership meetings, December 12, 1959, and January 9, 1960, ibid., Folder 16.

did not contract as much as women's, and new jobs were introduced and labeled "male" during this time. As women were laid off for increasingly longer periods of time, men with less or no seniority were hired. Local 662 successfully pressed Delco-Remy management in 1957 to sign an agreement stipulating that recalls of laid-off employees would be made according to the principle of noninterchangeable occupational group seniority but without reference to the separate-but-equal male and female job classifications that then comprised several occupational groups. In effect, the agreement gave women employed at Delco-Remy access to a larger number of jobs than women had at Oldsmobile in Lansing.[51]

Another important assault on the sexual division of labor occurred at the Dodge Main works in Hamtramck, Michigan, in the late 1950s. As part of its decentralization program and to a certain extent in an effort to rid itself of a particularly militant group of workers, Chrysler Corporation eliminated the wire room, an area in which eight hundred people, most of them female, assembled electrical systems for the cars produced at Dodge Main. Finding jobs for the women affected by the closing of the wire room required changing the basis for recall from departmental to plantwide seniority status. Despite resistance from plant managers and male workers, local leaders were successful in negotiating the elimination of the practice of de facto segregation from Dodge Main. Since Chrysler, in contrast to General Motors, did not also label jobs according to sex, the victory by Local 3, insofar as women's access to jobs was concerned, was of even greater consequence than the changes accomplished by Locals 602 and 662.[52]

51. Local 662 Seniority Agreement, February 1, 1957, Neal Edwards Collection, Box 3, Local 662 Agreements Folder; Memorandum of Understanding, February 1, 1957, ibid., Local 662 Demands Folder. Although it must be noted that Delco-Remy acceded to the combined seniority list in part because a provision was made for the retention of wage differentials based on sex, the local's commitment to gender equity was an important factor. In 1958 Delco-Remy threatened to throw out the single seniority list; local members in response voted overwhelmingly "in favor of equal seniority in this local" and to strike to retain the list. Management backed down. Minutes of meeting, March 29, 1958, UAW Local 662 Collection, Box 1, Courtney Minutes Notebook Folder, ALUA.

52. Jeffreys, *Management and Managed*, pp. 127–62; minutes of Executive Board meetings, October 13, 1955, and January 12, 1956, UAW Local 3 Collection (unprocessed), Box 2, Regular Executive Board Meetings 8/55–2/56 Folder, ALUA; minutes of Executive Board meeting, October 10, 1957, ibid., Regular Executive Board Meetings 1/57–10/57 Folder; minutes of Executive Board meeting, November 19, 1959, ibid., Regular Executive Board Meetings 10/59–2/61 Folder; minutes of Business meetings, September 29, 1957, and February 22, 1959, ibid., Box 4, Regular Business Meetings 3/57–11/59 Folder.

The evidence of local engagement with the problem of occupational segregation by sex in the 1950s and early 1960s offers a contrast to the prevailing view of the experience of American women in the postwar period. Noting the massive withdrawal of women from basic industries during reconversion and the postwar revival of the ideology of domesticity, scholars have emphasized the impermanence of the advances made by women workers during World War II. The principle of gender equity in the labor market and the workplace, according to these writers, quickly lost whatever approval it had gained during the war and remained out of favor until the feminist movement revived it in the late 1960s. Recent work has begun to explore the twenty years after 1945, revealing the survival and vitality of feminist goals and purposes. Although these studies have modified our understanding of the postwar era, they overlook the trade union as an arena for collective action in the interest of gender equity.[53]

The invisibility of women in unions in the 1950s is as much a product of the preoccupations of the postwar period as a measure of the inattentiveness of historians and other scholars. The ideal of domesticity and its middle-class bias not only masked the ever-increasing numbers of women in the labor force but especially obscured women in blue-collar jobs that were deemed both unfeminine and lower-class. Indicating the era's myopia with regard to wage-earning women, social scientists fascinated with postwar auto workers as the quintessential new members of an expanding middle class also failed to "see" women. The writings of Ely Chinoy, Bennett Berger, and Robert Blauner imply that auto workers and unionists were, by definition, male. Scholars such as Lee Rainwater, Richard Coleman, and Gerald Handel, who were explicitly interested in working-class women, focused on the wives of male blue-collar workers and looked at them only from their position within the home. The invisibility of women in industrial unions during the 1950s makes especially significant the growing support in the UAW not only for the principle of gender equality but for a particular vision of gender equality, one that

53. On World War II, see Karen Anderson, *Wartime Women* (Westport, Conn., 1981); D'Ann Campbell, *Women at War with America* (Cambridge, Mass., 1984); William Chafe, *The American Woman* (London, 1972). Recent assessments of gender advocacy in the postwar period include Harrison, *On Account of Sex*; Susan Hartmann, *The Home Front and Beyond* (Boston, 1982), pp. 143–61; Alice Kessler-Harris, *Out to Work* (New York, 1982), pp. 300–11; Rupp and Taylor, *Survival in the Doldrums*.

demanded that women and men be treated as alike rather than as different.[54]

To be sure, not everyone in the UAW who sympathized with the plight of women in the post–World War II period endorsed equal treatment as a strategy for improving the position of women in the auto labor force. The pervasiveness and extent of occupational segregation by sex made such women and men circumspect in their analyses and commitments. Fearing that women would lose even their limited place without the protection afforded by state laws and sex-based job classifications and seniority lists, some believed it was better for the UAW to defend and consolidate women's sphere than to erase its already constricted boundaries. At a regional women's conference sponsored by the Women's Bureau in 1955, women of Local 602 expressed their opposition to the UAW's demand for the abolition of separate seniority lists for women and men because they feared it would hasten their elimination from the plant. Suspecting a conspiracy between GM and some male unionists to drive them from the industry, the women were astounded that the Women's Bureau introduced and lobbied for the demand. The same cynical assessment of male attitudes and behavior threatened to undermine the efforts of Local 3 activists to save the jobs of the eight hundred women in the Dodge Main wire room. Some women complained when they gained access to all jobs in the plant because they were placed on jobs they deemed too heavy or difficult. Urging the women not to withdraw their support for the principle of plantwide seniority, Edie Van Horn, a chief shop steward and member of the Region 1–1A Women's Committee, promised that the local would protest any maliciously onerous job assignments but also explained that women would have to "take the bitter with the sweet" in their pursuit of both job security and sexual equality. In contrast to the Women's Bureau, which regarded any assertion of gender difference as an unacceptable affirmation of gender inequality, these propo-

---

54. Ely Chinoy, *Automobile Workers and the American Dream* (Garden City, N.Y., 1955); Bennett Berger, *Working-Class Suburb* (Berkeley, Calif., 1968); Robert Blauner, *Alienation and Freedom* (Chicago, 1964); Lee Rainwater, Richard Coleman, and Gerald Handel, *Workingman's Wife* (New York, 1959). The invisibility of women in blue-collar jobs meant that scant public attention was paid to their plight during the employment crisis of the late 1950s and early 1960s. A Bureau of Labor Statistics study of workers who lost their jobs through automation remarked with some surprise that women were especially hard hit by layoffs and discharges. BLS, *Case Studies of Displaced Workers: Experiences of Workers after Layoff*, Bulletin No. 1408 (Washington, D.C., 1964), pp. 7, 25, 32, 38.

nents rejected sex-blind treatment as detrimental to women and emphasized the ways in which it ironically could reinforce rather than subvert the marginality and invisibility of women workers.[55]

Despite the drawbacks, however, increasing numbers of auto unionists found the arguments of the Women's Bureau and other advocates for equal treatment compelling. The debate inside the UAW over contractual discrimination against married women reflects the shift in attitude about gender in the post–World War II period. In contrast to their stance in the 1930s, female auto unionists after World War II decried discrimination against married women as a violation of both the rights of all women to fashion their own lives and the democratic principles of industrial unionism. Just as they had in the 1930s, women after World War II did not claim that employment in auto plants was a fulfilling alternative to domesticity. "The number of women working for the sheer joy of working," explained Cecyle Carrigan, a Local 887 officer, "is at best infinitesimal." They argued, however, that a woman's decision to work was not the concern of the UAW. "Who is to say a woman should work or should not?" asked Mildred Szur of Local 174. "Where is our democracy in this country if a woman cannot be a free individual and make up her own mind? I think that when you start telling women you can or cannot work," Szur concluded, "you are infringing upon their civil rights, which I as a woman resent." In response to collusion between management and men in the locals to discriminate against them, married women invoked the fundamental precepts of trade unionism. "I can't see where and why if the company says we'd have to go after we were married where the membership and the union wouldn't fight for us also," Josephine DiChiera told the director of Region 2A. "There are some shady deals being pulled somewhere down the line," DiChiera contended. "We all want [to be] reimbursed on our Union dues we've paid. . . . It appears as though they're taking our money for nothing and fighting against us." These arguments appealed to unionists who regarded their organization as a vehicle for the achievement of individual freedom and social equality. "The right [of women] to determine their own destiny, their own life, is an essential point," one male delegate emphatically stated at the 1955 convention. "In the union movement we fight for every-

55. Jean Potter, Report to Membership on Region 1C Women's Conference, n.d. [1955?], Local 602 Collection, Box 25, Folder 33; Local 3 Regular Business Meeting, September 27, 1959, p. 2, Local 3 Collection (unprocessed), Box 4, Regular Business Meeting, 3/31/57–11/29/59 Folder.

thing that is democratic, allowing people to make their own decisions. They have a right to lead their own lives, and that is so
important a principle that it should not be underestimated and
should not be prevented from being carried out." The ideology of
egalitarianism and individual liberty implicit in industrial unionism
inspired some auto unionists to reassess their ideas about gender
relations and women's rights.[56]

A dramatic series of events that transpired in Local 663 in Anderson, Indiana, offers a final illustration of how the unemployment
crisis for women prompted many in the post–World War II period to
reconsider gender ideology and to endorse the position held by the
Women's Bureau and the National Advisory Council. Representing
the men and women employed on production at GM's Guide Lamp
plant, Local 663 experienced the same problem with unemployment
as did Local 662 across town. Employment fell at Guide Lamp from
4,300 workers in 1957 to 3,700 in 1963. In contrast to the situation in
Local 662, however, women at Guide Lamp initially encountered
much greater co-worker resistance to their demand for a single seniority list, which was rejected at several membership meetings between 1958 and 1960. Men were the principal opponents of a single
seniority list for Guide Lamp employees. Low-seniority men feared
more frequent layoffs, if not loss of employment, if the two lists were
combined. Other men, including the local's leaders, contended that
they would support a single list only if wage rates were equalized for
women and men, a disingenuous argument, since they were not at
all interested in pressing for equal pay. A commitment to the principle of gender hierarchy that was embedded in the practice of occupational segregation by sex enabled opponents of a combined seniority
list to assert, on the one hand, that "men are the 'breadwinners' and
should be retained in preference to women" and, on the other, that
separate seniority lists protected even married women against onerous job assignments. What made these claims credible, at least for a
while, was the opposition of high-seniority women to the institution
of a combined list. These women feared, not without reason, that
management would assign them to harder or dirtier jobs if they had

56. *1955 Convention Proceedings*, pp. 53, 56, 58; DiChiera to Ray Ross, May 18, 1953,
Mazey Collection, Box 35, Folder 9. In his 1963 study of shop stewards in Milwaukee
unions, Sidney Peck noted: "Most union stewards who defend the 'rights of women'
do so out of commitment to the equalitarian, democratic principles of class unionism.
They are not so much pro-feminine as they are class-conscious in their outlook." Peck,
The Rank-and-File Leader (New Haven, 1963), p. 198.

to compete with men for status. Thus the concern of high-seniority women about the impact of sex-blind treatment coincided with the view of men who essentially believed in the separate and unequal status of women.[57]

The coexistence of these two ideas, however, was temporary. From the outset, women who advocated the single seniority list based their argument on the principle of industrial unionism. An understanding of their rights as union members led them to the conclusion that women had a right to sex-blind treatment and that treatment based on the assertion of gender difference was a violation of that right. Seniority, they contended, not sex or marital status, "is the one and only thing that should be considered." Now, in the face of unemployment, the views of people such as the shop committee chair began to lose some of their legitimacy while the position advanced by advocates of a single list gained support. The vote on the single seniority list grew closer as time—and layoffs of women—went on. Whereas 90 percent of those voting at a meeting in February 1959 rejected the notion of a single list, only 61 percent of those voting in November of that year opposed the idea. In September 1960, when 169 new men were hired while 468 women with seniority dating back as far as 1946 were laid off, some of the women asked the chairman of the shop committee to file a grievance. Still unsupportive, he filed reluctantly only after the women complained to an international representative, who intervened in their behalf. Guide Lamp management turned down the grievance, claiming that the jobs being performed by the newly hired men were not "women's" jobs. After local union members rejected a single seniority list on November 13 by a vote of 382 to 324, a now-larger group of women filed an appeal with the IEB, charging that the local's adherence to separate seniority lists violated international policy. With more than 400 women still on layoff, 15 of them, frustrated by the slow pace of the grievance and appeal machinery, began picketing the Local 663 headquarters on December 8. "We are asking for fair play and the end of discrimination," the group explained in an advertisement in the *Anderson Herald*. "We will continue to protest and to picket our own local until it recognizes the rights of women workers."[58]

57. Zaban, "Internal Union Frictions," pp. 117–18; Local 663 *Lampmaker*, October 7, 1960.
58. *Delco Sparks*, November 28, 1960; Zaban, "Internal Union Frictions," pp. 123, 127–28; *Anderson Herald*, December 22, 1960.

The conflict having gone public, the international intervened again, this time in the person of Emil Mazey. Mazey first told the women that the IEB would not examine the appeal until the picket line was withdrawn. He learned, however, that the appellants were not the same women as the picketers, although both groups had the same complaint. The picketers did stop on January 11, 1961, since the IEB was scheduled to conduct its investigation by the end of the month. After holding hearings, the IEB told Local 663 finally to demand a combined seniority list during the UAW's upcoming negotiations with GM. Although the IEB did not condemn local leaders for their indifference, indeed hostility, to the women's concerns, the shop committee chair paid the price in the local elections in May, when he lost a reelection bid to a man backed by women seeking a single seniority list. Another indication of the increasing support among local unionists for sexual equality was the evidently widespread acceptance, even on the part of some opponents of a combined seniority list, of the women's picket line. Perceived as hardy, brave, and impressively militant, their action was deemed appropriate for aggrieved union members rather than, as Mazey had implied, antiunionist in effect if not in intent.[59]

A single seniority list was Local 663's principal demand in its negotiations with Guide Lamp in September 1961. Management resisted the demand for reasons ranging from its impracticality to its radicalism. The company negotiator stated it was "sociologically wrong for a woman to have job preference over a man who was the family breadwinner" and added that the call for one list was "outside agitated" by officials in the UAW's international headquarters in Detroit. An international representative averred that the UAW would not back down on the demand. The agreement was a compromise. It retained separate lists, thus satisfying management and those in Local 663 still opposed to a single list. But it included a provision that a woman could bump a lower-seniority man if she had performed the job before or could do it with minimal instruction. Although the

59. Zaban, "Internal Union Frictions," pp. 130–36. In a similar situation in 1951, Mazey severely chastised a group of women from Local 600 for setting up a picket line and speaking to the press to protest the dilatory response of local officers to a complaint of sexual discrimination at the Ford River Rouge complex. "I don't think that is proper conduct of a Union member whatsoever, because that kind of action doesn't do the Union any good. Any time the newspapers think that we are quarreling among ourselves," Mazey explained, "they will give it headlines and give us newspaper stories." Transcript of Local 600 hearing, September 26, 1951, pp. 97–98, Mazey Collection, Box 29, Folder 20.

agreement was far less than a victory for women in the plant, it is significant that those who wanted equal seniority for women favored the compromise and ratification of the entire collective-bargaining agreement. Those opposed to equal seniority for women also opposed the compromise and urged rejection of the contract. Indicating the now greater commitment to gender equality and equal treatment in the workplace, local members voted 794 to 496 to ratify the contract.[60]

The transformative process that took place in Local 663 in the late 1950s and early 1960s was not unique. As individuals and groups of people confronted the problem of unemployment in the auto industry and the circumscribed sphere for women, they too came to concur with the perspective and vision of the Women's Bureau and National Advisory Council. The coincidence of these trends had something of a cumulative effect; by the mid-1960s there was enough demand and support at the local level for achieving gender equality by means of equal treatment that UAW women leaders were able to play an important role in the rebirth of feminism. But until a different economic and political context provided a more conducive environment, advocates of women's rights had to be content with something less than a thoroughgoing and concerted effort to secure gender equity. During discussion of a women's rights resolution at the 1955 convention, Emma Murphy, a Local 3 officer with a history of activism on issues of concern to women auto workers dating back to the late 1930s, expressed the frustration felt by too few unionists in the postwar period. "I am burned up," Murphy asserted. "Year after year we come to convention and the same resolution is passed every time. We are just giving lip service to the women in industry," she remarked. "We go back for two years and the same thing happens over and over again."[61]

So despite the efforts to secure female employment, women did not attain equal status as auto workers during the postwar period. Patterns of job segregation changed little, and women remained clustered in a few, predominantly female occupations. The results of

60. Zaban, "Internal Union Frictions," pp. 136–47. The limits of the agreement were soon apparent. Approximately seventy women returned to the plant under its new terms. But more than one hundred were recalled when Local 663 negotiated to change a certain number of "men's" jobs to "women's" jobs, a strategy that reaffirmed the sexual division of labor. Real change did not occur until the federal government began to move against sexual discrimination in employment after 1964.

61. *1955 Convention Proceedings*, p. 58.

a 1963 study by the Bureau of Labor Statistics of automotive parts manufacturing were remarkably consistent with those of a similar study conducted in 1940. Although the 23,962 women in the 1963 survey were employed in twenty-four of forty job categories, half of them worked in just one category, Class C assembly, and 60.5 percent of all Class C assemblers were female. In the 1963 survey, 14 percent of the women were Class C inspectors and another 14 percent were light- and medium-punch-press operators; women constituted 52.8 percent and 31 percent, respectively, of all workers in these two classifications. In contrast, men were much more evenly distributed throughout the occupational structure in auto parts plants. None of the forty job categories contained more than 10 percent of the male labor force, and thirty-six of them each accounted for less than 6 percent. Only 8.6 percent of the 93,259 men included in the study, moreover, were Class C assemblers, and just 3.1 percent were Class C inspectors. The presence of women in 60 percent of the job categories in auto parts plants indicates the potential that existed for the greater integration of women into the industry's labor force. That potential, however, remained unfulfilled in the post–World War II period.[62]

62. The 1940 Bureau of Labor Statistics study indicated that women worked in thirteen of thirty-eight processing operations in the auto industry's parts division. Of the 27,801 women, 40 percent were engaged in small-parts assembly, and 58.5 percent of all small-parts assemblers were female. Another 4,854 women (17.5 percent) were inspectors, and 3,599 (12.9 percent) were punch-press operators; women composed 40.8 percent and 31 percent, respectively, of all workers in these two categories. BLS Bulletin No. 706, pp. 38–39; BLS Bulletin No. 1393, pp. 22–23.

CHAPTER FIVE

Feminism and Unionism: The UAW and the Challenge to Gender Inequality, 1963–1975

"If there had not been a few people like us around doing the kinds of things that we have done," Dorothy Haener observed in 1977, "much of what we have seen happen in the women's movement might not well have happened." Haener and others associated with the UAW Women's Department concluded, long before the fateful June 1966 meeting in Betty Friedan's Washington, D.C., hotel room which witnessed the birth of the National Organization for Women (NOW), that women needed an organization to press for implementation of federal antidiscriminatory legislation and to achieve social, political, and economic equality for women. Describing the reluctance of Mary Keyserling and other federal officials to use Title VII of the 1964 Civil Rights Act to challenge sexually discriminatory employment practices, Haener bitterly recalled the mounting frustration felt by women unionists in the mid-1960s. According to Haener, it was Dollie Lowther Robinson, a black trade unionist then working in the United States Women's Bureau, who first suggested, in a private discussion with a group of UAW women at least one year before the formation of NOW, that advocates of gender equality needed an "NAACP for women."[1]

1. Interview with Dorothy Haener, pp. 59–62, The Twentieth Century Trade Union Woman: Vehicle for Social Change Oral History Project, Institute of Labor and Industrial Relations, University of Michigan, Ann Arbor, Michigan, 1977. For Friedan's account of the formation of NOW, see Betty Friedan, *It Changed My Life* (New York, 1976), pp. 77–84.

The observations of Dorothy Haener indicate the importance of trade union women in shaping the agenda of the women's movement and contributing to its victories. In the 1960s high employment and the potential power of Title VII of the 1964 Civil Rights Act altered the context for the struggle to expand women's access to blue-collar jobs and provided the basis for a union assault on state laws regulating the employment of women. Speaking to the Women's Committee of UAW Region 1-1E in April 1970, Haener happily reported, "Professional women are beginning to admit that the women working in the shops were the most instrumental in getting Title VII of the Civil Rights Act into effect." The significance of this role, however, generally is overlooked in studies of the resurgence of feminism in the 1960s. Aware of the oversight, Haener herself remarked during an interview in 1977, "Somebody ought to write [this story] sometime because it's all sort of getting lost."[2]

The politics of feminism inside the UAW also require attention. The 1960s and early 1970s were punctuated by a series of outwardly impressive events: the 1964–1966 campaign to elect a woman to the International Executive Board (IEB), the UAW's endorsement of the Equal Rights Amendment (ERA) in the spring of 1970, the union's filing of sexual-discrimination charges with the Equal Employment Opportunity Commission (EEOC) against the Big Three auto producers in 1972, the first annual women's conferences at the UAW Educational Center in Black Lake, Michigan, and the election of Olga Madar as first president of the Coalition of Labor Union Women (CLUW) in 1974. Underlying these actions were two separate although mutually reinforcing developments: new directions for the twenty-five-year-old campaign for gender equality in the workplace and a fight for equality in the union, a battle that was not joined until the 1960s. The origins, character, and consequences of these trends indicate that not only did the UAW affect the feminist movement but feminism affected the union as well.

The prospects for achieving gender equity in the workplace improved with the passage in 1963 of the Equal Pay Act as an amendment to the 1938 Fair Labor Standards Act. The UAW participated in

---

2. Minutes of meeting, April 13, 1970, Women's Department–Lillian Hatcher Collection, Box 8, Folder 8, Walter P. Reuther Library, Archives of Labor and Urban Affairs, Wayne State University, Detroit, Michigan (hereafter cited as ALUA); Haener interview, p. 62.

the United States Women's Bureau's coalition campaign for passage of a federal equal-pay bill after World War II. That effort, however, failed on account of ineffective leadership, confusion over goals and purposes, business opposition, and national ambivalence about the role of women in American society. Social and economic obstacles began to dissipate in the late 1950s, and the campaign to enact equal-pay legislation gained a capable and important leader with the appointment of Esther Peterson as director of the Women's Bureau in 1961. Benefiting from the greater acceptance of female labor-force participation, the Kennedy administration's ties to organized labor, and the effective leadership of both Peterson and Arthur Goldberg, Kennedy's labor secretary, the Women's Bureau coalition finally won passage of equal-pay legislation. "For 15 years," Caroline Davis told Esther Peterson, "we have worked to secure passage of a law, and at a time had high expectations, only to have [them] dashed before we got very far. This is indeed a great accomplishment." Demanding the elimination of "this great moral, social and economic inequity that has been with us" since the first contract between the UAW and GM was signed in 1937, UAW locals in Kokomo and Anderson, Indiana, used the new federal statute to eliminate long-standing hourly wage differentials of as much as 8 cents for women employed on the same jobs as men at Delco Radio, Delco-Remy, and Guide Lamp. The Equal Pay Act similarly provided the UAW with the necessary leverage finally to secure equal pay for women workers in many other auto plants.[3]

Despite its importance, the Equal Pay Act alone could not equalize the status of women and men in the labor market. Knowing that employers often used any slight difference between men's and women's work to justify wage differentials, advocates of previous equal-pay bills had used such terms as *comparable work* requiring *comparable skills* rather than *equal work*. To assure passage of the bill in 1963, however, supporters agreed to eliminate job comparability as the standard for wage determination. Although advocates such as Dorothy Haener of the UAW believed the bill was better than

3. Cynthia Harrison, *On Account of Sex* (Berkeley, Calif., 1988), pp. 45–51, 89–105; Davis to Peterson, n.d. [May–June 1963], U.S. Women's Bureau Papers, Record Group 86, Box 1237, Equal Pay Folder, National Archives, Washington, D.C. (hereafter cited as RG 86/NA); *Delco Antenna*, November 1963, clipping in Bruce Kingery Collection, Series II, Box 2, Folder 1, ALUA; UAW Press Release, March 8, 1965, Walter P. Reuther Collection, Box 173, Folder 5, ALUA.

nothing, it applied only to the narrow spectrum of jobs performed by both women and men and thus was of limited use.[4]

The limits of the Equal Pay Act focused attention on Title VII of the 1964 Civil Rights Act as a means of addressing both the wage disparity between the sexes and the underlying problem of occupational segregation by sex. The absence of a federal commitment to eliminate sexual discrimination in employment, however, blunted the potential of even Title VII to improve the labor-market status of women. Although Title VII forbids discrimination on the basis of sex in all matters of employment, including compensation, Congress passed the Bennett amendment to the Civil Rights Act in anticipation of conflict between Title VII and the Equal Pay Act. The amendment allowed employers to differentiate on the basis of sex in wage determination if they adhered to the provision of the Equal Pay Act which permits as exceptions to the equal-pay principle wage differentials based on seniority, merit, differences in quantity or quality of production, or any factor other than sex. In so doing, Congress seemed to limit Title VII to the narrow equal-work standard of the Equal Pay Act. The applicability of Title VII to other forms of what some deemed employment discrimination, such as state laws regulating the employment of women, also was limited at first. Invited to suggest guidelines for the EEOC, the investigatory and conciliatory agency for Title VII complaints, Caroline Davis asked for "a policy saying that state laws affecting women cannot be used as a justification for discrimination against women." Hopes for prompt change were soon deflated. In a set of guidelines issued in November 1965, the commission skirted the question of whether the Civil Rights Act conflicted with state laws and essentially declared the federal law subordinate to state law, ruling that "the Commission will not find an unlawful employment practice where an employer's refusal to hire women for certain work is based on a state law which precludes the employment for such work, provided that the employer is acting in good faith and that the law in question is reasonably adapted to protect rather than to subject them to discrimination." In April 1966 the EEOC modified its position somewhat by allowing charges that state laws were discriminatory but warned that it would not rule on the merits of such cases.[5]

4. Harrison, *On Account of Sex*, pp. 96, 98; Elaine Johansen, *Comparable Worth* (Boulder, Colo., 1984), pp. 39–42.
5. Carl Brauer, "Women Activists, Southern Conservatives, and the Prohibition of Sex Discrimination in Title VII of the 1964 Civil Rights Act," *Journal of Southern History*

Advocates of gender equality in the UAW and other like-minded organizations picked up the gauntlet laid down by the EEOC. While unions such as the International Union of Electrical Workers (IUE) pressed for judicial and administrative recognition of the applicability of comparable worth under federal antidiscriminatory statutes, the UAW Women's Department sought ways to confirm the irrelevance and illegality of state laws applying only to women workers. Caroline Davis did not have to look too long or too far for evidence that female labor laws disadvantaged women in auto plants. A combination of factors produced growing discontent at the local level with what many regarded as these obstacles to equal opportunity for women. Although employment in basic industries such as the auto industry increased after the early sixties, women did not see themselves as benefiting equally from industrial expansion. Auto manufacturers did not hire women for new jobs, women in the plants were denied transfer to new or better-paying jobs, and women were denied overtime hours and premium pay. Women's relative sense of deprivation was intensified by the greater legitimacy accorded the idea of equal-employment opportunity by passage of the Equal Pay Act and the Civil Rights Act. Female labor laws became the target of those seeking the source of these inequities. By mobilizing and giving vent to these concerns, the Women's Department enhanced the status within the UAW of its own goals and purposes and laid the foundation for an assault on state laws regulating the employment of women.[6]

Although the applicability of the Equal Pay Act and Title VII remained in doubt, the two statutes did offer women workers in the

---

49 (February 1983): 37–56; Emily George, *Martha W. Griffiths* (Lanham, Md., 1982), pp. 148–52; Anne Draper to Franklin Delano Roosevelt, Jr., June 30, 1965, Katharine Pollack Ellickson Collection, Box 88, Folder 12, ALUA; text of statement by Stephen Schlossberg to EEOC at public hearings, May 2, 1967, Reuther Collection, Box 118, Folder 12; EEOC Guidelines, November 22, 1965, quoted in Jo Freeman, *The Politics of Women's Liberation* (New York, 1975), p. 186; text of Davis speech, August 19–20, 1965, Women's Department–Lillian Hatcher Collection, Box 2, Folder 4. In its April 1966 policy statement, the EEOC did promise to advise women of the time limits for filing a lawsuit challenging the statutes and reserved the right to participate in a suit as amicus curiae.

6. For union action in regard to comparable worth, see Winn Newman and Jeanne M. Vonhof, "'Separate but Equal'—Job Segregation and Pay Equity in the Wake of *Gunther,*" *University of Illinois Law Review* (1981): 269–331. The number of production workers in the transportation-equipment industry increased annually in the 1960s, from 992,700 in 1961 to 1,453,200 in 1969. Bureau of Labor Statistics (BLS), *Employment and Earnings, United States, 1909–75*, Bulletin No. 1312–10 (Washington, D.C., 1975), p. 300.

auto industry and elsewhere a means of contesting discrimination and occupational segregation by sex after 1963. When women were laid off from their jobs or refused better-paid positions by employers that cited state weight-lifting laws as reason for denying them recalls, transfers, and promotions, they cited the standard of gender equality implicit in these federal statutes. For example, when approximately 150 women employed as assemblers in the electronics division of Goodyear Aerospace in Akron, Ohio, were laid off in August 1966, management cited that state's weight-lifting law in refusing to allow the women to displace lower-seniority men on other jobs. Although the job to which the women sought transfer did not require constant lifting of parts of excessive weight, the company maintained that even the potential for abuse precluded their placement in it. Local 856 officers and the women in turn emphasized the greater importance of providing female workers with equal opportunity for employment and questioned the validity of the state law. A similar situation developed at the Apex Machine and Tool Company in Dayton, Ohio, when a woman requested transfer to a job as a turret lathe operator to which her seniority entitled her and which paid a minimum of $2.66 per hour. The company allowed her to transfer only into hand mill operation, a female-dominated classification that paid a maximum of $2.55 per hour, because turret-lathe operators occasionally lifted stock weighing more than twenty-five pounds and sometimes sharpened and dressed tools with emery or carborundum wheels, actions forbidden to female employees by state laws. Concerned by the way in which female labor laws contradicted standards of equality embedded in both the collective-bargaining agreement and federal law, Local 1040 appealed the woman's grievance to arbitration.[7]

Complaints about the adverse consequences of state laws restricting the number of hours women could be employed also increased in this period. To meet the growing demands in the 1960s of the Defense Department, American consumers, and corporate planners, plant managers in the auto and aerospace industries increased production by regularly scheduling overtime hours for blue-collar workers. Average weekly overtime hours for production workers in

7. Grievance A-4877, September 6, 1966, Women's Department–Lillian Hatcher Collection, Box 8, Folder 13; W. H. Smith to Caroline Davis, October 27, 1966, ibid., Hatcher report of meeting at Local 856, November 29, 1966, ibid.; Smith to Hatcher, December 9, 1966, ibid.; arbitrator's decision in Case No. 213 A-7, September 30, 1965, Reuther Collection, Box 172, Folder 13; Davis to Irving Bluestone, November 17, 1965, ibid.

the auto industry increased from 2.6 in 1960 to 6.2 in 1965; between 1961 and 1970 the figure did not fall below 3.2. While overtime carried the benefit of premium pay, it also was compulsory; and when the scheduling of overtime became extensive and recurring, some workers began to object to the practice. Women shared men's distaste for the compulsory character of overtime, especially if their often heavier domestic responsibilities conflicted with the obligation of working additional hours. But in states with laws limiting the number of hours women could be employed, women often were exempt from overtime requirements. Rather than see this as a status to be enjoyed, increasing numbers of women came to regard it as an obstacle to larger paychecks, better jobs, and, ultimately, gender equality.[8]

As the scheduling of overtime for plant workers became both more pervasive and more persistent in the mid-1960s, more and more women confronted the negative consequences of legal restrictions on the number of hours they could work in a day or a week. The most frequent complaint made by women was not only that male co-workers had the opportunity for additional income but that the men were receiving premium pay for the extra hours. Women employed on inspection at the Ternstedt plant in Elyria, Ohio, complained that whenever management scheduled overtime, male inspectors received three hours' pay for the extra two hours' work; but because state law forbade the employment of women more than eight hours per day, they did not have the opportunity for the overtime duty and the premium pay. "Over a period of time this could amount to considerable earnings to female employees," explained Renilda Dougherty. "This practice has been continuing for the past month," she added, "on an average of two or three times a week." Women denied overtime at GM's Fisher Body plant in St. Louis filed grievances contending that the collective-bargaining agreement forbade

8. BLS Bulletin No. 1312–10, p. 304; J. Ross Wetzel, "Current Developments in Factory Overtime," *BLS Employment and Earnings* 11 (May 1965): iii–xv; John Fenlon, "Patterns in Overtime Hours and Premium Pay," *Monthly Labor Review* 92 (October 1969): 42–46; Wetzel, "Long Hours and Premium Pay," *Monthly Labor Review* 88 (September 1965): 1083–88. In 1964, forty states and the District of Columbia had maximum daily or weekly hours' laws for women only in one or more occupations or industries. There was much diversity among the states in the character and scope of this coverage. See U.S. Women's Bureau, *1969 Handbook on Women Workers*, Bulletin No. 294 (Washington, D.C., 1969), pp. 270–73, for a detailed summary of laws concerning women's hours.

such discrimination on the basis of sex and that Title VII superseded a Missouri law restricing women workers to a nine-hour day.[9]

While the relative deprivation of take-home pay was reasonable cause for complaint, there were even more onerous consequences of hours-limitation laws. Women employed at a GM plant in Michigan, for example, were laid off because management temporarily required daily overtime in the department in which they worked and state law forbade the employment of women in excess of nine hours a day. A less obvious and more insidious result was the denial to women of transfer and promotional opportunities on the ground that the jobs occasionally entailed overtime. In 1965 four women working on spring assembly in the cushion department, one of the mere handful of jobs to which women were assigned at the Fisher Body plant in Pontiac, Michigan, sought transfer on the basis of their seniority to better-paying jobs in the all-male paint department. When management ignored the women's transfer applications and instead hired new male employees without seniority for that classification in the paint department, the women filed grievances. In the grievance hearing, Local 596 admitted that management had not violated the contract, which forbade discrimination on the basis of sex only insofar as intradepartmental, not interdepartmental, transfers were concerned. Local officers also acknowledged management's reminder that when women's upholstery jobs were moved from the cushion department to another plant in the mid-1950s, the union had agreed not to allow the women to transfer to other departments in the plant. But, the local contended, Title VII now superseded past agreements and practices, and women's right to transfer ought to be respected. After management rejected the grievance, the women filed a complaint with the EEOC, which investigated the charges in January 1966. Confronted with information that only one woman had been newly hired since 1958 and that not one black woman was currently employed in the plant, GM maintained that state laws were the basis for denying women access to all-male departments either as transfers or as new hires. GM admitted that women could perform some jobs within those departments without violating laws that regulated

9. EEOC Charge of Discrimination Form, May 3, 1968, Reuther Collection, Box 119, Folder 10; Roy Hartzell to Stephen Schlossberg, July 31, 1966, Women's Department– Lillian Hatcher Collection, Box 2, Folder 5; EEOC charges, Reuther Collection, Box 172, Folder 15; Bernard Ashe to Caroline Davis, May 9, 1969, Women's Department–Lillian Hatcher Collection, Box 3, Folder 6.

weight lifting, hours per week, and workplace safety, but their inability, for example, to work overtime contravened managerial prerogatives in organizing production.[10]

Women who contested female labor laws did not always enjoy the support of their fellow union members. After Local 101 negotiated the elimination of separate seniority lists for women and men employed at the Standard Screw Company to comply with Title VII, management laid off women while retaining men with less seniority on jobs the women could perform. Plant management denied the grievance filed by the local in behalf of the women, citing Ohio's weight-lifting law as justification for its refusal to recall the laid-off female employees. Infuriated by both the indifference of male local officers to their dilemma and the smug attitude of their employer, the women demonstrated outside the plant. The demonstration, the chairman of the local bargaining committee complained to Caroline Davis, "was embarrassing to both management and the union." Six women laid off by another Ohio company protested when they were forced to accept jobs paying less than those in a higher classification to which their seniority entitled them but which management claimed required frequent lifting of weights in excess of twenty-five pounds. The women complained that there were jobs within the classification which did not require frequent lifting of heavy weights and that their seniority rights were being violated. Local officers, however, delayed processing the women's grievances in deference to the concerns of younger men with less seniority who would have to take lower-paid jobs and to the complaints of other men with equal or greater seniority who believed they would have to take less desirable jobs in the classification, such as those entailing some lifting, to accommodate the women. To counter the women's assertion of their

10. Marge Liddy to Lillian Hatcher, November 30, 1965, Reuther Collection, Box 102, Folder 12; minutes of Appeal Committee hearing, December 16, 1965, ibid.; Richard Graham, "EEOC Decision in Liddy et al. vs. Fisher Body," February 2, 1966, ibid.; Lillian Hatcher to Caroline Davis, April 12, 1966, Women's Department–Lillian Hatcher Collection, Box 2, Folder 5. The EEOC found reasonable cause that GM did discriminate on the basis of sex in matters of hiring and promotion and that GM was "perhaps unintentionally—maintaining a wage rate differential structure based on sex by refusing to open lines of progression to women so as to qualify for higher rates of pay." The aggrieved women had sought transfer in part because wage rates in the cushion department were the lowest in the plant. The IUE used a similar line of reasoning in its landmark case against Westinghouse. See Newman and Vonhof, "Separate but Equal"; Ruth G. Blumrosen, "Wage Discrimination, Job Segregation, and Title VII of the Civil Rights Act of 1964," *University of Michigan Journal of Law Reform* 12 (Spring 1979): 397–502.

rights to equal opportunity, the men wrapped up the self-interested basis for their opposition in the ideological slogan "women's place is in the home" rather than at work. Eventually, an international representative from the Region 2A office negotiated with the company to allow women to perform the seven of seventy-one jobs in the classification which did not require the lifting and moving of parts exceeding twenty-five pounds in weight. Men working in the area remained hostile, an indication of the extent to which any serious challenge to occupational segregation by sex could potentially intensify gender conflict on shop floors and in union offices alike. Even the international representative was miffed, reporting that he had received "quite a bit of criticism from male employees for 'sticking my nose in the matter.' "[11]

Some women who protested the treatment accorded them were vindicated in the grievance procedure. Sometimes the overtime hours or weight-lifting requirements did not exceed state limits. A few persistent union representatives and receptive employers also negotiated settlements that enabled women to work in compliance with state law. Women in one auto-parts plant in Ohio, for example, were unable to work the two daily overtime hours required of fellow male employees on the weekday shift because Ohio mandated an eight-hour day for female employees. The law, however, did allow a six-day week, so the union convinced management that women could work an eight-hour shift on Sunday to share the available overtime. In some instances, state labor officials waived laws if in the judgment of all concerned the terms and conditions of employment were not excessive. It is difficult, if not impossible, to determine how many grievances involving female labor laws were thus resolved to the advantage of women workers. We also cannot know how many more women might have benefited if employers and union representatives had been more supportive of women's interests and more flexible and creative in organizing work. The nature and number of complaints about unresolved grievances which appear in the records of local unions, UAW departments, and union officers suggest that women experienced frustration more often than satisfaction at this level in their pursuit of equal-employment opportunity.[12]

11. Ray Webber to Caroline Davis, October 19, 1966, Reuther Collection, Box 172, Folder 17; Bernard Ashe to Dorothy Haener, December 1, 1966, ibid.; Haener to Mike Friedman, June 19, 1967, ibid.; Ashe to John Fillion, July 14, 1967, ibid.; William Garnes to Ray Ross, June 9, 1965, ibid., Box 252, Folder 26.
12. Caroline Davis to Leonard Woodcock, May 20, 1958, Leonard Woodcock Collec-

Appealing a grievance to arbitration, however, offered no greater likelihood of redress for women. Before 1965 arbitrators asserted either the propriety of employers in complying with state laws or the subordination of collective-bargaining agreements to state laws with which they were in conflict. After Title VII of the Civil Rights Act became effective in July 1965, arbitrators either ruled that sex was a bona fide occupational qualification for jobs occasionally requiring overtime or weight lifting in excess of state regulations, thus supporting employers' defense of hiring and placement practices, or simply claimed that they had no power to resolve conflicts between state and federal law. Despite dim prospects, more and more women pressed union officers to challenge management and to insist on women gaining equal access to jobs regardless of hours or weight-lifting limitations. Local union officials who were sympathetic to women's concerns, and even those who were not but who worried about union liability for discrimination, came to see the grievance procedure as a dead end and to wonder what avenue to follow in pursuit of gender equity. Local 780 officers, for example, protested when a woman accused them of collaborating with management to deny her grievance demanding an overtime assignment. They were sympathetic to women's plight, they explained, but felt the grievance procedure was pointless since Ohio law superseded collective-bargaining agreements. "It is our opinion that the state law is not permitting the women to work overtime," the local president maintained, "and we feel that the women in specific occupations and those in this department could work the ten hours without creating a hardship." "We definitely are in a bind on this problem," he commented.[13]

The increased agitation at the local level on the issue of female labor laws served the purposes of the Women's Department in several ways. First, the general expansion of employment in the auto industry as well as the more frequent scheduling of overtime in the plants provided a timely platform on which to launch a challenge to protective labor legislation for women. Second, the greater grassroots discontent helped legitimize the department's twenty-year-old call for union action against the laws. International leaders understood the power of the new federal laws to eliminate finally such

tion, Box 25, Folder 7, ALUA; Roy Hartzell to Stephen Schlossberg, July 31, 1966, Women's Department–Lillian Hatcher Collection, Box 2, Folder 5; Dorothy Haener to Caroline Davis, October 25, 1968, Reuther Collection, Box 172, Folder 20.

13. Stephen Schlossberg statement to EEOC, May 2, 1967, Reuther Collection, Box 118, Folder 12; Ira Ison to William Hodges, October 28, 1968, ibid., Box 119, Folder 10.

blatantly discriminatory contract features as separate seniority lists, sex-based job classifications, and sex-differentiated wage scales. Within months of the effective date of the Civil Rights Act, the IEB discussed the implications of Title VII for the treatment of women in seniority provisions in collective-bargaining agreements and agreed that each international representative who was responsible for servicing local unions would be obligated to review seniority provisions in contracts and "promptly" initiate efforts to "negotiate corrections" if violations of the law were found. Many top union leaders, however, seemed unaware of the problem of protective labor legislation insofar as it concerned workers in plants under their jurisdiction. Caroline Davis complained to Irving Bluestone, Walter Reuther's administrative assistant, in November 1965 that Ray Ross, the director of Region 2A, "didn't approve of us doing anything about the state laws. He believes they protect women and that's that. I did my best to enlighten him over the phone, but the most I could get out of him was that 'of course he didn't want to see discrimination practiced against any one, male or female.'" By the fall of 1966, however, local discontent in regard to Title VII and female labor laws had become so widespread that it reached the offices of many of the regional directors and department chiefs who together occupied the majority of seats on the IEB. The sheer number of complaints had overwhelmed local union officers, compelling international leaders to confront the obstacles posed by state laws regulating the employment of women and to devise policies and strategies for dealing with them.[14]

Many shared the view of Stephen Schlossberg, a UAW attorney who believed that grievance and arbitration procedures were "fruitless" because managements inevitably claimed that they were bound not to employ women in violation of state laws. The EEOC complaint process was not much more satisfying. On the one hand, its procedural deadlines were not synchronized with those of the union grievance procedure; women's grievances could and did fall through the cracks. On the other hand, although the EEOC might find evidence of discrimination, it would not overrule state laws in this period. Warning that there were no "guarantees of success," Schlossberg nevertheless urged the UAW to take the EEOC at its word and

14. Walter Reuther to Officers and IEB Members, January 21, 1966, Reuther Collection, Box 79, Folder 3; Davis to Bluestone, November 17, 1965, ibid., Box 172, Folder 13; Tony Connole to Irving Bluestone, November 11, 1966, ibid., Box 81, Folder 15; Bluestone to Stephen Schlossberg, December 5, 1966, ibid.; Bluestone to Connole, December 12, 1966, ibid.

seek a test case "to litigate all the way to the Supreme Court" if necessary. "Lose or win," Schlossberg asserted, the UAW should "clear the air." A second method advanced was to seek the amendment or repeal of the objectionable state codes, those "undesirable relics of a past era." Both approaches received the endorsement of a majority of IEB members. Most immediately, in 1967 the Women's Department participated in campaigns in two states containing large concentrations of female auto unionists to amend hours-limitation laws so that women might work overtime; the department also lobbied for repeal of Michigan's hours-limitation law. Ten years earlier, Caroline Davis had been chastized by international officers for stating to women in an Ohio local union that the UAW ought to seek amendment of that state's restrictive hours-limitation law. The contrast with the same leaders' sanction of political activism after 1966 indicates the importance of local pressure in legitimizing the agenda of the Women's Department.[15]

The Women's Department's litigative and legislative efforts to challenge protective labor laws for women and to assert the power of Title VII placed its leaders in the vanguard of the renascent feminist movement. Department leaders and their supporters on the local and regional women's committees for many years had endorsed sex-blind treatment as a strategy for achieving equality in the workplace. Their rejection of the idea that gender differences required different treatment for women and men in society generally and the labor market specifically coincided with the emerging view of nonunionists such as Betty Friedan that sex roles were not immutable and that the sameness of women and men should serve as the basis of sexual equality. It is not surprising, therefore, that Caroline Davis and Dorothy Haener were founders of NOW and that the UAW provided clerical services for the new organization. But UAW feminists at the same time placed themselves at odds with the labor movement. The AFL-CIO was a leading antagonist of ERA forces, and its unwavering commitment both to female labor laws and the principle of protection implicit in the legislation caused problems for those in the labor movement who were questioning the necessity, utility, and wisdom of such coverage. Women unionists, for example, were scourged for joining the attack on protective labor legislation during the June 1966

15. Schlossberg to Bluestone, December 9, 1966, ibid.; UAW, *President's Report to the Twenty-first Constitutional Convention, May 4–10, 1968,* pt. 2, pp. 155–56; Caroline Davis to Leonard Woodcock, May 20, 1958, Woodcock Collection, Box 25, Folder 7.

meeting of the various state commissions on the status of women because they "created the impression that labor is either divided or no longer concerned about these labor standards." Out of loyalty to the labor movement and in recognition of the lack of consensus even within the UAW, the union withdrew from NOW in 1968. But the conflict inside the house of labor could not be resolved to the satisfaction of union feminists such as Davis and Haener, and open revolt was inevitable.[16]

The challenge to protective legislation for women workers was the principal strategy adopted by the UAW in the 1960s for securing equality of opportunity for women workers. The Equal Pay Act and Title VII made the elimination of blatant forms of sexual discrimination in contracts not only easier but legally imperative. The October 1967 amendment of President Johnson's Executive Order 11246 to require federal contractors not to discriminate on the basis of sex and to undertake affirmative-action programs to rectify the effects of past discrimination was another long-sought means of securing equality.[17] But more subtle forms of discrimination persisted. Departmental or occupational group seniority arrangements, for example, could be discriminatory in effect if not in intent by denying women equal access to employment. Occupational segregation by sex also masked wage imparities between male and female auto workers. These were difficult problems, and the obstacles to solving them loomed large. On the one hand, narrow judicial and administrative interpretations of federal antidiscriminatory statutes were inadequate for a thoroughgoing attack on the sexual division of labor in the auto industry. On the other hand, there was much evidence that men still regarded women as threats to wage standards and as competitors for jobs. Since the prospects of securing the active support of the male majority for an extensive revision of women's place in the industry were dim, the Women's Department focused its energy and resources on removing the impediments to equal opportunity posed by female

16. Harrison, *On Account of Sex*, pp. 37, 199–200, 205; Olya Margolin to Andrew Biemiller, quoted, ibid., p. 195; Leila Rupp and Verta Taylor, *Survival in the Doldrums* (New York, 1987), pp. 144–53. The UAW disaffiliated from the AFL-CIO in 1968 over differences in foreign policy, civil rights, organizational drives, and other union and political issues. Although I have not found any direct evidence to support such an argument, it is possible that this action freed the UAW from any obligation to oppose the ERA and contributed to its endorsement of the amendment in 1970. John Barnard, *Walter Reuther and the Rise of the Auto Workers* (Boston, 1983), pp. 177–98.

17. Harrison, *On Account of Sex*, pp. 198, 201–2; Freeman, *The Politics of Women's Liberation*, p. 191.

labor laws. It seemed easier to press for change in the political arena outside the UAW than to mobilize enough enthusiasm and action within the organization to eliminate gender inequality in the labor market.

It is ironic that in deciding to take the path of least resistance, the Women's Department stumbled into a hornet's nest of controversy. The challenge to hours-limitation laws was the most nettlesome issue. By seeking women's access to overtime hours and pay, those who advocated repeal of state statutes regulating the employment of women appeared to be working at cross purposes with those in the UAW who demanded relief from mandatory overtime. The seemingly contradictory aims of the two forces within the UAW gave rise to debate, principally among women, over feminism and unionism. The most interesting critics of repeal believed that sexual discrimination was wrong and that the UAW ought to press for its elimination. Their challenge demonstrates the persistent divisions among UAW women over the meaning of gender equality.

The most concerted effort to challenge the drive for repeal of hours-limitation laws was made by women of UAW Local 3. The local, which represented production workers at Chrysler's huge auto works in Hamtramck, Michigan, had a history of militancy in behalf of gender equality. The most notable instance occurred in the late 1950s, when, in response to the elimination of jobs held by eight hundred women, the local successfully pressed for the integration of women into traditionally male jobs. More recently, the Local 3 Women's Committee had castigated Dodge Main management for denying women jobs, in violation of Title VII, and had vowed to use union, state, and federal resources to "assert the rights of women as first-class human beings." The same women who mobilized collective actions to demand equal opportunity for women in hiring, however, so vehemently disagreed with the effort to repeal Michigan's hours limitation law that they joined forces with others in the state to lobby against repeal, and filed a lawsuit for an injunction to stay implementation of a decision by the Michigan legislature to suspend the hours limitation statute.[18]

Local 3 women opposed repeal partly on feminist grounds and partly on class grounds. They defended the interests of women in

18. "Local 3 Women's Committee Protest Discrimination in Hiring of Women," *UAW Women's Department Special Bulletin*, January–February 1966, p. 5; Dorothy Haener to Caroline Davis, September 4, 1968, Reuther Collection, Box 172, Folder 19; *Detroit News*, December 28, 1968.

unorganized occupations, who, they asserted, needed the protection against harsh working conditions that the state law provided. They also underscored the difficult situation in which even UAW women who were self-supporting heads of households with small children or invalid husbands would find themselves if compelled to work in excess of their regularly scheduled shifts. Local 3 women, however, also argued that the hours limitation law for women offered "a small measure of protection against inhuman work schedules" and that it should be retained until legislation that made overtime voluntary on the part of the employee was passed or until a voluntary-overtime provision was incorporated into collective-bargaining agreements. Repeal the hours-limitation law for women but overlook the need for a voluntary-overtime provision, they warned, and all workers would be "left to the mercy of unscrupulous employers," which would demand more labor from some employees while laying off others or refusing to hire new, job-hungry workers to assume the increased production load. "How can we hope to see an end to compulsory overtime for all workers," asked Edith Fox of Local 3, "if we now favor repeal? How can we hope to realize our goal of a 30 hour week at 40 hours pay, when we insist on repeal of the 54 hour limit in exchange for no limits—resulting in possibly 10 or 12 hour days, six to seven day weeks?" The Women's Department, Local 3 activists charged, was playing a dangerous and destructive game, since re-peal of the hours-limitation law would undermine rather than en-hance efforts to achieve a voluntary-overtime act and thus would benefit employers at the expense of workers. The implication was that by condemning women to brutal working conditions, advocates of repeal were betraying not only feminism but unionism and class solidarity as well.[19]

Others in the UAW came forward to criticize the position taken by the Women's Department and by extension the international union. Emily Rosdolsky, an international staff member, indicated her dis-tress about the campaign for repeal in a letter to Walter Reuther. Claiming that the poorest and most exploited working women would be the most negatively affected by repeal, Rosdolsky noted that "the traditional concerns of the labor movement in this country and other countries for protecting women from excessively long hours of work

19. *Dodge Main News*, November 23, 1968, February 28, 1969, December 6, 1969, and March 7, 1970; "Attention: Women Members of Local 3," flyer, n.d. [February 1969], Mildred Jeffrey Collection, Box 42, Folder 5, ALUA.

is still valid" and warned that "it would be harmful to the image of the UAW if it seemingly ignores the interest of these working women to pursue what it believes to be in the interest of its own members." Rosdolsky echoed the concern of Local 3 women about the lack of legislative or contractual protection against compulsory overtime for all workers regardless of sex and urged Reuther not to advocate "the repeal of a law which shields at least women against such shocking work practices." Like the Local 3 group, Rosdolsky argued from a feminist position grounded in a working-class perspective. "Even though we would all prefer it if men enjoyed the same protection," she concluded, the principle of gender equality advanced by repeal would be cold comfort to a woman forced to work against her will for sixty or seventy hours per week.[20]

Supporters of the repeal effort were quick to poke holes in such arguments. Responsibility for the lack of voluntary-overtime legislation and contract clauses, they noted, lay not with the UAW, which called for them, but with state legislators and private employers who opposed them. A feminist with a working-class perspective, moreover, could support repeal. "Nothing is more disturbing," Dorothy Haener of the Women's Department said in reference to Rosdolsky and the Local 3 Women's Committee, "than their ability to drip tears of blood . . . to retain protective laws for the overworked, overburdened, underpaid women while, without any indignation, they tacitly accept and ignore the refusal of employers to hire them on $3.50 an hour jobs using these same laws as justification." The critics of repeal, however, had raised an important question about the consequences of one strategy for achieving equality in the workplace. Advocates of sex-blind treatment had never adopted an extremist stance. *How to Be Equal though Different—Working Women Today* read the title of a 1963 Women's Department pamphlet. Laws that "really are protective," stated Stephen Schlossberg in 1967, "need to be preserved." Legislation mandating separate restrooms, job modifications for pregnant workers, and maternity leaves were acceptable because they were based "on biological facts not stereotypes," he explained. But because these issues conflicted with the view that women and men were equal as human beings, they had been muted in the pursuit of gender equality and the elimination of female labor laws. The Local 3 Women's Committee and Emily Rosdolsky, how-

20. Rosdolsky to Reuther, March 3, 1969, Reuther Collection, Box 119, Folder 11.

ever, forced opponents of female labor laws to confront such inconsistencies and to reassert their positions.[21]

In response to this challenge, advocates of repeal offered arguments and strategies that promoted class and gender interests simultaneously. The very existence of hours-limitation laws for women only, they contended, divided workers and precluded solidarity. Moreover, Ann Lefebvre of Local 148 in Long Beach, California, noted that employers and politicians tricked male workers into endorsing female labor laws as a defense of conventional gender ideology but then used the same laws to justify excessive compulsory overtime. "Who," she asked rhetorically, "is discriminated against? We the women with protective laws, or you, the men that make the laws and are penalized [if you] won't work ten hours a day, seven days a week?" Others argued for the extension of hours-limitation laws to men as an expedient solution to the problem. "I don't believe that state laws should be used to discriminate against women," asserted Marlea Stefanski at the 1968 convention. "I don't think they should use the working hour sections to deprive us of income." But, she added: "I don't think they should work you guys to death, either. So if one segment of this society is going to be governed by the number of hours that they can work, I think this should apply to all workers." Frances Rogers of Ford Local 600 criticized men "who will work until the sweat just comes right off of them and they are just about ready to bleed" for undermining union action against excessive overtime. Although she preferred to see the hours limitation law for women repealed in the interest of gender equality and individual freedom, Rogers said she also would accept an extension of the law to men as an alternate way of addressing the problem of mandatory overtime without reinforcing occupational segregation by sex. "This way we can see that we [all] are benefiting and none of us should have to work these long backbreaking hours."[22]

As UAW women indicated in their arguments, the matter of hours of employment was not just a women's issue but one for all union members. The response of men to the problem of compulsory over-

21. Haener to Walter Reuther, April 18, 1969, Reuther Collection, Box 173, Folder 2; Irving Bluestone to Dorothy Haener, June 18, 1963, ibid., Box 172, Folder 12; Schlossberg statement, ibid., Box 118, Folder 12.

22. UAW, *Proceedings, Special UAW Collective Bargaining Convention, April 20–22, 1967* (hereafter cited as *1967 Special Convention Proceedings*), p. 103; UAW, *Proceedings, 21st Constitutional Convention, May 4–10, 1968* (hereafter cited as *1968 Convention Proceedings*), pp. 130–32.

time also indicates the potential of the hours issue to subvert the customarily marginal status of women's concerns. Some men criticized mandatory overtime because it prevented all auto workers from fulfilling domestic responsibilities, an argument reminiscent of that originally made for legal protection of working women. The 1967 collective-bargaining convention, for example, adopted a resolution asserting that "the end purpose of industrial and economic activity" was "to lift the human family to new heights of economic well-being and to enhance the quality of human life" and condemning employers that regarded workers as "tools of production, to be . . . pushed about at management whim as if they belonged to the corporations and had no separate and prior life of their own." The resolution also contended, "For many of our members, compulsory, excessive overtime is a great personal inconvenience which keeps them from their families and prevents their taking care of matters of personal or family concern."[23]

Male auto unionists, however, never integrated the debate over female labor laws with the debate over excessive and compulsory overtime. Women themselves made such connections in the course of their own discussions, and the text of the Women in the UAW resolution adopted during the 1970 convention asserted that the UAW should "make every effort to have maximum hours of work . . . extended to all workers by legislation on the federal and state level." But a different resolution stating the union's legislative goals and also adopted by the delegates contained no reference to extending to men the protection of hours-limitation laws. Even men who believed that protective labor laws discriminated against women in favor of men did not suggest that both sexes would benefit from such laws. Immediately after Frances Rogers called for the extension to men of hours-limitation laws during discussion of the Women in the UAW resolution at the 1968 convention, Doug Griffith of Local 148 declared that such legislation for women "violates the rights of our women workers" and asked the convention "to go on record in support of equal rights for women on this point of overtime, that women should have the same choice of overtime that our male workers do."[24]

The solutions proposed by union men to the problem of excessive, compulsory overtime also tended to reinforce the marginal status of

23. *1967 Special Convention Proceedings*, p. 90.
24. *1968 Convention Proceedings*, p. 132; UAW, *Proceedings, 22nd Constitutional Convention, April 1970*, p. 278.

women in the UAW. The principal strategy advocated was, as Ray Ashby of Local 659 put it, to "make overtime so expensive to management that they themselves will turn it down for us." Specifically, this meant seeking an increase in the legal penalty for overtime from the standard time-and-a-half to double or triple time and negotiating a substantial increase in wage rates. These solutions, while not intrinsically related to gender in meaning or implication, sustained the position of those men who, in commenting on the issues raised by excessive hours and mandatory overtime, not only mourned the passing of the traditional "family wage" but desired its return. One male delegate at the 1967 collective-bargaining convention implored union leaders to negotiate a wage increase that would enable men to resist the lure of overtime pay and would restore the standard of the family wage. "I remember back in the '30s," he began, "when the Bureau of Labor Statistics used to print the income of the average American worker. It was the average American worker. It was the individual worker. It was the family head. Today they don't do that anymore. They print the income of the family unit. The old man is working, the old lady is working. Maybe the old man is working overtime. We have forgotten what it is . . . to live on a 40 hour pay." The delegate clearly understood the "average American worker" and "the family head" to be male. To emphasize the inadequacy of a (male) wage to support a family, he offered the example of "a young fellow that is working 40 hours, he hasn't got a wife that is working, he isn't working any overtime . . . [and] he isn't moonlighting." That man "can't make ends meet." "Now, how can we honestly tell people they should give up their overtime," the delegate contended, "when they can't live on a 40 hour week?" "The fat is there on the corporations," he concluded. "They got it. It is up to us to get out there and get it. And if we don't, shame on us." Although the absence of the 170,000 women then employed in the auto industry from this man's vision of the moral purpose of unionism is especially glaring, the invisibility of women in the language and perspective of male auto unionists was not unusual. During the same convention discussion, Local 980 delegate Robert Richardson condemned excessive, compulsory overtime, explaining, "Children of the workers in the shop are disturbed . . . because they do not see their fathers enough." To be sure, not all male auto unionists in the 1960s still shared the once pervasive assumption that auto workers were ipso facto male. Nor did all men who commented on the problem of excessive, compulsory overtime justify the necessity of higher pay in terms of a defense of the family wage. But neither did anyone during the course of these discussions counter formulations that rested on a view of women as reproducers of the labor force, dependents of men, and secondary wage earners.[25]

The trend of administrative and judicial interpretations of the relationship of Title VII to state laws rendered moot much of the debate over hours limitation laws. In August 1969 the EEOC announced that state laws restricting employment opportunities for women conflicted with Title VII. Confirming this statement of policy, the Michigan attorney general in January 1970 ruled specifically that Title VII superseded the still-contested state statute limiting the number of hours women could be employed. At its biannual convention several months later, the UAW became the first union in the nation ever to endorse the ERA. Although the Women's Department may have appeared to Local 3 activists and Emily Rosdolsky to have had the international leadership in its hip pocket, Caroline Davis and Dorothy Haener knew better. Certainly the position on gender equality which they had advanced since the late 1940s gained adherents in the 1960s and was firmly embedded in UAW policy by the 1970s. But the discrepancy between policy and practice remained. Mindful of the UAW's rhetorical commitment to advance the principle of gender equality, Paul Schrade, director of the union's California region, criticized what he deemed the too tepid response of GM Department director Leonard Woodcock to the EEOC's statement in August 1969 regarding female labor laws. "After many years of struggle," Schrade began, Woodcock "recognizes the problems, yet, suggests only that . . . we *may* want to file selective cases. . . . Shouldn't we have a more positive position and strategy from the IEB to break into this area of discrimination against women?" Asked how UAW leaders responded to the Women's Department's attack on protective labor laws for women, Dorothy Haener admitted that when the union "got publicity because you're far out in front and so forth and liberal, they liked that, but when this really started hitting close to home, they tended not to be all that happy with it." "The leadership has never been terribly happy with having these concepts implemented," Haener added, "especially when it hits them personally." Undertones of bitterness, frustration, and betrayal color even Haener's correspondence and memorandums from this period, confirming the retrospective observations about the marginality of the Women's Depart-

25. *1967 Special Convention Proceedings*, pp. 99, 65, 87–88.

ment that she made in a 1977 interview. Such comments suggest the extent to which the IEB's endorsement of the Women's Department's quest to abolish female labor laws may have been more a matter of convenience than an expression of shared concern about the sexual division of labor and woman's place in the plants. The department's decision to seek the elimination of state laws did, after all, take the heat off UAW leaders to challenge gender hierarchy and inequality in the workplace more aggressively and to acknowledge that responsibility for these problems lay with the union as much as with employers or government.[26]

The UAW's endorsement of the ERA and the amendment's implicit definition of gender equality was a bittersweet victory not only for the Women's Department and its allies but for women auto workers in general. The UAW in fact made almost no progress toward the goal of voluntary overtime after state laws restricting the number of hours women could be employed were found to be in conflict with Title VII. In this respect, the critics of the Women's Department who had argued that the union's renunciation of the principle of protection embodied in female labor laws contradicted its call for legislation making overtime voluntary for all employees proved both astute and prescient. It is particularly ironic that the Women's Department and union feminists began calling for a national child care policy only after women workers complained that the persistent scheduling of mandatory overtime wreaked havoc with individual child-care arrangements. In evaluating the UAW's response to the problem of excessive, mandatory overtime, it is important to observe that many workers wanted overtime and resisted attempts to eliminate or even curtail it. But the lassitude of UAW leaders in regard to the matter also indicates ironically how a certain definition of gender equality can reinforce the marginality of women. Having decided that gender equality means that women should be treated like men, male UAW leaders did not consider that men could be treated like women and receive legal protection from excessive overtime.[27]

26. Freeman, *Politics of Women's Liberation*, p. 187; Leonard Woodcock to All GM Local Unions, August 28, 1969, Reuther Collection, Box 217, Folder 10; "Women Hail Jobs Ruling," *Solidarity*, October 1969, p. 15; Woodcock to GM Locals in Michigan, March 19, 1970, Woodcock Collection, Box 12, Folder 9; Schrade to Walter Reuther, September 18, 1969, Reuther Collection, Box 217, Folder 10; Haener interview, p. 64; Haener to Walter Reuther, April 18, 1969, Reuther Collection, Box 173, Folder 2; Haener to Caroline Davis, September 4, 1968, ibid., Box 172, Folder 19.
27. William Serrin, *The Company and the Union* (New York, 1974), pp. 328, 334–37.

The sense of isolation felt by UAW feminists in the 1960s and the persistent marginality of issues regarded as women's indicated the importance of challenging sexual discrimination in the union as well as in the plants. Women activists were not oblivious to the constraints imposed by male prejudice on female participation and power in the union. But until the sixties they tended to regard the organization as the only vehicle for achieving equality for women in the workplace and thus were reluctant to criticize it. In the 1960s and 1970s a variety of factors prompted women to assess the union more critically and to see it as part of the problem at the same time as it offered a solution. The favorable climate for political and social reform, concern about discrimination on the basis of ascriptive and descriptive traits, the resurgence of feminism and the emergence of new allies outside the UAW and the labor movement, the rejection of biological determinism in regard to sex roles, and even the new orientation of working women, more of whom aspired to careers in the labor movement, all encouraged women in the UAW to reconsider their place within the institution.

The campaign for a woman on the IEB reflected these new concerns. Launched in the winter of 1964, it culminated in the election of Olga Madar as board member at large in May 1966. The idea for the campaign was not new; it dated back at least as far as 1937, when Katherine Wilk decried the absence of women from the IEB during the second UAW convention. More recently, the idea had been bantered about by union activists since the Women's Bureau had attained departmental status in 1955. The decision actually to mount a campaign was made in part because advocates of racial equality had successfully pressed for black representation on the board in 1962. To avoid the impossible task of fielding a black candidate with sufficient support to win election to the IEB by unseating a regional director or one of the top international officers, civil rights activists convinced union leaders to propose a constitutional change expanding the IEB to include the new post of board member at large. Some women believed the same favor would be extended to them in 1964. With no action forthcoming and emboldened by the earlier success of black unionists, a group comprising the women holding international staff positions at Solidarity House decided in January 1964 to demand the same consideration.[28]

28. Madar notes for February meeting with IEB, n.d., Olga Madar Collection (unprocessed), Box 1, 1964 Attempt Folder 1, ALUA; *Detroit News*, March 1, 1964; Vera Lentine to Walter Reuther, February 29, 1964, Reuther Collection, Box 70, Folder 6.

A new political strategy only partly accounts for the effort to elect a woman to the IEB in 1964. An equally important motivation was the growing concern with the paltry number of women in international staff positions. Women represented 12.5 percent of the UAW's 1.2 million members in 1964, but only ten of the seven hundred international representatives were female. Meeting with Walter Reuther to inform him of the plan to push for election of a woman to the IEB, Olga Madar applauded the UAW's progress in providing equal opportunity for women in the plants and the local unions. But, she explained, "the fact that we [can] get all UAW women staff except for the two in the field in [this room] without crowding" indicated the relative lack of progress at the international level. Describing the absence of women on the international staff as "blinding," Frances Parks of Grand Rapids, Michigan, told the delegates to the 1964 convention: "It is time to discontinue the policy of this Union in practicing personal prejudice against women. We are not second class citizens and no longer should we tolerate the double standards in our Union." Contrary to those who blamed the low number of female staffers on women's inexperience, proponents such as Parks charged discrimination. "Even where the ability of the woman member is equal [to] and in many cases exceeds that of a male member," Parks stated, "the woman member is bypassed strictly because of her sex." Campaign leaders argued for the election of a woman to the board as a practical short-run solution to the problem, a female board member being more likely to offer women staff positions. In the long run, they hoped that the successful performance of a woman on the IEB and of women staffers would change the minds of male union leaders about the abilities of women and convince them to begin hiring women. Appealing to UAW leaders' pride in the organization, advocates also contended that the election of a woman to the IEB would fulfill the UAW's commitment to social progress and promote its public image as a proponent of social justice. The request for female representation on the IEB should not be deemed "unusual," said Madar to the board in February, "because you have long said that you believe in the equality we are asking for." "You must practice what you preach," Nadine Brown, a black civil rights activist from Chrysler-Jefferson Local 490 in Detroit, told the male convention delegates.[29]

29. Madar notes for February 4, 1964, meeting with Reuther, n.d., Madar Collection (unprocessed), Box 1, 1964 Attempt Folder 1; "You Can't Ignore the Facts of Life!!!" flyer, n.d. [February 1964], Women's Department–Lillian Hatcher Collection, Box 2,

The group of women who initiated the campaign in 1964 were not without supporters inside and outside Solidarity House. Not surprisingly, women unionists expressed their accord. "I am with you 100%," wrote Doris Thom, recording secretary of Local 95 in Janesville, Wisconsin. "It is something which has been *needed* for some time." Thelma Cummins reported to Olga Madar that all three convention delegates from Local 941 in Elkhart, Indiana, "agreed it was time" to elect a woman to the IEB. "I declined nomination to run for delegate to the Convention," Cummins ruefully concluded. "Now I wish I were going." Meetings held at Detroit-area UAW locals to mobilize support among the rank and file drew hundreds of unionists, most of them women. One held for Local 212 members resulted in a petition signed by 221 people, 87 percent of whom were female. But men were not uniformly hostile. The male president of Local 850 in Buffalo, New York, thought the request for election of a woman to the IEB "just" and offered "to lend any support to this movement that I possibly can." Daniel Giesin, president of the Dana Unit of Local 889 in Ecorse, Michigan, informed Walter Reuther of his group's unanimous endorsement of the effort to add a woman to the board and averred, "Women's participation means added strength to the Union." In another unanimous decision, the executive board of Chrysler Local 51 in Detroit voted "for the cause of the women," reported local recording secretary Stanley Kuprey, partly because Dorothy Knight, a Local 51 officer and leader of the campaign to elect a woman to the IEB, "made it very clear that a woman, if elected to the International Board[,] would by no means represent only women. She would work the same as any Board Member." Of the forty-two UAW members of the Macomb County, Michigan, AFL-CIO Council who signed a petition in support of the election of a woman to the IEB, all but one were male. Campaign leaders also were careful to seek the advice and support of the UAW's black activists. Willoughby Abner, Luther Slinkard, Nadine Brown, Buddy Battle, and Octavia Hawkins were among those prominent black auto unionists who actively supported the campaign to further integrate the IEB. Lacking IEB endorsement, the group turned for support to the National Steering Committee (NSC), an assembly of local presidents

Folder 3; Edith Van Horn to Olga Madar, February 7, 1964, Woodcock Collection, Box 35, Folder 9; Vera Lentine to Walter Reuther, February 29, 1964, Reuther Collection, Box 70, Folder 6; UAW, *Proceedings, 19th Constitutional Convention, March 1964* (hereafter cited as *1964 Convention Proceedings*), pp. 385–86, 430.

and other union leaders which determines the substance and direction of UAW conventions. Although the committee as a whole preferred to postpone action on the proposal until the convention, at least seven NSC members promised to approve the plan and another thirteen vowed to speak in favor of the plan at the steering-committee meeting. Finally, even Walter Reuther supported the plan and was "extremely helpful," according to Madar, offering the group encouragement as well as practical advice.[30]

But despite the support, the attempt to elect a woman to the IEB failed in 1964. The late starting date of the campaign contributed to its defeat. Beginning a scant eight weeks before the convention was scheduled to commence in March, the group had inadequate time fully to mobilize support among those leaders who determined convention actions. The character and extent of opposition to the campaign also did not bode well. An oft-repeated argument was that any qualified candidate, regardless of sex, would be elected to any position in the UAW. The absence of women from the IEB, then, reflected not prejudice but the lack of qualified women. Moreover, to specify the sex of a board member, opponents claimed, was to practice discrimination. Others contended more boldly that women simply were unqualified by nature for union leadership. Although Reuther approved the effort to elect a woman, several of his fellow top officers, including Emil Mazey, UAW secretary-treasurer, and Leonard Woodcock, a union vice-president and director of the UAW GM Department, did not. Mazey publicly lampooned the campaign, telling a *Detroit News* reporter: "Women have equality—plus. They've been seeking equal rights for centuries. One of these days they'll get it and it'll serve 'em right." Others were even less kind, criticizing women as "pussycats" unsuited to the difficult "manly" work required of board members, such as organizing and collective bargaining. Others, from whom support was expected, either did not come through or were less than enthusiastic. Some NSC members, for example, expressed

30. Responses from Local 850 and Doris Thom, Madar Collection (unprocessed), Box 1, 1964 Attempt Folder 1; Thelma Cummins to Olga Madar, February 26, 1964, ibid.; Giesin to Walter P. Reuther, March 4, 1964, Reuther Collection, Box 70, Folder 6; Macomb County petition, n.d., attached to Darlene Metz to Walter Reuther, March 5, 1964, ibid.; Stanley Kuprey to Walter Reuther, March 5, 1964, ibid.; National Steering Committee Commitments, n.d. [1964], Madar Collection (unprocessed), Box 1, 1964 Attempt Folder 2; *Detroit News*, March 1, 1964; Local 212 list, n.d., Madar Collection (unprocessed), Box 1, 1964 Attempt Folder 2; Madar 1964 calendar, entry for February 4, 1964, ibid., Folder 1; Lillian Hatcher notes on February 14, 1964, meeting with black leaders, Women's Department–Lillian Hatcher Collection, Box 10, Folder 8.

their verbal support but then refused to declare their position publicly and urged delay. Campaign leaders also suspected that members of the influential Trade Union Leadership Council (TULC), formed in 1958 to bring blacks into leadership positions in unions and politics, withheld support from the effort to elect a woman to the IEB. Madar, recalling her own less visible, behind-the-scenes advocacy of the TULC effort to desegregate the all-white IEB in 1962, gave council leaders the benefit of the doubt, concluding in a letter to Horace Sheffield that they may have acted similarly "when our production was staged." But the TULC had "a limited concept of equitable representation on labor's policy making boards," Madar charged. "Throughout the events of these past two months," she complained, "I had the sensation that I had seen the 'play' before but some of the cast were missing or missed their cues and did not appear on stage." Perhaps the most bitter pill to swallow was the silence of Walter Reuther. He may have expressed his favor in private, but the UAW president refused to indicate his support in public. Consoling themselves that at least Reuther had not openly criticized the campaign, campaign leaders attracted two hundred women and twenty men to a meeting at the end of the convention. They formed a new organization to be led by unionists outside Solidarity House, christened the new group Help Equalize Representation (HER), and vowed to win in 1966.[31]

The campaign to elect a woman to the IEB was successful in 1966. Organizers were careful not to make the same mistakes twice. To demonstrate the extent of support among men and within the rank and file, Gino Serafini, president of Local 51, joined HER as vice-chairman, and Local 51 was designated the group's headquarters. HER's steering committee was enlarged to include representatives from every region in the UAW; a special effort was made to include at least one man for every three women. HER began in the fall of 1965 to press Reuther and the IEB for early consideration of its intents and purposes. Reminding them of the unfavorable light in which the male leadership was cast at the 1964 convention following its rejection of a female presence on the board, HER officers Joanne Wilson, a

31. David Cooper to Olga Madar, February 28, 1964, Reuther Collection, Box 70, Folder 6; *Detroit News*, March 8, 1964; Madar datebook entry for February 11, 1964, Madar Collection (unprocessed), Box 1, 1964 and 1965–66 Folder; *1964 Convention Proceedings*, pp. 385–86, 430; *Toronto Telegram*, June 19, 1964, clipping in Reuther Collection, Box 103, Folder 16; Madar to Sheffield, n.d. [March 1964], Madar Collection (unprocessed), Box 1, 1964 Attempt Folder 1; *Detroit News*, March 26, 1964.

white woman from Region 2B, and Elizabeth Jackson, a black woman from Ford Local 600 (the largest local in the UAW), confessed that they were "torn between the need to launch our campaign and the realization that our action might precipitate unfavorable publicity for our Union." HER suggested in December that Reuther and the IEB avoid the possibility of bad blood and bad press by recommending early on both the addition of a member-at-large position to the board and the nomination of a woman as a candidate for the new spot. Although Reuther and a majority of the board favored the plan, they declined to take action so soon.[32]

In the five months before the May 1966 convention, HER sought to demonstrate the extent of support for the project. In contrast to his earlier detachment, Reuther worked more closely with HER, suggesting strategies for the campaign; he also was not reticent this time in professing his endorsement of the plan to union leaders. In February the UAW president went so far as to solicit from HER the names of women leaders for possible nomination, another action that assured HER activists of the better prospects for this campaign. HER took advantage of the greater amount of time available in this campaign to solicit local union endorsements of the plan on a wider scale than had been possible in 1964. The group also carefully courted NSC members in anticipation of their consideration of the proposal to increase the number of member-at-large slots and to nominate a woman as candidate for the new position. In April HER was rewarded for its persistence and perseverance when the IEB voted sixteen to eight with one abstention to recommend the addition of a member-at-large seat to the board. The intent, explained Leonard Woodcock, was "to enlarge the administrative team of the International Union to meet the increasing challenge that we face in this world of great social change and to make us better armed as a total Union to meet all of the problems we face as America's most progressive Union." Although expressed in an awkward and defensive manner, the announcement practically ensured the election of a woman to the IEB. "Through your leadership and foresight," glowed Edie Van Horn to Walter Reuther, "the UAW women are 'UPWARD BOUND.' Thank you."[33]

32. Joanne Wilson and Elizabeth Jackson to Walter Reuther, December 6, 1965, Reuther Collection, Box 103, Folder 16.

33. Olga Madar to HER officers, October 21, 1965, Reuther Collection, Box 103, Folder 16; HER officers' notes for meeting with Walter Reuther, n.d. [December 1965–January 1966], ibid.; Madar to Reuther, February 11, 1966, ibid.; *Detroit News*, February

The next hurdles were to gain convention approval of the constitutional change and then actually to elect a woman to the board. The
first was surmounted after thirty-five minutes of debate by a six-to-
one vote. Although the character of the comments made by men who
opposed the plan indicated the persistent extent of resistance, serious
conflict arose only with the matter of nominations for the new position. HER preferred that one of the women on the staff of the international union receive the nod, partly to counter claims that no woman
had sufficient experience to sit on the IEB. By convention time the
leading candidates were Caroline Davis, Edie Van Horn, Florence
Peterson, and Olga Madar. Because of her position as long-time
director of the Women's Department, Davis had the inside track. Van
Horn, who had led the fight to integrate women into male-dominated
jobs at Dodge Main in the late 1950s, was a comparative newcomer to
Solidarity House, having joined the Citizenship Department in 1963.
Peterson had longer tenure on the international staff than Van Horn
and, because of her work in the union's retirees' program, had support from a different constituency than the other candidates. Although Madar had little collective-bargaining experience—a distinct
liability for a board member—she was one of only three women with
experience directing international departments (the other two being
Caroline Davis and Mildred Jeffrey). But many argued that a woman
from the local level rather than the international staff deserved the
nomination. Some people who opposed the Solidarity House candidates actually disapproved of the very idea of a woman on the IEB or
resented the administration's heavy hand in directing convention
actions. But others, who staunchly supported the principle of female
representation, advocated a local candidate because they believed
there were women outside Solidarity House who had greater experience representing workers on the shop floor and in negotiating
contracts and who thus were better qualified to serve on the IEB.
Carolyn Maggio, Odessa Komer, Genevieve Nestor, and others who
were promoted as local union candidates had compiled impressive
leadership records and enjoyed the support of large local and re-

27, 1966; Elizabeth Jackson and Gino Serafini to [local union leaders], March 16, 1966,
ibid.; UAW, *Proceedings, 20th Constitutional Convention, May 16–21, 1966* (hereafter cited
as *1966 Convention Proceedings*), p. 135; Van Horn to Reuther, April 21, 1966, Reuther
Collection, Box 103, Folder 16. I have not seen any completely reliable tallies of the
IEB's voting on the election of a woman to the board. One source indicated that Ken
Robinson, Pat Patterson, Leonard Woodcock, Pat Greathouse, Patrick O'Malley, Martin Gerber, Ray Ross, and Ray Berndt opposed the motion. Notes, n.d. [April–May
1966], Madar Collection (unprocessed), Box 1, HER Folder.

gional memberships. If nothing else, the candidacies of such women attested to the significance of the UAW—despite its androcentrism—as an arena for women's activism. After Caroline Davis declined consideration for personal reasons, Olga Madar emerged as the Solidarity House candidate. In the interest of unity and, as Maggio explained, to prevent a man from slipping into the new seat on the board, all but one of the other female prospects endorsed Madar. Beverly Gibson, a delegate from the Canadian region, claimed to run as a fifth candidate for a member-at-large position to protest the alleged attempt by the administration to improve its public image by instating a token woman on the IEB. Her candidacy merely consolidated much of the anti-Reuther and antifeminist opposition to Madar as a Solidarity House nominee, and Gibson lost the election, although she had the satisfaction of having forced the first convention roll-call vote since 1955.[34]

The campaign to elect a woman to the IEB was a turning point for advocates of gender equality in the UAW. Heretofore concerned chiefly with discrimination against women in the plants, union leaders such as Olga Madar, Florence Peterson, and Dorothy Haener had themselves only recently recognized the problem of sexual discrimination at the top levels of the union itself. These women were not naive; those who had battled unionists as well as employers over women's right to fair and equal treatment were especially aware of the power of prejudice against women. They tended, however, to regard themselves and their own careers as exceptional. Believing themselves to be able, skilled, and effective unionists, they assumed that their appointments to the international staff were based on their individual qualifications. If prejudice impinged on their careers, it was only insofar as they were able to transcend it. Women's horizons within the UAW, however, were limited. Most importantly, appointments providing experience with national-level collective bargaining, the heart of the UAW's policy and practice, were denied them. As each woman confronted the obstacles to upward career mobility within the UAW, she began to see herself as affected by the same

34. Caroline [Davis] to Walter [Reuther], n.d. [May 1966], Reuther Collection, Box 103, Folder 16; *Detroit Free Press*, May 8, 17, 18, and 31, 1966; *Toledo Blade*, May 15 and 16, 1966, clippings in Madar Collection, Folder 1, ALUA; *Flint Journal*, May 17 and 19, 1966, ibid.; *Globe and Mail*, May 20, 1966, ibid.; *Detroit News*, May 20, 1966; *1966 Convention Proceedings*, pp. 86–91, 266–76. The results of the roll-call vote were 10,650.999 for Ken Bannon (incumbent); 10,674.655 for Nelson Jack Edwards (incumbent); 10,663.337 for Douglas Fraser (incumbent); 8,273.601 for Madar; and 2,818.684 for Gibson.

attitudes that circumscribed woman's place and derogated her status in auto plants. This collective process of revelation had in large part prompted the effort to elect a woman to the IEB. The rejection of women's claim to female representation on the board reinforced their sense of grievance and inspired them to continue the campaign after March 1964. "Let this convention floor be the launching pad to place the UAW women in orbit," Edie Van Horn announced, "to stop the sometimes subconscious, but, nevertheless, relegation of our women members—to place them in orbit throughout the staff of every region of this UAW and on the International Board in 1966."[35] Quite apart from the practical benefits to be won from electing a woman to the board, the symbolic importance of the movement's goal came to serve as a rallying point for supporters of women's rights and gender equality in the UAW in the 1960s.

The campaign to elect a woman to the IEB was significant for other reasons as well. In a positive sense, it unified the forces favoring gender equality in the UAW, provided them with an important victory, and demonstrated the existence of a large pool of talented and militant women leaders at the local level. But in a negative sense, the campaign also starkly exposed what women were up against insofar as attitudes were concerned. The convention debates made clear that some auto unionists rejected the idea of union recognition of women as a group because it violated their belief that the interests of one group should not be promoted at the expense of all. Although this argument served as a defense of male prerogatives for some, it was a fundamental article of working-class and union faith for others. The dismissal of the demand for a female presence on the board as well as for a larger fight to achieve gender equality also reflected the view— not only of auto unionists but of most Americans in the early to middle 1960s—that discrimination on the basis of sex either did not exist or was not as widespread, pervasive, and objectionable as discrimination on the basis of race. Some unionists doubted the ability of women to lead or to stand up to employers. Another view frequently expressed during the campaign was that women simply were uninterested in the union and did not actively participate in it. According to this perspective, since women evinced so little interest in the organization at the local level, they did not need special representation on the IEB or on the international staff. This argument also implied that the vast majority of the UAW's 170,000 female members

35. *1964 Convention Proceedings*, p. 424.

were content with the treatment accorded them by the union (if not also by employers) and did not share the sense of grievance that the few outspoken leaders claimed for them. The argument was specious in at least one important respect; the moans of local and international leaders in this period about poor attendance at union meetings attested to the fact that most men did not participate in the union either. But these claims demanded a response. In this way, the political challenge to male dominance of the IEB prompted consideration of the relationship of women to unionism and assessment of the strategies that were being employed to increase women's participation in the union.

Since its inception in 1944, the Women's Department had been responsible for increasing the level of women's involvement in the union. To this end, the department had engaged principally (although not exclusively) in gender-specific organizing. The assumption was that women regarded the androcentric union as an unfriendly environment and needed their own institutional spaces, such as women's committees or women's conferences. Although creating a place for women was a short-term goal of such organizing, the longer-term purpose was to provide women with both the practical skills and the confidence to further integrate themselves into the union. Women did use the groups and meetings as a jumping-off point for other activities. And some women's committees led bold actions reminiscent of the World War II and reconversion period; the Local 596 Women's Committee, for example, launched the attack in 1965 which culminated in the EEOC finding reasonable cause for the complaint that GM practiced widespread discrimination at the Fisher Body plant in Pontiac, Michigan. Women's committees, however, whether by choice or by request, often assumed responsibility for local fund raising, charitable activities, and social events. Such tasks were not in themselves detrimental; they minimally provided women with a sense of useful purpose. But these functions could become an end in themselves instead of a means to greater or different activities, thus confirming rather than challenging the auxiliary or marginal status accorded women and their activities by many male unionists. Some activists also suggested that excessive reliance on gender-specific organizing could hurt more than help the cause of women in the UAW because it encouraged men to believe that women's committees were not only the best but the only place for women in the union. Similarly there was concern that UAW leaders used the Women's Department to ghettoize women and to serve as window-dressing for the leaders' merely rhetorical commitment to gender equity. Florence Peterson, for example, thinks Caroline Davis reinforced the assumption that any woman on the international staff should work for the Women's Department by protesting whenever new female appointees were not assigned to her department. Although Davis's actions likely also reflected her constant frustration with limited resources and a too-small staff, Peterson's observation suggests the limits of gender-specific organizing and indicates one dimension of the dilemma that confronts women in a male-dominated institution.[36]

An alternate strategy was to bypass the gender-specific organizations and gain access to the existing structure. This effort required that women participate in meetings as members, seek office on union committees and local executive boards, and, as one woman asserted, demand respect as "UAW members instead of female members." Such a strategy, however, was not necessarily any more likely to facilitate female participation in the union. Not only did women have to learn how to navigate the treacherous waters of local union politics but they also had to confront all the widely held negative attitudes about their abilities and interests. Bette Murphy, whose involvement in Local 148 spanned several decades, claims that women like herself "weren't afraid of the devil himself." Local women leaders "had to be that way," Murphy explains, "because we were having a harder time throughout the years being accepted by the men."[37]

On the basis of its own experience in the 1950s, the Women's Department understood the limits of an approach based on assertions of gender sameness. The Republican ascendancy of the post–World War II era and organized labor's political misfortunes generated a great deal of concern about the political behavior of the rank and file. Women as wives and as workers came in for special criticism, since social scientists claimed that they as a group voted Re-

36. Mildred Jeffrey to Walter Reuther, May 15, 1946, Reuther Collection, Box 89, Folder 2; 1949 Convention Proceedings, p. 9; Caroline Davis to E. T. Michael, February 27, 1959, UAW Region 8 Collection, Box 20, Folder 15, ALUA; Kenneth Robinson to Lillian Hatcher, January 6, 1958, UAW Region 1D Collection, Box 35, Women's Department Folder, ALUA; UAW, Proceedings, 18th Constitutional Convention, 1962, pp. 444–47; interview with Lillian Hatcher, pp. 92–95, Twentieth Century Trade Union Woman Oral History Project; Gabin interview with Florence Peterson, October 17, 1985.

37. 1966 Convention Proceedings, p. 89; interview with Bette Murphy, pt. 1, p. 165, Rosie the Riveter Revisited: Women and the World War II Work Experience Oral History Project, California State University, Long Beach. For interesting insights into women's experience in local union politics, see Haener interview; interview with Odessa Komer, pp. 55–61, ibid.

publican more than men did. This observation confirmed the view widely held not only in the labor movement but throughout gender-conscious postwar society that women, because of their domestic orientation, were naturally more conservative and apolitical than men. To prove both the sameness of male and female members and the loyalty of women to the organization, the Women's Department tried mightily to politicize union women in this decade. Tremendous amounts of time and energy were spent, at the expense of the department's commitment to addressing women's job concerns, encouraging women not only to vote but to participate in electoral politics by distributing campaign literature, canvassing the electorate, and staffing Democratic headquarters. With relief as well as jubilation, Caroline Davis and Edie Van Horn, who coordinated the participation of Detroit-area women in the 1960 and 1962 elections, reported that pollsters and political scientists had found that more women than men voted for John F. Kennedy and other Democratic Party candidates. But the proof of women's equality did not translate into equal treatment or equal access. "Shouldn't we more fully realize the importance of developing and including women in our own organization, on all levels, all year round?" Van Horn queried in her report on the 1960 national election effort. "It is shocking to realize that our Citizenship and Education staff are exclusive 'male only' divisions," she continued. "This exclusive 'maleness' is downright unhealthy and weakens the strength of our union." The situation had not improved by 1962. "Shouldn't our special efforts to arouse women in political campaigns be a year-round proposition?" Van Horn asked. "When we strive to organize women into political activity, *must we operate like a sound truck*? . . . Turning the switch on and then off around election time?"[38]

If neither approach to activizing women was entirely successful, perhaps the key was to combine the approaches and then confront the obstacle posed by union men. Neither strategy as it was implemented before the mid-1960s directly challenged men's power and

38. CIO-PAC Planning Committee for Women's Conference minutes, June 2, 1953, UAW Political Action Department: Roy Reuther Files, Box 48, Folder 29, ALUA; Report on CIO-PAC Women's Conference, January 21, 1954, ibid., Box 49, Folder 1; Mildred Jeffrey, "CIO Family Participation Conference," n.d. [December 1955], ibid., Folder 2; Mildred Jeffrey to Roy Reuther, December 29, 1955, ibid.; Lillian Hatcher to Caroline Davis, December 6, 1960, Women's Department–Lillian Hatcher Collection, Box 1, Folder 15; Van Horn report, January 30, 1961, UAW Citizenship Department: Roy Reuther Files, Box 34, Folder 25, ALUA; Van Horn report, n.d. [December 1962], ibid., Box 37, Folder 7.

control in the union. Gender-specific organization could indeed marginalize women if they passively accepted their separate and unequal sphere. A gender-neutral strategy also was doomed if the problem of personal and institutional discrimination was not addressed. With the election of Olga Madar to the IEB, both strategies in combination and underlaid with a new willingness to criticize rather than accept male prerogatives helped to facilitate an upsurge in women's union activism. Women's conferences increased in number and frequency, and their content was altered. Instead of fashion shows and speeches by local judges on the problem of juvenile delinquency and by international officers on the importance of women stuffing envelopes and answering telephones at campaign headquarters in election years, there were workshops on plant problems such as as unequal pay, seniority violations, and maternity leaves. In response to demand from local women, more classes offering instruction in the grievance procedure, collective bargaining, and parliamentary procedure were given by the Women's Department and the regional offices. Another sign of increased union activism on the part of women was their greater attendance at regional women's conferences. The 1971 Detroit-area regional women's conference attracted 250 participants, twice as many as attended in the 1960s.[39]

Women's greater interest in workplace-oriented programming was accompanied by greater discontent with their exclusion from positions of power and influence. The National Advisory Council (NAC) to the Women's Department gave vent to its concerns in its 1967 recommendations to the IEB. Urging the board to take greater strides toward achieving the goal of equal opportunity for women in the plants, the NAC criticized union men for themselves practicing discrimination. "While women have become accustomed to rejection by their plant foremen," the representatives from all regions of the union stated, "they had come to expect different treatment from their union." But "the reluctance and resistance to affording them an equal opportunity to advancement in the union is causing many of our sisters to conclude that management men and union men are much alike in their reluctance to promote women." Encouraging the IEB to increase its appointment of women to staff positions, the NAC also requested "that women be given assignments and responsibilities in all areas of union interest rather than those considered to be only of

39. The material on women's conferences on which this paragraph is based is in Women's Department–Lillian Hatcher Collection, Boxes 5–9.

interest to women." Although oblique, the request indicated that women were themselves rejecting their ghettoization in the Women's Department and community service departments such as Recreation, Retirees, and Consumer Affairs. Eighteen months later, delegates to the Detroit-area regional women's conference recommended that the IEB "reevaluate" its record in promoting women in staff positions and that the UAW begin endorsing female unionists as candidates for political office and as appointees to government and public service agencies.[40]

In June 1972 the second international UAW women's conference was held at the UAW Educational Center in Black Lake, Michigan, twenty-eight years after the first meeting was convened in Detroit. Anticipating approximately 200 delegates, organizers were unprepared for the overflow crowd of 450 women from all over the United States and Canada. During the three-day conference, at a variety of workshops on employment subjects such as hiring practices, wages, seniority, and maternity leaves, delegates learned what the UAW, the federal government, and the women's movement had done and were doing for women. Hoping to inspire the UAW's 200,000 women members, Olga Madar took the opportunity provided by the conference to announce that she would not seek reelection to the IEB when her current term expired in 1974 and that she would spend her two remaining years in office encouraging women to increase their political participation within the union so that they themselves could determine her replacement. "I have no political constituency," Madar explained. "I feel women should develop one and pick their next vice-president rather than have the leadership do it." Calling for more "woman power" in the labor movement and in American politics, Caroline Davis declared: "Women are rebelling against discrimination. We are organizing. We are protesting. We are going to revolutionize society."[41]

The conference was a watershed event for women and the UAW. The turnout and the tone and substance of discussion over the course of the weekend demonstrated that the female membership cared about gender equality as much as top women leaders claimed they did. Conference delegates also effectively challenged male officers,

40. NAC recommendations, April 11, 1967, Reuther Collection, Box 172, Folder 16; resolutions, October 27–29, 1968, Women's Department–Lillian Hatcher Collection, Box 6, Folder 1.

41. Frances D'Hondt, "Women Have Their Say," UAW, Solidarity, September 1972, p. 3; Detroit News, June 25 and 26, 1972; Detroit Free Press, June 26, 1972.

such as Emil Mazey, who still held that the underrepresentation of women in the union's leadership ranks reflected women's disinterest rather than discrimination against them. "There is a difference between the opportunity of seeking leadership and the actual will of women to seek leadership," Mazey asserted in an interview in the month following the conference. But when he offered the example of an all-male bargaining committee in a local with a majority female membership, Mazey undermined his own position by also implying that women as a group were less able than men to stand up to the pressures of collective bargaining. "At the point they do and they show they have some ability," Mazey contended, "they will be elected." Such testimony to the persistent power of male prejudice against women simply confirmed the charges that women had been leveling at the UAW with increasingly greater force since the early 1960s.[42]

By the 1970s union feminists such as Dorothy Haener no longer felt so isolated and lonely. The development of a popular movement for gender equality in the plants and in the union greatly enhanced the status of these now historic goals. Although the union feminists all shared a commitment to the union as an advocate of their interests as workers, the movement was composed of people from different generations and backgrounds. The membership lists of the NAC and the regional women's committees in the 1970s include the names of retired World War II union pioneers such as Gertrude Kelly and Stella Deakins, of women who entered the industry in the 1950s as young wives intending—as so many married women did in the postwar era—to work only temporarily, and of younger women born after World War II who never doubted that their lives would be shaped by a permanent relationship to employment. Odessa Komer, who succeeded Olga Madar on the IEB and assumed responsibility for the Women's Department when Caroline Davis retired, remarked in the mid-1970s: "The most spirited women at our women's conferences . . . are very young women. They get on that floor and when they get through I just sit there and say 'Thank God.'" Contrasting her own generation to the younger one, Komer stated, "They're brought up different now."[43]

Komer may have been too self-deprecating in her observations

42. *Detroit News*, July 2, 1972.

43. Program, Women's Biennial Conference, Regions 1–1E, October 14–16, 1973, Women's Department–Lillian Hatcher Collection, Box 7, Folder 5; Komer interview, p. 45; *New York Times*, March 25, 1974.

about women who came of age in post–World War II America. The preference of auto-union women in the 1970s for the term *chairperson* instead of *chairman* does indicate the greater willingness of younger women to challenge convention. The new concern with sexual harassment in the workplace, too, not only was evidence and consequence of the greater integration of women in the plants but also reflected the impact of feminism, which provided the critique of such offensive behavior. Union women "were the first women's libbers," explained Olga Madar in 1974, but their fights for equal pay, single seniority lists, and other forms of equality did not move out into other areas. "The women's movement," Madar said, "gave an impetus to our moving ahead." The feminist movement outside the UAW certainly legitimized the union movement and provided fresh ideas and insights. But most striking are the similarities between past and present within the UAW. The emphasis on sex-blind treatment, so consistent with the history of gender advocacy in the UAW, underlay the successful effort in the 1970s, for example, to have pregnancy treated in gender-neutral terms as a medical disability insofar as insurance benefits, leaves of absence, and job-recall rights were concerned. Madar's comments notwithstanding, it is important to recognize the extent of continuity in the goals and purposes of women activists in the UAW from the 1940s through the 1970s.[44]

The formation of the Coalition of Labor Union Women (CLUW) in 1974 in many respects culminated the history of gender politics in the UAW. Interest in a union women's organization dated back to the late 1960s. Women from a number of unions, including the UAW, met informally in 1968 to discuss the lack of trade-union organization among women, the necessity of women becoming more active in union affairs, and the importance of meetings for trade-union women to discuss common problems. An organization called United Union Women, which included representatives of the Communications Workers of America, the Amalgamated Meat Cutters and Butcher Workmen, and the UAW, held a conference on working women's issues in Chicago in November 1969, but the group was short-lived. The situation became more favorable in the early 1970s.

44. National Advisory Council to the Women's Department, February 1974, Women's Department–Lillian Hatcher Collection, Box 10, Folder 12; UAW Administrative Letter, vol. 33, letter no. 1, 1981; Caroline Davis to All Women's Committee Chairwomen and Members, October 27, 1972, Women's Department–Lillian Hatcher Collection, Box 10, Folder 12; Leonard Woodcock to Officers and Regional Directors, October 31, 1972, ibid.; Instructions to International Representatives on Filing EEOC Charges Concerning Pregnancy, n.d. [October 1972], ibid.

In 1973 eight trade-union women, including Edie Van Horn and Olga Madar, arranged a Midwest regional conference of women unionists that attracted two hundred women. Interest was great enough to justify the calling of a national conference in March 1974, which was attended by more than three thousand women from fifty-eight unions. The largest single contingent at the founding convention of CLUW was from the UAW, and Olga Madar was elected president of the new organization. The goals and purposes of CLUW were synonymous with those of UAW women. Committed to advancing the position of women both as workers and as unionists, CLUW vowed to organize women workers, to demand sex-blind treatment in the workplace, and to encourage women to become more active and to gain a larger share of power and influence in the unions. Feminism clearly was influential in the formation of CLUW. "One result of this meeting," president-elect Madar said, "is that fewer and fewer union women will be saying 'we are not women's libbers.' By coming here, they have proved that they are." But as its slogan, "A Woman's Place Is in Her Union," indicates, CLUW asserted the importance of unionism as the principal vehicle for improving the status of working women. "We're trade-unionists first," Joyce Miller, an Amalgamated Clothing Workers leader and CLUW officer, said in 1975. "We are loyal to our unions. Within that framework, we want to advance the role of women."[45]

In choosing to work within the established framework of the still male-dominated labor movement, CLUW limited in certain ways its commitment to feminist principles. The resulting tension was apparent within CLUW and the UAW when the manufacturing sector began its decline and women and minority men—those with the least

45. Notes on Informal Meetings of Trade Union Women, Esther Peterson Collection, Box 20, Sept. 7–Minutes Folder #1, Schlesinger Library, Radcliffe College, Cambridge, Mass.; Esther Peterson to Lillian Hatcher, October 11, 1968, Women's Department–Lillian Hatcher Collection, Box 3, Folder 3; United Union Women material, ibid., Box 16, Folder 11; Edith Van Horn to Olga Madar, January 4, 1973, Coalition of Labor Union Women Collection, Box 2, Folder 1, ALUA; Barbara Wertheimer to Olga Madar, July 3, 1973, ibid., Folder 3; CLUW Agenda Committee memo, January 18, 1974, ibid., Box 1, Folder 1; CLUW Proposed Statement of Purpose, March 1974, ibid.; *New York Times*, March 25, 1974; *U.S. News & World Report*, March 17, 1975. On CLUW, see Diane Balser, *Sisterhood and Solidarity* (Boston, 1987), pp. 151–210; Philip Foner, *Women and the American Labor Movement from World War I to the Present*, (New York, 1980), pp. 516–36; Ruth Milkman, "Women Workers, Feminism and the Labor Movement since the 1960s," in Milkman, ed., *Women, Work, and Protest* (Boston, 1985), pp. 300–322; Nancy Seifer and Barbara Wertheimer, "New Approaches to Collective Power: Four Working Women's Organizations," in Bernice Cummings and Victoria Schuck, eds., *Women Organizing* (Metuchen, N.J., 1979), pp. 152–83.

seniority and in some sense the most to lose—were laid off in massive numbers. Despite the position adopted by NOW that the seniority principle was discriminatory in effect, CLUW leaders, like those in the UAW, defended seniority rights when they conflicted with the principles of affirmative action. "More women are losing their jobs who are in unorganized work places and do not have the protection of the seniority," Olga Madar maintained in a letter to Karen DeCrow, president of NOW, "than the number of women being laid off who are in organized work places and have the protection of seniority systems which, by the way, also protect their right to recall in line with their seniority." As they had since the 1940s, UAW women (and now their peers in CLUW) chose to emphasize gender sameness and equal treatment, in part because the strategy seemed most compatible with the preference in unions for gender-neutral class goals and purposes. The debate over affirmative action and seniority in the mid-1970s demonstrates the complex and contingent character of the process by which trade union women negotiate the competing although not necessarily mutually exclusive terms of feminism and unionism.[46]

Despite the massive layoffs of 1975, women in the UAW undeniably had made progress in the decade since the Equal Pay Act was passed. Once derided as "no woman's land," the UAW claimed 300,000 women as members; their 21 percent share of the total membership was a post–World War II high. The greater integration of women in the industry, rather than new organizing, largely accounted for the increase in the UAW's female membership. The entrance of women into the skilled trades was a major victory that received a great deal of attention within and without the industry. But equally as significant was the less obvious phenomenon of women gaining access to a larger proportion of unskilled production jobs. Women's share of the labor force in the transportation-equipment industry increased from 9 percent in 1971 to 13 percent in 1977. Under pressure from the UAW, the Department of Labor, and the EEOC, and despite the severe depression in the early 1980s which permanently contracted employment in the auto industry, the percentage of women among all employees in the industry continued to grow in the eighties. The ever-increasing involvement of women in the union

46. *Business Week*, February 16, 1974; CLUW Resolution on Affirmative Action and Seniority, May 31, 1975, Coalition of Labor Union Women Collection, Box 14, Folder 11; Madar to DeCrow, May 5, 1975, ibid., Folder 12.

despite the membership losses sustained during the depression offers additional testimony to the significance of the changes that
occurred in the 1960s and 1970s. Although the number of UAW
women fell to 150,000 at the end of the 1980s, the number of women
in the top four local union offices increased from 806 in 1973 to 1,500 in
1988; and the number of female local union presidents nearly doubled, from 77 in 1973 to 144 in 1988. By pressing the demand for
gender equality and equal treatment in the workplace and in the
union, UAW women and their allies not only accomplished a great
deal but established a legacy that endures.[47]

47. Percentages of Women in the UAW, n.d. [1973], Madar Collection (unprocessed), Box 3, UAW Local Women Officers Folder; "From Rosie the Riveter to Dolly the
Diemaker," *Solidarity*, December 1971, pp. 6–7; Janice Neipert Hedges and Stephen E.
Bemis, "Sex Stereotyping: Its Decline in Skilled Trades," *Monthly Labor Review* 97 (May
1974): 14–22; Bureau of Labor Statistics (BLS), *Employment and Earnings, United States,
1909–78, Bulletin 1312–11* (Washington, D.C., 1979), p. 351; BLS, *Supplement to Employment and Earnings, July 1984* (Washington, D.C., 1984), p.126; BLS, *Supplement to
Employment and Earnings, July 1987* (Washington, D.C., 1987), p. 80; *New York Times*,
November 26, 1980, and October 19, 1983; "A Woman's Work Is Never Done," *Solidarity*, March 1989, pp. 8–13. For discussion of the greater integration of women into
auto jobs during the 1970s and 1980s, see *Detroit Free Press*, May 27, 1973; *Business Week*,
August 14, 1978; Mary L. Walshok, *Blue-Collar Women* (Garden City, N.Y., 1981);
Richard Feldman and Michael Betzold, eds., *End of the Line* (New York, 1988). In
contrast to the classic interpretation of trends in female employment in manufacturing, the greater integration of women in the auto industry in the 1960s and 1970s
appears not to have been the consequence of the increasing mechanization or simplification of production processes. See BLS, *Technological Trends in Major American
Industries*, Bulletin No. 1474 (Washington, D.C., 1966), pp. 97–102; BLS, *Technological
Change and Its Labor Impact in Five Industries*, Bulletin No. 1961 (Washington, D.C.,
1977), pp. 23–33.

Conclusion

In 1944 Steve Kane criticized the women in his Chicago UAW local for "constantly ask[ing] for higher pay on the same basis as the men, instead of simply trying to maintain equality among the women." In May 1970 Olga Madar told the Senate Subcommittee on the Equal Rights Amendment that the UAW favored "equal treatment for men and women" and sought the removal of "all the legal impediments to the equal treatment of Americans, regardless of sex."[1] Nearly thirty years of change in the social position of women, the definition and status of the idea of equality, and the attitude of the UAW toward the principle of gender equity separated these two statements. Taken together, however, the comments of Kane and Madar indicate the problems and prospects for women in the auto industry and the UAW. The rejection of gender equality in 1944 helped prompt the clear endorsement of it by the early 1970s. But the choices made by UAW women in melding feminism and unionism limited options at the same time that they created opportunities.

Change in the orientation of female labor activism was in some respects overdue by the 1930s. As Thomas Dublin, Susan Levine, and Mary Blewett have shown, union feminists in the nineteenth century accepted and argued from the principle of gender differ-

1. UAW, *Proceedings, First Annual Education Conference* (Detroit, 1944), p. 101; Catharine Stimpson, ed., *Women and the "Equal Rights" Amendment* (New York, 1972), p. 210.

ence.[2] By the early twentieth century, however, the mechanization of production and the concomitant decline in skill levels had eroded the basis for their proud assertions of feminine power and autonomy. But the independent female labor activists who had galvanized the Knights of Labor and the Daughters of St. Crispin were uncomfortable with the Women's Trade Union League and its emphasis on women's dependent position within the family and need for protection, and the American Federation of Labor did not welcome women. A new approach was needed, one that asserted equality across alleged occupational differences between women and men and that recognized female independence. Middle-class feminists also began to shift away from an emphasis on recognizing gender differences and toward equal treatment, but contact between them and union women was minimal. The circumstances of the 1930s, therefore, seemed propitious. The New Deal labor codes generally applied equally to both sexes, and the new industrial unions opened their doors to women. Commitment to the principle of gender equality, however, was limited in this period. CIO unionists believed that both women and men should be organized and that women's position merited as much militant protection as men's, but they also still assumed that the sexes were not only different but unequal. Because the unions' understanding of the position of women was based on an assumption of both gender difference and gender hierarchy, women in unions such as the UAW were marginalized. Their interests in protection from sexual harassment and in safer working conditions and higher wages were advanced, but their interests in equal wages and equal access to employment were not, since the latter implied a notion of gender equality that few endorsed in the 1930s.

The potential for change, however, was present. Drawing on the egalitarian ideology implicit in industrial unionism, women sought to challenge the authority of gender hierarchy. Gender hierarchy at work also began to lose legitimacy as World War II and reconversion exposed the arbitrary character of occupational segregation by sex. The unemployment crisis of the late 1950s further undermined the principle, at least in regard to some jobs. Equal-employment policy combined with the evidence of women's desire and ability to perform so-called male jobs continued to erode the power of the sexual divi-

2. Thomas Dublin, *Women at Work* (New York, 1979); Susan Levine, *Labor's True Woman* (Philadelphia, 1984); Mary Blewett, *Men, Women, and Work* (Urbana, 1988).

sion of labor. Paralleling and reinforcing the trends in the workplace was the gradual (although by no means complete) decline of gender hierarchy outside the workplace. The increasing significance of employment for married women, evident in the working class before it was apparent in the middle class, undermined the family-wage ideology and asserted female economic independence, at least insofar as the equal importance of women's wage earning to working-class family survival was concerned. Once women were viewed as individual economic actors, as behaving like men, gender equality was easier to accept even in its broader implications. In some respects it was inevitable that gender equality would be incorporated into the ideology of industrial unionism.

By demonstrating the significance of unions as arenas for collective action in the interest of gender equality, this study of gender politics in the UAW complicates the history of feminism in the twentieth century. Scholars trace its development from the suffrage campaign through the conflict over the Equal Rights Amendment to the civil rights movement and *The Feminine Mystique*. The framework provided by these events focuses primarily on the activities of middle-class white women. Wage-earning women play no active role in the events and debates that compose the standard historical narrative. Admittedly, the word *feminism* was not part of the vocabulary of UAW women and men until the 1970s. But the absence of the term has led to the mistaken assumption that working-class women and men simply are antifeminist. Auto unionists may not have used the word; however, they not only debated the issue of gender equality in the period known as the doldrums of American feminism but also significantly shaped the agenda of the new feminist movement and contributed some of its principal victories.

The evidence, moreover, indicates that the UAW was not unique. Once we expand the narrow focus on feminism per se, we can see that working women and men in other industries and unions also weighed and debated the issue of gender equality after the 1930s. The labor movement clearly did not universally endorse the idea. "I have a great bone to pick with the organized labor movement," declared Bessie Hillman, wife of former Amalgamated Clothing Workers president Sidney Hillman and herself a vice-president of the union, in 1961. "They are the greatest offenders as far as discrimination against women is concerned. Today women in every walk of life have bigger positions than they have in organized labor." The negative response of male labor-movement officials to the election of Olga Madar to the UAW International Executive Board in 1966 illustrates some of the obstacles to women's advancement in unions. At a loss to explain the UAW's action, one man said, "Beats me why Walter did it." Dismissing the idea that women themselves might have demanded the position, the man speculated lamely, "Maybe he thought it'll help organize women white-collar workers." Nor did all who asserted the idea of equality prefer sex-blind treatment as a means of securing equality in the workplace. Conflict over female labor laws in particular divided union feminists in the 1950s and 1960s just as it divided other feminists. Indeed, the Coalition of Labor Union Women was not really possible until Title VII was found to contravene such laws. The vitality of the issue of gender equality as well as the evidence of wage-earning and union women's efforts to achieve it after the 1930s, however, indicate that unions served as "social spaces" for working-class women to address issues of gender, just as civil rights and new-left organizations did for young, middle-class women in the 1960s. They also suggest the need for a wider vision of the history of feminism and the feminist movement since the ratification of the Nineteenth Amendment.[3]

Even as this book demonstrates the importance of unions for working-women's collective action, it also indicates the distinctive character of the feminism that emerged in the labor movement. As gender advocacy developed in the UAW, it entailed challenging sexual discrimination in the workplace. The elimination of gender inequality in the home, in marriage, or in the social arena outside the plants was not an explicit part of that agenda. UAW feminists did not speak the language of sexual politics or understand the slogan "the personal is the political," at least not through the early 1970s. This characteristic makes it unsurprising that Dorothy Haener was a founding member of the Women's Equity Action League, a group that regarded the National Organization for Women as too distracted by divisive per-

3. AFL-CIO, Problems of Working Women: a Summary Report of a Conference Sponsored by the Industrial Union Department, AFL-CIO (Washington, D.C., 1961), p. 49; Business Week, May 28, 1966; U.S. Women's Bureau, Report of Conference on Unions and the Changing Status of Women Workers, Held at Rutgers University, October 17, 1964 (Washington, D.C., 1964); Sara Evans, Personal Politics (New York, 1979), pp. 212–32; Dolores Janiewski, "Seeking 'a New Day and a New Way': Black Women and Unions in the Southern Tobacco Industry," in Carol Groneman and Mary Beth Norton, eds., To Toil the Livelong Day (Ithaca, 1987), p. 178; Vicki Ruiz, Cannery Women, Cannery Lives (Albuquerque, 1987), pp. xviii, 81, 97, 121.

sonal issues and too radical.[4] The job orientation of trade-union feminism owes much to the circumstances that gave rise to it. The mere experience of sexual inequality was in itself an insufficient spur to feminist consciousness. Additional crucial factors were the ideology of equality embedded in the principle of industrial unionism and the antidiscriminatory employment policies advanced by unions such as the UAW. These forces rooted unionists' sense of inequity in the workplace and did not encourage or inspire wider visions of equality. Since the union was to be the agent of change, and since unions tend to focus on the workplace, nonworkplace concerns were regarded and treated as peripheral even by union feminists themselves.

The role played by the union and the workplace in the development of trade-union feminism attests to the importance of the employment experience in shaping the attitudes and behavior of working-class women.[5] At the same time, it is apparent that different work environments have different effects. Ruth Milkman, for example, has argued for the importance of industry and occupational structure in shaping the configuration of the sexual division of labor and the terrain of conflict between labor and management.[6] Similarly, such differences prompt a variety of responses and diverse goals and strategies for obtaining equality for women in the workplace. Because women held such a limited occupational space in the auto industry, they sought principally to integrate women into men's jobs. The International Union of Electrical Workers and the United Electrical Workers, in contrast, pioneered the concept of equal pay for jobs of comparable worth, in large part because women already occupied a significant share of the jobs in the industry. The extent to which different industry structures and workplace contingencies define the issues and the strategies for unions and women challenges the view

4. Arlene Daniels, "w.e.a.l.: The Growth of a Feminist Organization," in Bernice Cummings and Victoria Schuck, eds., Women Organizing (Metuchen, N.J., 1979), pp. 133–51.
5. For discussion of the importance of the work experience for working-class women, feminist consciousness, and collective action, see Louise Tilly, "Paths of Proletarianization: Organization of Production, Sexual Division of Labor, and Women's Collective Action," Signs 7 (Winter 1981): 400–417; Myra M. Ferree, "Working Class Feminism: A Consideration of the Consequences of Employment," Sociological Quarterly 21 (Spring 1980): 173–84; and Sherna Gluck, Rosie the Riveter Revisited (Boston, 1987), 259–70. For a different, more negative, view, see Leslie Tentler, Wage-Earning Women (New York, 1979); Lillian Rubin, Worlds of Pain (New York, 1976).
6. Ruth Milkman, Gender at Work (Urbana, 1987).

that attributes the subordinate status of women within organized labor to the power of patriarchy.[7] Too dichotomous and ahistorical an explanation, patriarchy cannot account for divisions among women, for instances of men's action in their class as well as their gender interests, or for change over time. Admittedly, unions in general and union men in particular can be as much a part of the problem of women's separate and unequal status as employers. UAW women, for example, felt compelled to demonstrate their loyalty to the organization and to their class, even at the expense of advancing women's gender interests or seeking allies outside the labor movement. Too, although the UAW was one of the first unions to endorse a policy of sex-blind treatment for women in the workplace, it did not fully abandon other commitments to gender difference and gender hierarchy. For these reasons, progress in achieving equality for women at work and in the union was slow. Although unionism delimits feminism, however, it does not preclude it.

Since the mid-1970s, the momentum behind feminist labor activism has shifted away from the UAW. The unionization of the service sector in the 1960s and 1970s brought thousands of women into the labor movement. Although they were organized into unions as part of a broader effort to unionize specific occupational groups that happened to be heavily female, an unintended consequence of this organizing activity was that as women became a significant part of unions' membership, they became increasingly active participants, gaining leadership posts and placing women's issues on their unions' agendas. The UAW was no longer one of the few unions in the field. In the 1970s gender-specific organizations of working women also emerged as putative expressions of a distinctive women's culture. Groups such as 9 to 5 not only advanced the idea of gender difference while espousing the goal of gender equality but tried to keep a critical distance from established labor organizations; UAW feminists were uncomfortable with such approaches. Another indication of the shift away from the UAW's leadership of the trade-union women's movement and its emphasis on equal treatment is the interest in and the status of the idea of comparable worth. Advanced as a strategy for redressing the persistent disparity between the wages of women and

7. Heidi Hartmann, "Capitalism, Patriarchy, and Job Segregation by Sex," *Signs* 1 (Spring 1976): 137–69.

men, comparable worth acknowledges occupational segregation by sex but rejects the principle of gender hierarchy on which the division of labor is based. Comparable worth, like the notion of a unique women's culture, has been hailed as both more effective and more radical than the strategies developed by UAW feminists in improving women's status in the labor market and the labor movement and in achieving gender equality.[8]

These alternate solutions, however, are not necessarily more likely to produce change or to resolve the tensions between feminism and unionism. The idea of comparable worth, for example, is not a panacea for working-women's problems. Although it does not in and of itself threaten men's jobs the way that a demand for equal access to employment does, comparable worth does provoke gender conflict. In some situations, for example, blue-collar men have objected to the demands by white-collar women for a comparable-worth policy because they stand to lose relative to women and because job-evaluation techniques tend to be biased against blue-collar jobs. For women, comparable worth has benefited chiefly those in female-dominated professional and managerial occupations in the public sector. Pay equity is a distant goal for the mass of women in clerical and service jobs, since the cost of closing the gap between men's and women's wages is great. Comparable worth also seems to offer no relief to women employed in industries characterized by intense competition, low profits, and low capital investment; comparable-worth advocates have focused on intraindustry wage differentials and have not yet addressed the problem of interindustry disparities. Some also argue that an exclusive reliance on comparable worth ultimately will reinforce rather than challenge occupational segregation by sex. As conflict over pregnancy disability leaves, comparable worth, and gender-

---

8. Ruth Milkman, "Women Workers, Feminism and the Labor Movement since the 1960s," in Milkman, ed., *Women, Work, and Protest* (Boston, 1985), pp. 300–322; Nancy Seifer and Barbara Wertheimer, "New Approaches to Collective Power: Four Working Women's Organizations," in Cummings and Schuck, eds., *Women Organizing*, pp. 152–83; Nancy Gabin, "The Issue of the Eighties: Comparable Worth and the Labor Movement," *Indiana Academy of the Social Sciences Proceedings, 1988* 23 (February 1989): 51–58; Alice Kessler-Harris, "The Just Price, the Free Market, and the Value of Women," *Feminist Studies* 14 (Summer 1988): 235–50; Roslyn Feldberg, "Women and Trade Unions: Are We Asking the Right Questions?" in Christine Bose, Roslyn Feldberg, and Natalie Sokoloff, eds., *Hidden Aspects of Women's Work* (New York, 1987), pp. 299–322.

specific organizing indicates, feminists in unions as well as outside them still are torn between demanding either special treatment for women or equal treatment with men. In the persistent debate, the UAW maintains its historic stature, helping to define goals and purposes, strategies, and approaches. That the debate continues speaks to the prospects for as well as the dilemma of combining feminism and unionism.

Bibliography

Manuscript Sources

Archives of Labor and Urban Affairs. Wayne State University. Detroit, Michigan.
George F. Addes Collection
Ken Bannon Collection
Charles Beckman Collection
Joe Brown Collection
Joseph Chrapkiewicz Collection
Neal Edwards Collection
Katherine Pollack Ellison Collection
Leo Fenster Collection
Richard T. Gosser Collection
Claude E. Hoffman Collection
Mildred Jeffrey Collection
Bruce Kingery Collection
Olga Madar Collection (unprocessed)
Olga Madar Collection
Norman Matthews Collection
Ernest J. Moran Collection
Walter P. Reuther Collection
Cecil C. Roeder Collection
Howard R. Smith Collection
R. J. Thomas Collection
Leonard Woodcock Collection

UAW Chrysler Department Collection

UAW Citizenship Department: Roy Reuther Files
UAW Education Department: Victor Reuther Collection
UAW Fair Practices and Anti-Discrimination Department Collection
UAW Fair Practices and Anti-Discrimination Department–Women's Bureau Collection
UAW Ford Department Collection
UAW General Motors Department Collection
UAW International Executive Board Collection (unprocessed)
UAW International Executive Board Collection
UAW Political Action Department: Roy Reuther Files
UAW Public Relations Department: Frank Winn Collection
UAW Region 1D Collection
UAW Region 3 Collection
UAW Region 8 Collection
UAW Region 10 Collection
UAW Research Department Collection
UAW War Policy Division Collection
UAW War Policy Division–Women's Bureau Collection
UAW Washington Office: Donald Montgomery Collection
UAW Women's Department: Lillian Hatcher Collection

UAW Local 3 Collection (unprocessed)
UAW Local 9 Collection
UAW Local 15 Women's Committee Collection
UAW Local 45 Collection
UAW Local 51 Collection
UAW Local 78 Collection
UAW Local 154 Collection
UAW Local 156 Collection
UAW Local 212 Collection
UAW Local 230 Collection
UAW Local 236 Collection (unprocessed)
UAW Local 400 Collection
UAW Local 410 Collection
UAW Local 506 Collection
UAW Local 599 Collection (unprocessed)
UAW Local 599 Collection
UAW Local 600 Collection
UAW Local 602 Collection
UAW Local 662 Collection
UAW Local 771 Collection (unprocessed)

Coalition of Labor Union Women Collection
Jewish Labor Committee Collection
Michigan AFL-CIO Collection

Automotive History Division. Detroit Public Library. Detroit, Michigan.
    Records of the Automotive Council for War Production
Department of Labor Library. U.S. Department of Labor. Washington, D.C.
    President's Commission on the Status of Women Files
Ford Motor Company Archives. Dearborn, Michigan.
    Accession 435: Production–World War II
    Accession 735: Factory Counts
    Accession 958: George Heliker Papers
Library of Congress. Washington, D.C.
    Records of the National Women's Trade Union League
Michigan Historical Collections. Bentley Library. University of Michigan.
    Ann Arbor, Michigan.
    Josephine Fellows Gomon Papers
    Martha Wright Griffiths Papers
National Archives and Records Service. Washington, D.C.
    Record Group 86: U.S. Women's Bureau Papers
Schlesinger Library. Radcliffe College. Cambridge, Massachusetts.
    Mary Anderson Papers
    Alice K. Leopold Papers
    Frieda S. Miller Papers
    Esther Peterson Papers
    President's Commission on the Status of Women Papers

Interviews

Ford Motor Company Oral History Project. Ford Motor Company Archives.
    Dearborn, Michigan.
    H. S. Ablewhite, William P. Baxter, Frank Vivian
Life and Times of Rosie the Riveter Film Transcript. Tamiment Institute Library.
    New York University. New York, New York.
    Wanita Allen
Rosie the Riveter Revisited: Women and the World War II Work Experience.
    Oral History Resource Center. California State University. Long Beach,
    California.
    Marie Baker, Clella Juanita Bowman, Flora Chavez, Alma Dotson, Videll
    Drake, Mildred Eusebio, Maria Fierro, Mern Freige, Fanny Christina Hill,
    Marguerite Hoffman, Josephine Houston, J. K., Eva Lowe, Mary Luna,
    Lillian March, Betty Murphy, Mildred Owen, Lupe Purdy, Alicia Shelit,
    Addie Stangeland, Margaret White, Women's Counselors: Emilie Cook
    and Susan Laughlin
Twentieth Century Trade Union Woman: Vehicle for Social Change Oral
    History Project. Institute of Labor and Industrial Relations. University of
    Michigan. Ann Arbor, Michigan.
    Caroline Davis, Dorothy Haener, Lillian Hatcher, Mildred Jeffrey, Odessa
    Komer, Dorothy and Henry Kraus, Olga Madar, Florence Peterson

UAW Oral History Project. Institute of Labor and Industrial Relations. University of Michigan, Ann Arbor, and Wayne State University, Detroit.
George F. Addes, John W. Anderson, Charles K. Beckman, J. A. Beni, Raymond H. Berndt, Norman W. Bully, Jess Ferrazza, Bert Foster, Catherine Gelles, Josephine Gomon, Pat Greathouse, Carl Haessler, Joseph Hattley, John K. McDaniel, Andrew B. Montgomery, Ken Morris, Stanley Nowak, William Oliver, Leon Pody, Walter Quillico, May Reuther, Harry E. Ross, Raymond Vess, Leonard Woodcock, Lawrence Yost
Women's History Coalition Oral History Project. Anderson Public Library. Anderson, Indiana.
Loma Berkebile, Nellie Hancock, Geneva Hartley, Rosemary McGuire, Ina Meeks, Helen Russell, Juanita Stultz

Interviews by author
Mildred Jeffrey. August 1, 1983.
Dorothy and Henry Kraus. April 21, 1986.
Florence Peterson. October 17, 1985.
Lillian Sherwood. October 17, 1985.
Sandy Stiles. February 20, 1986.
Priscilla Young. February 21, 1986.

Government Publications

Dewey, Lucretia M. "Women in Labor Unions." *Monthly Labor Review* 94 (February 1971): 42–48.
Fenlon, John. "Patterns in Overtime Hours and Premium Pay." *Monthly Labor Review* 92 (October 1969): 42–46.
Hedges, Janice Neipert, and Bemis, Stephen E. "Sex Stereotyping: Its Decline in Skilled Trades." *Monthly Labor Review* 97 (May 1974): 14–22.
Hooks, Janet *Women's Occupations through Seven Decades*. U.S. Women's Bureau Bulletin No. 218. Washington, D.C.: Government Printing Office, 1947.
Pidgeon, Mary Elizabeth. "Women Workers and Recent Economic Change." *Monthly Labor Review* 65 (December 1947): 666–71.
Raphael, Edna E. "Working Women and Their Membership in Labor Unions." *Monthly Labor Review* 97 (May 1974): 27–33.
Tolles, N. A., and LaFever, M. W. "Wages, Hours, Employment, and Annual Earnings in the Motor-Vehicle Industry, 1934." *Monthly Labor Review* 42 (March 1936): 521–53.
U.S. Bureau of Labor Statistics. *Case Studies of Displaced Workers: Experiences of Workers after Layoff*. Bulletin No. 1408. Washington, D.C.: Government Printing Office, 1964.
——. *Employment and Earnings, United States, 1909–75*. Bulletin No. 1312-10. Washington, D.C.: Government Printing Office, 1976.

——. *Employment and Earnings, United States, 1909–78*. Bulletin No. 1312-11. Washington, D.C.: Government Printing Office, 1979.

——. *Handbook of Labor Statistics, 1947*. Bulletin No. 916. Washington, D.C.: Government Printing Office, 1947.

——. *Handbook of Labor Statistics, 1950*. Bulletin No. 1016. Washington, D.C.: Government Printing Office, 1951.

——. *Industry Wage Survey: Motor Vehicles and Parts, April 1969*. Bulletin No. 1679. Washington, D.C.: Government Printing Office, 1971.

——. *Industry Wage Survey, Part I—Motor Vehicles, Part II—Motor-Vehicle Parts: April 1963*. Bulletin No. 1393. Washington, D.C.: Government Printing Office, 1964.

——. *Supplement to Employment and Earnings, July 1984*. Washington, D.C.: Government Printing Office, 1984.

——. *Supplement to Employment and Earnings, July 1987*. Washington, D.C.: Government Printing Office, 1987.

——. *Technological Change and Its Labor Impact in Five Industries*. Bulletin No. 1961. Washington, D.C.: Government Printing Office, 1977.

——. *Technological Trends in Major American Industries*. Bulletin No. 1474. Washington, D.C.: Government Printing Office, 1966.

——. *Wage Chronology: Chrysler Corporation, 1939–64*. Report No. 198. Washington, D.C.: Government Printing Office, 1964.

——. *Wage Chronology: Ford Motor Company, 1941–64*. Report No. 99. Washington, D.C.: Government Printing Office, 1965.

——. *Wage Chronology: General Motors Corporation, 1939–63*. Report No. 185. Washington, D.C.: Government Printing Office, 1964.

——. *Wages and Hours of Labor in the Motor-Vehicle Industry: 1925*. Bulletin No. 438. Washington, D.C.: Government Printing Office, 1927.

——. *Wages and Hours of Labor in the Motor-Vehicle Industry: 1928*. Bulletin No. 502. Washington, D.C.: Government Printing Office, 1930.

——. *Wage Structure of the Motor-Vehicle Industry*. Bulletin No. 706. Washington, D.C.: Government Printing Office, 1942.

U.S. Bureau of National Affairs. *War Labor Reports*. 28 vols. Washington, D.C.: Government Printing Office, 1942–46.

U.S. Bureau of the Census. *Biennial Census of Manufactures: 1935*. Washington, D.C.: Government Printing Office, 1938.

——. *Sixteenth Census of the United States: 1940. Manufactures, 1939*. Vol. 1. Washington, D.C.: Government Printing Office, 1942.

——. *Sixteenth Census of the United States: 1940. Population*. Vol. 3. Washington, D.C.: Government Printing Office, 1943.

——. *Seventeenth Census of the United States: 1950. Population*. Vol. 4. Washington, D.C.: Government Printing Office, 1956.

——. *Eighteenth Census of the United States: 1960. Population*. Vol. 2. Washington, D.C.: Government Printing Office, 1963.

——. *Nineteenth Census of the United States: 1970. Population*. Vol. 1. Washington, D.C.: Government Printing Office, 1973.

U.S. Employment Service. *Job Specifications for the Automobile Manufacturing Industry, June 1935.* 3 vols. Washington, D.C.: Government Printing Office, 1935.

U.S. National Labor Relations Board. *Decisions and Orders of the National Labor Relations Board.* Washington, D.C.: Government Printing Office, 1936–   .

U.S. National War Labor Board. *Termination Report of the National War Labor Board.* 3 vols. Washington, D.C.: Government Printing Office, 1947.

U.S. President's Commission on the Status of Women. *Report of the Committee on Private Employment.* Washington, D.C.: Government Printing Office, 1964.

U.S. Women's Bureau. *Changes in Women's Employment during the War.* Special Bulletin No. 20. Washington, D.C.: Government Printing Office, 1944.

——. *1969 Handbook on Women Workers.* Bulletin No. 294. Washington, D.C.: Government Printing Office, 1969.

——. *Report of Conference on Unions and the Changing Status of Women Workers, Held at Rutgers University, October 17, 1964.* Washington, D.C.: Government Printing Office, 1964.

——. *Women as Workers: A Statistical Guide.* Washington, D.C.: Government Printing Office, 1953.

——. *Women Workers in Flint.* Bulletin No. 67. Washington, D.C.: Government Printing Office, 1929.

——. *Women Workers in Ten War Production Areas and Their Postwar Employment Plans.* Bulletin No. 209. Washington, D.C.: Government Printing Office, 1946.

"Wages and Hours of Labor in the Motor-Vehicle Industry, 1932." *Monthly Labor Review* 36 (June 1933): 1365–75.

Wetzel, J. Ross. "Current Developments in Factory Overtime." *BLS Employment and Earnings* 11 (May 1965): iii–xv.

——. "Long Hours and Premium Pay." *Monthly Labor Review* 88 (September 1965): 1083–88.

Books

Anderson, Karen. *Wartime Women: Sex Roles, Family Relations, and the Status of Women in World War II.* Westport, Conn.: Greenwood Press, 1981.

Arnow, Harriette. *The Doll Maker.* New York: Macmillan, 1954.

Babson, Steve. *Working Detroit: The Making of a Union Town.* Detroit: Wayne State University Press, 1986.

Baer, Judith A. *The Chains of Protection: The Judicial Response to Women's Labor Legislation.* Westport, Conn.: Greenwood Press, 1978.

Balser, Diane. *Sisterhood and Solidarity: Feminism and Labor in Modern Times.* Boston: South End Press, 1987.

Barnard, John. *Walter Reuther and the Rise of the Auto Workers.* Boston: Little, Brown, 1983.

Berger, Bennett M. *Working-Class Suburb: A Study of Auto Workers in Suburbia.* Berkeley: University of California Press, 1968.

Bernstein, Irving. *Turbulent Years: A History of the American Worker, 1933–41*. Boston: Houghton Mifflin, 1970.

Blackwelder, Julia Kirk. *Women of the Depression: Caste and Class in San Antonio, 1929–1939*. College Station: Texas A & M University Press, 1984.

Blauner, Robert. *Alienation and Freedom: The Factory Worker and His Industry*. Chicago: University of Chicago Press, 1964.

Blewett, Mary. *Men, Women, and Work: Class, Gender, and Protest in the New England Shoe Industry, 1780–1910*. Urbana: University of Illinois Press, 1988.

Brody, David. *Workers in Industrial America: Essays on the Twentieth Century Struggle*. New York: Oxford University Press, 1981.

Buffa, Dudley. *Union Power and American Democracy: The UAW and the Democratic Party, 1935–72*. Ann Arbor: University of Michigan Press, 1984.

Campbell, D'Ann. *Women at War with America: Private Lives in a Patriotic Era*. Cambridge: Harvard University Press, 1984.

Chafe, William. *The American Woman: Her Changing Social, Economic, and Political Roles, 1920–1970*. London: Oxford University Press, 1972.

——. *Women and Equality*. Oxford: Oxford University Press, 1977.

Chinoy, Ely. *Automobile Workers and the American Dream*. Garden City, N.Y.: Doubleday, 1955.

Clive, Alan. *State of War: Michigan in World War II*. Ann Arbor: University of Michigan Press, 1979.

Cochran, Bert. *Labor and Communism: The Conflict That Shaped American Unions*. Princeton: Princeton University Press, 1977.

Cooper, Patricia. *Once a Cigar Maker: Men, Women, and Work Culture in American Cigar Factories, 1900–1919*. Urbana: University of Illinois Press, 1987.

Cott, Nancy. *The Grounding of Modern Feminism*. New Haven: Yale University Press, 1987.

Dublin, Thomas. *Women at Work: The Transformation of Work and Community in Lowell, Massachusetts, 1826–1860*. New York: Columbia University Press, 1979.

Dunn, Robert W. *Labor and Automobiles*. New York: International Publishers, 1929.

Dye, Nancy Schrom. *As Equals and as Sisters: The Labor Movement and the Women's Trade Union League of New York*. Columbia: University of Missouri Press, 1980.

Evans, Sara. *Personal Politics: The Roots of Women's Liberation in the Civil Rights Movement and the New Left*. New York: Vintage Books, 1980.

Feldman, Richard, and Betzold, Michael. *End of the Line: Autoworkers and the American Dream*. New York: Weidenfeld and Nicholson, 1988.

Ferree, Myra, and Hess, Beth. *Controversy and Coalition: The New Feminist Movement*. Boston: Twayne Publishers, 1985.

Fine, Sidney. *The Automobile under the Blue Eagle*. Ann Arbor: University of Michigan Press, 1963.

——. *Sit-Down: The General Motors Strike of 1936–1937*. Ann Arbor: University of Michigan Press, 1969.

Foner, Philip. *Women and the American Labor Movement from World War I to the Present*. New York: Free Press, 1980.

Frank, Miriam, Ziebarth, Marilyn, and Field, Connie. *The Life and Times of Rosie the Riveter: The Story of Three Million Working Women during World War II*. Emeryville, Calif.: Clarity Educational Productions, 1982.

Freeman, Jo. *The Politics of Women's Liberation*. New York: Longman Publishers, 1975.

Friedan, Betty. *It Changed My Life: Writings on the Women's Movement*. New York: Random House, 1976.

Friedlander, Peter. *The Emergence of a U.A.W. Local, 1936–1939: A Study in Class and Culture*. Pittsburgh: University of Pittsburgh Press, 1975.

Galenson, Walter. *The CIO Challenge to the AFL: A History of the American Labor Movement, 1934–41*. Cambridge: Harvard University Press, 1960.

Gartman, David. *Auto Slavery: The Labor Process in the American Automobile Industry, 1897–1950*. New Brunswick, N.J.: Rutgers University Press, 1986.

George, Emily. *Martha W. Griffiths*. Lanham, Md.: University Press of America, 1982.

Glaberman, Martin. *Wartime Strikes: The Struggle against the No-Strike Pledge in the UAW during World War II*. Detroit: Bewick Editions, 1980.

Gluck, Sherna Berger. *Rosie the Riveter Revisited: Women, the War, and Social Change*. Boston: Twayne Publishers, 1987.

Goldfarb, Lyn. *Separated and Unequal: Discrimination against Women Workers after World War II (The UAW 1944–54)*. A Union for Radical Political Economics Pamphlet. Washington, D.C.: Union For Radical Political Economics, 1976.

Halpern, Martin. *UAW Politics in the Cold War Era*. Albany: State University of New York Press, 1988.

Harbison, Frederick, and Dubin, Robert. *Patterns of Union-Management Relations: United Automobile Workers (CIO), General Motors, Studebaker*. Chicago: Science Research Associates, 1947.

Harris, Howell John. *The Right to Manage: Industrial Relations Policies of American Business in the 1940s*. Madison: University of Wisconsin Press, 1982.

Harrison, Cynthia. *On Account of Sex: The Politics of Women's Issues, 1945–1968*. Berkeley: University of California Press, 1988.

Hartmann, Susan. *The Home Front and Beyond: American Women in the 1940s*. Boston: Twayne Publishers, 1982.

Hawes, Elizabeth. *Hurry Up Please It's Time*. New York: Reynal and Hitchcock, 1946.

——. *Why Women Cry or Wenches with Wrenches*. New York: Reynal and Hitchcock, 1943.

Hoffman, Claude E. *Sit-Down in Anderson: UAW Local 663, Anderson, Indiana*. Detroit: Wayne State University Press, 1968.

Hole, Judith, and Levine, Ellen. *Rebirth of Feminism*. New York: Quadrangle Books, 1971.

Honey, Maureen. *Creating Rosie the Riveter: Class, Gender, and Propaganda during World War II*. Amherst: University of Massachusetts Press, 1984.

Howe, Irving, and Widick, B. J. *The UAW and Walter Reuther*. New York: DaCapo Press, 1973.

Janiewski, Dolores. *Sisterhood Denied: Race, Gender, and Class in a New South Community*. Philadelphia: Temple University Press, 1985.

Jeffreys, Steven. *Management and Managed: Fifty Years of Crisis at Chrysler*. Cambridge: Cambridge University Press, 1986.

Johansen, Elaine. *Comparable Worth*. Boulder, Colo.: Westview Press, 1984.

Jones, Jacqueline. *Labor of Love, Labor of Sorrow: Black Women, Work, and the Family from Slavery to the Present*. New York: Basic Books, 1985.

Kaledin, Eugenia. *Mothers and More: American Women in the 1950s*. Boston: Twayne Publishers, 1984.

Keeran, Roger. *The Communist Party and the Auto Workers Unions*. Bloomington: Indiana University Press, 1980.

Kennedy, Susan Estabrook. *If All We Did Was to Weep at Home: A History of White Working-Class Women in America*. Bloomington: Indiana University Press, 1979.

Kessler-Harris, Alice. *Out to Work: A History of Wage-Earning Women in the United States*. New York: Oxford University Press, 1982.

Komarovsky, Mirra. *Blue-Collar Marriage*. New York: Vintage Books, 1967.

Kraus, Henry. *The Many and the Few: A Chronicle of the Dynamic Auto Workers*. Los Angeles: Plantin Press, 1947.

Kruchko, John. *The Birth of a Union Local: The History of UAW Local 674, Norwood, Ohio, 1933–1940*. Ithaca: New York State School of Industrial and Labor Relations, Cornell University, 1972.

Levine, Susan. *Labor's True Woman: Carpet Weavers, Industrialization, and Labor Reform in the Gilded Age*. Philadelphia: Temple University Press, 1984.

Lichtenstein, Nelson. *Labor's War at Home: The CIO in World War II*. Cambridge: Cambridge University Press, 1982.

Linton, Thomas E. *An Historical Examination of the Purposes and Practices of the Education Program of the UAW, 1936–1959*. Ann Arbor: University of Michigan School of Education, 1965.

Macdonald, Robert M. *Collective Bargaining in the Automobile Industry*. New Haven: Yale University Press, 1963.

McPherson, William Heston. *Labor Relations in the Automobile Industry*. Washington, D.C.: Brookings Institution, 1940.

Marquart, Frank. *An Auto-Worker's Journal: The UAW from Crusade to One-Party Union*. University Park: Pennsylvania State University Press, 1975.

Meier, August, and Rudwick, Elliott. *Black Detroit and the Rise of the UAW*. Oxford: Oxford University Press, 1979.

Meyer, Stephen, III. *The Five Dollar Day: Labor Management and Social Control in the Ford Motor Company, 1908–1921*. Albany: State University of New York Press, 1981.

Milkman, Ruth. *Gender at Work: The Dynamics of Job Segregation by Sex during World War II*. Urbana: University of Illinois Press, 1987.

——, ed. *Women, Work, and Protest: A Century of U.S. Women's Labor History*. Boston: Routledge and Kegan Paul, 1985.

Mortimer, Wyndham. *Organize! My Life as a Union Man*. Boston: Beacon Press, 1971.

National Manpower Council. *Womanpower*. New York: Columbia University Press, 1957.

Northrup, Herbert R. *The Negro in the Automobile Industry*. Philadelphia: University of Pennsylvania, 1968.

Peck, Sidney. *The Rank-and-File Leader*. New Haven: College and University Press, 1963.

Peterson, Joyce Shaw. *American Automobile Workers, 1900–1933*. Albany: State University of New York Press, 1987.

Polenberg, Richard. *War and Society: The United States, 1941–1945*. Philadelphia: J. B. Lippincott, 1972.

Rainwater, Lee, Coleman, Richard P., and Handel, Gerald. *Workingman's Wife: Her Personality, World, and Life Style*. New York: Oceana Publications, 1959.

Reuther, Victor. *The Brothers Reuther and the Story of the UAW*. Boston: Houghton Mifflin, 1979.

Rubin, Lillian. *Worlds of Pain: Life in the Working-Class Family*. New York: Basic Books, 1976.

Ruiz, Vicki. *Cannery Women, Cannery Lives: Mexican Women, Unionization, and the California Food Processing Industry, 1930–1950*. Albuquerque: University of New Mexico Press, 1987.

Rupp, Leila. *Mobilizing Women for War: German and American Propaganda, 1939–1945*. Princeton: Princeton University Press, 1978.

Rupp, Leila, and Taylor, Verta. *Survival in the Doldrums: The American Women's Rights Movement, 1945 to the 1960s*. New York: Oxford University Press, 1987.

Scharf, Lois. *To Work and to Wed: Female Employment, Feminism, and the Great Depression*. Westport, Conn.: Greenwood Press, 1980.

Schatz, Ronald. *The Electrical Workers: A History of Labor at General Electric and Westinghouse*. Urbana: University of Illinois Press, 1983.

Seidman, Joel. *Labor from Defense to Reconversion*. Chicago: University of Chicago Press, 1953.

Seifer, Nancy. *Nobody Speaks for Me! Self-Portraits of American Working Class Women*. New York: Simon and Schuster, 1976.

Serrin, William. *The Company and the Union*. New York: Vintage Books, 1974.

Slichter, Sumner, Healy, James, and Livernash, E. Robert. *The Impact of Collective Bargaining on Management*. Washington, D.C.: Brookings Institution, 1960.

Snyder, Carl Dean. *White-Collar Workers and the UAW*. Urbana: University of Illinois Press, 1973.

Stieber, Jack. *Governing the UAW*. New York: Wiley, 1962.

Stimpson, Catharine, ed. *Women and the "Equal Rights" Amendment: Senate Subcommittee Hearings on the Constitutional Amendment, 91st Congress*. New York: R. R. Bowker, 1972.

Tax, Meredith. *The Rising of the Women: Feminist Solidarity and Class Conflict, 1880–1917*. New York: Monthly Review Press, 1980.

Tentler, Leslie. *Wage-Earning Women: Industrial Work and Family Life in the United States, 1900–1930*. New York: Oxford University Press, 1979.

Walshok, Mary L. *Blue Collar Women: Pioneers on the Male Frontier*. Garden City, N.Y.: Anchor Books, 1981.

Wandersee, Winifred D. *Women's Work and Family Values, 1920–1940*. Cambridge: Harvard University Press, 1981.

Ware, Susan. *Beyond Suffrage: Women in the New Deal*. Cambridge: Harvard University Press, 1981.

———. *Holding Their Own: American Women in the 1930s*. Boston: Twayne Publishers, 1982.

Wertheimer, Barbara, and Nelson, Anne. *Trade Union Women: A Study of Their Participation in New York City Locals*. New York: Praeger Publishers, 1975.

Zelman, Patricia. *Women, Work, and National Policy: The Kennedy-Johnson Years*. Ann Arbor: UMI Research Press, 1982.

Zieger, Robert. *American Workers, American Unions, 1920–1985*. Baltimore: Johns Hopkins University Press, 1986.

———. *Madison's Battery Workers, 1934–1952*. Ithaca: New York State School of Industrial and Labor Relations, Cornell University Press, 1977.

Articles

Anderson, Karen. "Last Hired, First Fired: Black Women Workers during World War II." *Journal of American History* 69 (June 1982): 82–97.

Asher, Nina. "Dorothy Jacobs Bellanca: Women Clothing Workers and the Runaway Shops." In Joan Jensen and Sue Davidson, eds. *A Needle, a Bobbin, a Strike: Women Needleworkers in America*. Philadelphia: Temple University Press, 1984, pp. 195–226.

Bernstein, Barton. "The Automobile Industry and the Coming of the Second World War." *Southwestern Social Science Quarterly* 47 (June 1966): 22–33.

———. "Walter Reuther and the General Motors Strike of 1945–46." *Michigan History* 49 (1965): 260–77.

Blumrosen, Ruth G. "Wage Discrimination, Job Segregation, and Title VII of the Civil Rights Act of 1964." *University of Michigan Journal of Law Reform* 12 (Spring 1979): 397–502.

Bodnar, John. "Power and Memory in Oral History: Workers and Managers at Studebaker." *Journal of American History* 75 (March 1989): 1201–21.

Boryczka, Ray. "Militancy and Factionalism in the United Auto Workers Union, 1937–1941." *Maryland Historian* 8 (Fall 1977): 13–25.

Brauer, Carl. "Women Activists, Southern Conservatives, and the Prohibition of Sex Discrimination in Title VII of the 1964 Civil Rights Act." *Journal of Southern History* 49 (February 1983): 37–56.

Clive, Alan. "Women Workers in World War II: Michigan as a Test Case." *Labor History* 20 (Winter 1979): 44–72.

Cobble, Dorothy Sue. " 'Practical Women': Waitress Unionists and the Controversies over Gender Roles in the Food Service Industry, 1900–1980." *Labor History* 29 (Winter 1988): 5–31.

Cook, Alice. "Women and American Trade Unions." *Annals of the American Academy of Political and Social Science* 375 (January 1968): 124–32.

Daniels, Arlene. "Conclusion." In Alice H. Cook, Val R. Lorwin, and Arlene Kaplan Daniels, eds. *Women and Trade Unions in Eleven Industrialized Countries*. Philadelphia: Temple University Press, 1984, pp. 312–16.

——. "w.e.a.l.: The Growth of a Feminist Organization." In Bernice Cummings and Victoria Schuck, eds. *Women Organizing: An Anthology*. Metuchen, N.J.: Scarecrow Press, 1979, pp. 133–51.

Dickason, Gladys. "Women in Labor Unions." *Annals of the American Academy of Political and Social Science* 251 (May 1947): 70–78.

Dobija, Jane. "Voices of Struggle: Working Women in Detroit." *Ms.*, September 1982, p. 21.

Feldberg, Roslyn. "Women and Trade Unions: Are We Asking the Right Questions?" In Christine Bose, Roslyn Feldberg, and Natalie Sokoloff, eds. *Hidden Aspects of Women's Work*. New York: Praeger Press, 1987, pp. 299–322.

Ferree, Myra M. "The Women's Movement in the Working Class." *Sex Roles* 9 (1983): 493–505.

——. "Working Class Feminism: A Consideration of the Consequences of Employment." *Sociological Quarterly* 21 (Spring 1980): 173–84.

Fonow, Mary Margaret. "Occupation/Steelworker: Sex/Female." In Laurel Richardson and Verta Taylor, eds. *Feminist Frontiers: Rethinking Sex, Gender, and Society*. New York: Random House, 1983, pp. 274–79.

Freedman, Estelle. "Separatism as Strategy: Female Institution Building and American Feminism, 1870–1930." *Feminist Studies* 5 (Fall 1979): 512–29.

Freeman, Joshua. "Delivering the Goods: Industrial Unionism during World War II." *Labor History* 19 (Fall 1978): 570–94.

Gabin, Nancy. "The Issue of the Eighties: Comparable Worth and the Labor Movement." *Indiana Academy of the Social Sciences Proceedings, 1988* 23 (February 1989): 51–58.

Greenwald, Maurine Weiner. "Working-Class Feminism and the Family Wage Ideal: The Seattle Debate on Married Women's Right to Work, 1914–1920." *Journal of American History* 76 (June 1989): 118–49.

Hartmann, Heidi. "Capitalism, Patriarchy, and Job Segregation by Sex." *Signs* 1 (Spring 1976): 137–69.

Hartmann, Susan. "Women's Organizations during World War II: The Interaction of Class, Race, and Feminism." In Mary Kelley, ed. *Woman's Being, Woman's Place*. Boston: G. K. Hall, 1979, pp. 313–28.

Hield, Melissa. "Union-Minded: Women in the Texas ILGWU, 1933–1950." *Frontiers* 4 (Summer 1979): 59–70.

Jacoby, Robin. "Feminism and Class Consciousness in the British and American WTULS, 1890–1925." In Berenice Carroll, ed. *Liberating Women's History*. Urbana: University of Illinois Press, 1976, pp. 137–60.

——. "The Women's Trade Union League and American Feminism." *Feminist Studies* 3 (Fall 1975): 126–40.

Janiewski, Dolores. "Seeking 'a New Day and a New Way': Black Women and Unions in the Southern Tobacco Industry." In Carol Groneman and Mary Beth Norton, eds. *"To Toil the Livelong Day": America's Women at Work, 1780–1980*. Ithaca: Cornell University Press, 1987, pp. 161–78.

Jennings, Ed. "Wildcat! The Wartime Strike Wave in Auto." *Radical America* 9 (1975): 77–105.

Kesselman, Amy. "Hidden Resistance: Women Shipyard Workers after World War II." In Christine Bose, Roslyn Feldberg, and Natalie Sokoloff, eds. *Hidden Aspects of Women's Work*. New York: Praeger, 1987, pp. 283–98.

Kessler-Harris, Alice. "The Debate over Equality for Women in the Work-place: Recognizing Differences." In Laurie Larwood, Ann Stromberg, and Barbara Gutek, eds. *Women and Work: An Annual Review*. Vol. 1. Beverly Hills, Calif.: Sage Publications, 1985, pp. 141–61.

——. "The Just Price, the Free Market, and the Value of Women." *Feminist Studies* 14 (Summer 1988): 235–50.

——. "Organizing the Unorganizable: Three Jewish Women and Their Union." *Labor History* 17 (Winter 1976): 5–23.

——. "Where Are the Organized Women Workers?" *Feminist Studies* 3 (Fall 1975): 92–110.

Klehr, Harvey. "Female Leadership in the Communist Party of the USA." *Studies in Comparative Communism* 10 (Winter 1977): 394–402.

Komer, Odessa, and Johnson, Gloria. "Education for Affirmative Action: Two Union Approaches." In Barbara Wertheimer, ed. *Labor Education for Women Workers*. Philadelphia: Temple University Press, 1981, pp. 204–16.

Levine, Susan. "Labor's True Woman: Domesticity and Equal Rights in the Knights of Labor." *Journal of American History* 70 (September 1983): 323–49.

Lichtenstein, Nelson. "Auto Worker Militancy and the Structure of Factory Life, 1937–1955." *Journal of American History* 67 (September 1980): 335–53.

McPherson, William H., and Luchek, Anthony. "Automobiles." In Harry A. Millis, ed. *How Collective Bargaining Works*. New York: Twentieth Century Fund, 1942, pp. 571–630.

May, Martha. "The Historical Problem of the Family Wage: The Ford Motor Company and the Five Dollar Day." *Feminist Studies* 8 (Summer 1982): 399–424.

Milkman, Ruth. "American Women and Industrial Unionism during World War II." In Margaret Randolph Higgonet, Jane Jenson, Sonya Michel, and Margaret Collins Weitz, eds. *Behind the Lines: Gender and the Two World Wars*. New Haven: Yale University Press, pp. 168–81.

——. "Organizing the Sexual Division of Labor: Historical Perspectives on 'Women's Work' and the American Labor Movement." *Socialist Review* 49 (January–February 1980): 95–150.

——. "Women's History and the Sears Case." *Feminist Studies* 12 (Summer 1986): 375–400.

——. "Women's Work and the Economic Crisis: Some Lessons from the

Great Depression." *Review of Radical Political Economics* 8 (Spring 1976): 73–97.

Miller, Marc. "Working Women and World War II." *New England Quarterly* 53 (March 1980): 42–61.

Newman, Winn, and Vonhof, Jeanne M. " 'Separate but Equal': Job Segregation and Pay Equity in the Wake of *Gunther*." *University of Illinois Law Review* (1981): 269–331.

O'Farrell, Brigid. "Women and Nontraditional Blue Collar Jobs in the 1980s: An Overview." In Phyllis Wallace, ed. *Women in the Workplace*. Boston: Auburn House Publishing, 1982, pp. 135–65.

Quick, Paddy. "Rosie the Riveter: Myths and Realities." *Radical America* 9 (1975): 115–32.

Reeves, Nancy. "Women at Work." In Bert Cochran, ed. *American Labor at Midpassage*. New York: Monthly Review Press, 1959, pp. 133–43.

Robinson, Donald Allen. "Two Movements in Pursuit of Equal Opportunity." *Signs* 3 (Spring 1979): 413–33.

Schaffer, Robert. "Women and the Communist Party, USA, 1930–1940." *Socialist Review* 9 (May–June 1979): 73–119.

Seifer, Nancy, and Wertheimer, Barbara. "New Approaches to Collective Power: Four Working Women's Organizations." In Bernice Cummings and Victoria Schuck, eds. *Women Organizing: An Anthology*. Metuchen, N.J.: Scarecrow Press, 1979, pp. 152–83.

Sexton, Patricia Cayo. "A Feminist Union Perspective." In B. J. Widick, ed. *Auto Work and Its Discontents*. Baltimore: Johns Hopkins University Press, 1976, pp. 18–33.

Skeels, Jack. "The Background of UAW Factionalism." *Labor History* 2 (Spring 1961): 158–81.

Skold, Karen Beck. "The Job He Left Behind: American Women in the Shipyards during World War II." In Carol Berkin and Clara Lovett, eds. *Women, War, and Revolution*. New York: Holmes and Meier, 1980, pp. 55–75.

Straub, Eleanor. "U.S. Government Policy toward Civilian Women during World War II." *Prologue* 5 (Winter 1973): 240–54.

Strom, Sharon Hartman. "Challenging 'Woman's Place': Feminism, the Left, and Industrial Unionism in the 1930s." *Feminist Studies* 9 (Summer 1983): 359–86.

Thomas, Mary Martha. "Rosie the Alabama Riveter." *The Alabama Review* 39 (July 1986): 196–212.

Tilly, Louise. "Paths of Proletarianization: Organization of Production, Sexual Division of Labor, and Women's Collective Action." *Signs* 7 (Winter 1981): 400–17.

Tobias, Sheila, and Anderson, Lisa. "What Really Happened to Rosie the Riveter: Demobilization and the Female Labor Force, 1944–47." *MSS Modular Publications* 9 (1973).

Trey, Joan Ellen. "Women in the War Economy—World War II." *Review of Radical Political Economics* 4 (July 1972): 40–57.

Yeghissian, Patricia. "Emergence of the Red Berets." *Michigan Occasional Papers in Women's Studies* 10 (Winter 1980).

Unpublished Works

Fehn, Bruce. "Women of the United Packinghouse Workers of America, 1946–1956." Unpublished paper in author's possession.
Fonow, Mary Margaret. "Women in Steel: A Case Study of the Participation of Women in a Trade Union." Ph.D. dissertation. Ohio State University, 1977.
Lichtman, Sheila. "Women at Work, 1941–1945: Wartime Employment in the San Francisco Bay Area." Ph.D. dissertation. University of California–Davis, 1981.
Meyer, Stephen. "Shop Culture, Shop Stewards, Shop Grievances: Sources of Labor Militancy at Allis-Chalmers in the 1930s and 1940s." Paper presented at the Social Science History Association Conference, Bloomington, Indiana, November 1982.
Meyerowitz, Ruth. "Women in the UAW, 1935–1945." Manuscript in author's possession, n.d.
——. "Women Unionists and World War II: New Opportunities for Leadership." Paper presented at the Organization of American Historians Meeting, San Francisco, California, April 1980.
Posner, Leslie P. "Male-Female Worker Relations in a Traditionally Male Industrial Setting: The Case of the First Women Workers in a 'Company-Town' Steel Mill." Ph.D. dissertation. University of Pittsburgh, 1979.
Rose, Margaret. "Women and the United Farm Workers: A Study of Chicana and Mexicana Participation in a Labor Union, 1950 to 1980." Ph.D. dissertation. University of California–Los Angeles, 1988.
Wigderson, Seth. "The Evolution of Service Unionism: The U.A.W. as a Case Study." Paper presented at the Social Science History Association Meeting, Washington, D.C., October 29, 1983.
——. "The UAW in the 1950s: Development of a Service Union." Paper presented at the Southern Labor History Conference, Atlanta, Georgia, September 1982.
Zimmelman, Nancy. "The UAW Women's Auxiliaries: Activities of Ford Workers' Families in Detroit, 1937–1949." Master's thesis. Wayne State University, 1987.

Index

Library of Congress Cataloging-in-Publication Data

Gabin, Nancy Felice.
  Feminism in the labor movement: women and the United Auto Workers, 1935–
1975/Nancy F. Gabin.
    p. cm.
  Includes bibliographical references.
  ISBN 0-8014-2435-6 (alk. paper).—ISBN 0-8014-9725-6 (pbk.: alk. paper)
    1. Women in trade-unions—United States—Case studies. 2. International Union,
United Automobile Workers of America—History. I. Title.
HD6079.2.U5G33 1990
331.4'8292'0973–dc20   90-1571